RANJEET

13 INSIDER
TRADING SECRETS
THAT WILL
BLOW YOUR MIND

13 INSIDER TRADING SECRETS THAT WILL BLOW YOUR MIND

By Ranjeet Singh

TIP 10 –
HOW REALLY INDEPENDENT ARE IFAS? 103

TIP 9 –
PUMP & DUMP 127

TIP 8 –
MARKET MANIPULATION – THE HOUND OF
HOUNSLOW   167

TIP 7 –
PIE IN THE SKY EVALUATION   187

TIP 6 –
PRINCIPAL DEALING   219

TIP 5 –
"LEARN TO TRADE" SCAM   257

TIP 4 –
BOILER ROOM SCAMS   289

TIP 3 –
THE EQUITY INVESTOR SCANDAL (EIS)   343

TIP 2 –
BONDS 393

TIP 1 –
DISCRETIONARY FUND MANAGER (DFM)   451

PREFACE

I am no Author

Before I begin to share with you what I know, allow me to share with you, what I don't know.

I don't know how to write professionally. I'm not a writer, I'm not an accomplished author, and I have had no training, formal or otherwise, about how to write a book. I have no ghost-writer, no co-author and apart from a proof-reader who checked for spelling errers, I have had no help.

Every word on every page in this book is written by me. Everything you are about to read comes either directly from what I have witnessed myself, or from credible sources I trust. It is served to you unfiltered and raw; it's not exaggerated or embellished in any way.

I promise you that this book is worthy of both my time and yours. My time to write it and your time to read it.

I'm also incredibly proud of the finished piece. Not because of the words that I have written, but because of the impact those words may have in helping the most vulnerable people in our society.

I'm an FCA qualified professional and chartered wealth manager. Over the past 25 years, I've written hundreds of stock market articles and research papers, as well as produced hundreds of educational videos and webinars. I've created countless pieces of educational content, including extensive online courses and trading programmes teaching people how to grow their wealth and increase their financial intelligence.

I've spoken at many presentations, given key note speeches, and appeared on various investor stages over the years. I've written for newspapers, investor columns and appeared as a financial analyst and commentator for CNBC, Bloomberg and other television programmes at least a hundred times.

I've spoken to and helped many tens of thousands of people with their investments over almost three decades. I've analysed data, information, spreadsheets, portfolios and market news. I have given recommendations, advice and help on how to achieve financial goals.

I've written a lot of things and I've spoken about them even more.

And I continue to do all of the above today.

But I know that what you're about to read in this book is quite possibly the single most important piece of professional work that I've ever produced.

It's more important than anything I've done in my career before and it may be the most important thing that I will ever do.

People of a certain age often talk about their legacy and what they hope to leave behind. I'm not sure if I'm at that stage in my life just yet, but I might look back in a few years and realise that this was my legacy, the thing that I was remembered by;

the one piece of work that had the most powerful impact in this world.

That's because this isn't about making money in the stock market; it's about something far more important than that. I'm going to show you how not to lose money.

I'll show you how not to lose your life savings, your pension, your cash, your job, your house, your health, your sanity and yes, even your life.

The insider trading secrets exposed in this book are real- life financial scams that happen in the City every day. Every year, lives are destroyed by professional scammers.

It's time we all knew what really goes on, so that we may protect ourselves and our loved ones.

In particular, I hope that with God's will, this book will somehow find its way into the hands of that 80-year-old widower that I will never meet, and never know. He was about to invest his life savings into a scam.

By some small miracle, he was able to read this book just in time, and stopped himself from making the worst decision of his life.

If just for him, it will have all been worth it.

Who am I and why should you care?

In 2008, I founded my own stock broking and portfolio management firm which I still run today. However, this book has nothing to do with my business or my position as an FCA regulated person. I write this book from my own personal opinion and perspective.

Looking back, it's been a long and eventful journey, and it's one that I'm incredibly grateful for. For nearly thirty years, I have worked in the City of London for numerous investment firms and in a plethora of different roles.

For the first few years of my career, after I left Brunel University in West London, I traded currencies, futures, indices and options. It sounds impressive but it wasn't really. I was just playing around, learning the game.

I went on to work in many different roles, including a stock analyst, researcher and technical chartist, market commentator, broker, trader and eventually an investment portfolio manager. Again, it all sounds very impressive, but it really wasn't. Anybody could have done the same with an opportunity and the right training.

Whilst working for different companies, and on different training programmes, I was lucky enough to experience back-office operational positions, as well as middle-office trade support roles. This helped me to understand the full picture of the investment cycle, something that most front office traders never get to see.

Because I run my own business, I continue to work at a very high level in compliance and anti-money laundering. I'm also professionally qualified in senior risk management. I work with compliance firms and still, to this day, I'm actively involved in developing and implementing internal procedures, as well as regulatory policies, to protect my investors.

Over the years, I've made a lot of money and lost a lot of money, but I've never been a big trader.

I've spent most of my working life in sales and broking rather than trading. Perhaps that's just as well, because I've made some pretty poor decisions in my life. I've made poor decisions in property, business, tax, and personal relationships. Those decisions have cost me a lot of stress, time and money.

I've also been scammed so I know how it feels to be on the receiving end.

My work and experience have varied considerably because of how many times I've moved company. As a child, I've never been able to sit still, either figuratively or literally speaking. That spilled over into my working life; in my twenties, I was constantly jumping from one firm to another; sometimes out of choice, but usually against my own free will. Either I was made redundant, or my contract was terminated because I was acting like a fool.

I've worked at massive multi-billion-pound global investment banks, like Deutsche Bank and the Royal Bank of Scotland, right the way down to the tiniest of one-man broker firms. I've worked at commercial foreign exchange houses, futures trading firms, penny share specialists, CFD brokerages, option and derivative companies, and a number of stockbroker houses. I've traded multi-million-pound accounts for high net worth investors, and I've traded accounts with less than a thousand pounds.

For the majority of my career, more than 20 years and counting, I've traded and brokered almost exclusively in equities as a stockbroker. During that time, I have had the great fortune of meeting and forging great relationships with many hard-working and committed professionals in that financial space.

This includes other brokers, traders, chartered accountants, tax experts, compliance consultants, financial advisors, equity issuers, market makers, custodians, analysts, researchers, company directors, partners, traders, fund managers and many others.

This book is not about any of them.

I also regularly speak to very wealthy property millionaires and very high net worth investors. This book isn't about them either.

This book is not about anybody in particular; it's about a broken system, not about the people.

It's quite simple really.

Amongst all the hustle and bustle, amongst all the billions of pounds moving from one product to another, from one firm to another, and from one country to another, there is a deep-set level of corruption.

Now it's time for the world to finally see it.

Beautiful London hides a Dirty Truth

Scams will never stop. They've been happening for thousands of years. It's just that the financial scams in the City of London are the biggest and most horrific of them all. They affect everybody.

Look up when you're next stood outside Liverpool Street Train Station, or when you find yourself at the Bank of England, or if you're standing outside a coffee shop on Cannon Street. Or maybe you were sight-seeing at St Paul's Cathedral, but you ventured off and ended up in one of the little pebbled alleys.

If you ever find yourself there, just stand still, stop what you're doing, and look up.

What do you see?

It's an incredible view, isn't it?

Tall glass skyscrapers, glamorous investment banks, and beautifully designed buildings are intertwined with some of the world's most iconic monuments and incredible architecture, all steeped in medieval history. Then look at the floor where you are standing. You can almost imagine the horses trotting down the cobbled streets as they head towards the fruit market in centuries gone by.

There is a wonderful contrast of the very old and the very new in the City of London.

I've been fortunate to work there for my entire adult life and its beauty still never fails to amaze me. I still catch myself pausing and looking up at the amazing landscape above me.

There's an indescribable energy as some of the most talented, intelligent, hungry and successful people in the world hurriedly congregate in boardrooms, meeting rooms, coffee shops, restaurants and pubs to share ideas and innovations. They are forever driving forward; thinking, collaborating, pushing boundaries and breaking new ceilings.

It's a melting pot of amazing buildings, roads, architecture, and people.

But hidden behind this seemingly beautiful face of the City, runs many deep and! dirty secrets.

These secrets lie in the City's dark underworld.

It is to be expected; with money comes corruption. That's why London is the number one city in the world where the biggest criminals operate, where the largest crimes are committed. From shiny, leather briefcases stuffed with cash to multi-million-pound bank electronic transfers.

The Square Mile is awash with criminality.

This doesn't mean that all institutions are rotten or that all City traders are bad.

There are many people who work very hard to do the best for their investors and their clients. They are the unsung heroes.

There are many traders, bankers, financial advisors, analysts, market, brokers and salespeople who do wonderful jobs. They provide an amazing service to their clients, to the people, to the public.

They don't rip people off. They take care of them and they do their best for them.

But there are always a few who don't; and now you're about to find out who they are.

Global Pandemic

Corruption is not just here in the UK but all over the world.

This game has no geographical boundaries or language barriers. It doesn't favour a particular, country or religion. It doesn't discriminate against age or gender.

Money and corruption flow freely.

From empires and kingdoms thousands of years ago to the modern-day financiers, there is one eternal, unbreakable truth; where there is cash, there is cheating. The two are intrinsically interwoven, joined at birth.

The difference between today and what happened historically, is that with each passing year, the corruption is more deceitful and better disguised than ever before. Today, you really have no idea who is your friend and who is your foe.

Where there is illicit money, not far behind are heinous crimes that are so cruel that they are hard to imagine.

Drug abuse, parties, sex orgies, drug-dealing, terrorism,

political blackmail, religious cults, satanic worshipping, masonic groups, child trafficking, pedophilia and much more.

There's a lot of stuff that goes on that nobody dares to talk about. I don't know enough about that to write a book on it, and as I value my life, perhaps that's not a bad thing. But I can tell you that it does happen.

It happens in a lot of places that you wouldn't even imagine, like Hollywood. It's a sick world. Just know that the narrative mainstream media portrays, is false. People are slowly waking up to this fact but most of the world remains asleep.

They are especially oblivious to what goes on in the financial markets because it's so closely guarded by the criminals. There's too much money at stake for the bubble to burst and the corruption is happening in every major financial city in the world.

It just so happens that London is at the epicentre of it all.

But that's not where this story begins. For that, I need to take you to Coventry.

From Coventry to the City

Before we begin, I want to share with you a little bit about my own journey. If you are to derive any value from this book, then you need to trust what I'm about to tell you. In order for you to trust me, you need to know me. By the end of this chapter, I hope we will have become good friends.

I was born in 1974 in Coventry, a working-class industrial city in the West Midlands. My grandparents came to the UK as immigrants in the early 1950s from Panjab in India, desperately searching for a better life for their children away from poverty. They didn't know it then but that arduous four-week slow boat trip to the UK would be the beginning of a new era that would change the course of British and Indian history forever.

It linked the two countries together and transformed the British landscape.

My grandparents travelled with nothing more than a small suitcase of clothes and a few Indian rupees, which were worth literally just a few UK shillings. We often hear about the guy who came to seek his fortune with 'just the shirt on his back'.

Well, that was the true story for both of my grandfathers. It was the true story for thousands of other immigrants just like them. They all came with just a shirt, a dream and a smile.

At the time, my mother and father were only 12 and 15 years old respectively.

My mother had no formal education, apart from just three years as a young child in India where she learned to read and write Panjabi. Girls weren't allowed to study. It was frowned upon in the culture. So, instead, as a young child she worked milking the cows, tending the cattle, and making dung patties for fuel. It was hard work for a ten-year-old child.

When she came to the UK, her life didn't get any easier. As a twelve-year-old, she would sit and stare out of the top bedroom window but was never allowed to go out, not even to play. Having two young daughters of my own of a similar age, the contrast between my mother's life and theirs is so stark that it saddens me. I wish my mother could have had the freedom to play like my children have.

It was common for groups of immigrants from different families to share tiny, terraced houses. Uncles, aunts, grandparents, brothers, sisters and wailing babies, all thrown together into a melting pot - that's how my parents lived. Crammed like sardines; five people to a tiny room with shared makeshift beds and mattresses strewn across the floor.

A single toilet outside for up to twenty people and a steel bucket filled with cold water for showers.

They got by with the little money that they could muster working in tough, manual jobs, like steel factories or the local textile firm, with low pay and poor working conditions. A lot of the work was dangerous but there were barely any health and safety rules back then, especially for immigrants.

But that wasn't the worst part.

It was the racism and exclusion that was hard to bear. Even though it was the UK Government that had warmly invited overseas immigrants to help rebuild the country after World War II, the local English residents were not too keen. They saw my grandparents as a threat; a threat to their jobs, to their culture, to their way of life - and they made their feelings known.

I remember it very well, growing up in the late '70s and early '80s; the National Front, the skinheads with the Doc Marten steel-cap boots, the red bomber jackets. The words 'Paki's Out' graffitied on every second shop window that I'd walk past, or the words "Go Home" spray painted on people's garages.

Just last week, I asked my ten and thirteen year old daughters if they had heard of the word 'Paki'. They looked at me very confused. I was shocked. By their age, I had heard that word a thousand times. How things have changed.

That was just life back then and I didn't think anything of it. I didn't feel hard done by. I didn't feel bad. I just didn't know any different; nobody did.

Besides, it was even more difficult for my grandparents and yet they were always very thankful. Despite the difficulties, they were still much better off in this land of opportunity, than those they had left behind in Panjab. They were happy to absorb the racism, the suffering and the sacrifices so that their children would one day have a chance of living a better life than they did.

I'm living proof that those sacrifices paid off in the end and if they're reading this from somewhere above, then I'd like to dedicate this book to them. To my grandparents, to my parents and to all of the immigrants who willingly suffered to give their children a better life.

At the tender age of just fourteen, my mother married my father, who was only seventeen himself at the time, in an arranged marriage. She had never met him, had never spoken to him, and had never even seen a photo. That's how it was in those days.

My mother had to lie at the local Registry Office because she was obviously below the legal age of consent for marriage. By the time she was sixteen, she was already a mother with my eldest sister, and by the age of eighteen, my brother was born. Shortly afterwards, she had another daughter and then, as the youngest of the four kids, I finally made my first appearance into this world.

Instead of remaining a child, my mother had to grow up fast. She became a wife, a full-time mother and a home keeper. She became a cook and cleaner not only for my father and her children, but also for the extended family, including uncles, grandparents, nephews and nieces and anybody else who decided to rock up to the house.

Worst of all, her mother-in-law, my grandmother, wasn't very nice to her; something that I learned about much later in life. My Dad also had his moments of selfishness as he was prone to a drink, or three.

Cinderella had nothing on my dear Mum.

My father worked as a bus driver but there wasn't enough money in the house. So, my mother got a job and worked long, hard hours in a cooker factory from dawn to dusk. We didn't have money for nice things.

One day, as a small child, I remember opening the fridge and reaching in to take a slice of ham when my mother, with tear- filled eyes stopped me. She explained that meat was expensive, and that the ham was only for my father, so he could be strong when he went to work. I still remember that vividly. It breaks my heart to think what my mother must have felt to say those words to me.

We lived a simple life.

We didn't have after school clubs, private schooling, private tuition, personal swimming lessons, car video entertainment systems, a live-in housekeeper, a cleaner, a personal trainer, gym membership, multiple holidays abroad each year, skiing trips, or any of the things that my children have today.

We didn't even have holidays. My first holiday was when I was sixteen when we went back home to Panjab for the first time.

But like most poor kids, I knew no different. All my friends were the same as me and I had a great childhood.

My summer holidays were spent playing football in the park until 10pm every night, until it was too dark to see the ball. I loved every minute of it.

The day that changed my life

I was naturally gifted at school but a little bit naughty, getting into trouble sometimes. When I was nine years old, I was suspended from primary school for a week for misbehaving, but I couldn't tell my parents. So, I ended up just hanging around the school gates until bell-time.

My best friend was much worse than me, but we had a great time together; exploring, playing, and messing about - we were as thick as thieves. I hadn't seen or spoken to him in nearly forty years, but just last year I recognized his photo on the front page of a local newspaper. He had been jailed for eight years for sexual assault, blackmail, and impersonating a police officer.

When I was eleven years old, I remember my dad teaching me how to put on my school tie. It was my first day at secondary school. It was a special day. He was so proud of me and I was so happy. So, here I was heading into 'big school'; a new life, a new adventure. I was going to make my dad so proud, I thought.

But it never happened.

Just three weeks after proudly tying that beautiful Windsor knot for me, my dad was dead. At the age of just forty, he died from a massive heart attack. He had previously survived two serious cardiac arrests but the third one got him.

It was a shock for everybody, except my mom. The doctor had told my dad that he had just six months to live and so mom was already preparing for what was coming next.

What followed was a very difficult time for the family; a period of hardship, uncertainty and fear.

At the time we had a small grocery shop in a very rough area of Coventry called Hillfields. It, was notorious for gangs, drugs, prostitution, gun-crime and murder. My brother was just nineteen years old at the time and after my dad's sudden departure, he now found himself the head of the household. It wasn't long before he was caught up in all of the chaos and fighting, trying to protect the family's livelihood as drug-dealers and gangsters came into the shop refusing to pay, walking out with food and drink.

My mother left her job in the cooker factory to protect her son. She protected us all and single-handedly raised us like a true heroine.

How things have changed now. Looking back, my life is unrecognisable from the time when I was a child; even more unrecognisable if my grandparents had never come to this country.

For thousands of years, my ancestors, have followed the same simple lives. They have ploughed the lush, green fields and tended to their livestock.

I've been to Panjab several times and love nothing more than sitting on the farm just staring out onto the land; listening to the quietness and serenity of what I feel is really still my home. I listen to the stories of my uncles and my cousins. I picture myself standing there, tending to the cattle and crops just as they do today.

It's all a million light years away from the busy, crazy London life that I lead now. As God would have it, my destiny was to work in the hustling, bustling financial heart of the greatest city in the world. Clearly, he had other plans for me. The cows can wait.

So, now I'm surrounded by rushing commuters, billion-pound skyscraper buildings, Michelin-starred restaurants as well as the smell of money and capitalism.

Had it not been for that single boat adventure which my grandparents were brave enough to take, I wouldn't be here today; and you wouldn't be reading this book.

Maybe it was supposed to be this way; so that one day I would have the opportunity of helping potentially millions of people around the world by sharing what I now know.

Thank you for taking a moment to learn about my journey.

I do hope that we are now one step closer to becoming friends, and that you can trust me.

Now, let's begin to answer the questions you came here for.

TIP 13 –
INSIDER TRADING

'Insider trading' is when you act on information that has not yet been made public with the intention of making money.

Even though the penalties for insider trading are harsh, it doesn't stop people from doing it, because there is so much money to be made. This is especially true if you are close to the original source of the information. By the time any information filters its way down to the public, loses its value and sensitivity.

You see, all action takes place at the top of the tree and that's where huge amounts of money is being made. The people of privilege are creaming the money from the top, just because they can. This leaves the retail investor fighting amongst other retail investors for the pitiful scraps that are left over.

A retail investor can be described as any normal, average person. There is mum, your dad, your brother, your sister, your friend, your work colleague... and you. Basically, it's 99% of society.

On the other side of that coin sits the professional investor. He's your financial advisor, stockbroker, tax expert, investment manager, fund manager, trader or anybody else who works in the financial industry.

As you'll find out, the professionals are the biggest scammers and it's them you have to watch out for. That makes sense as they know the game the best; and they know how to play it to win.

It's also true that the majority of professionals are men, which is why you'll notice that I make reference to 'he' and 'him'.

As to insider trading, that's played almost exclusively by the professional men.

To think of it in another way, insider trading is like Chinese Whispers.

The message is clear to begin with and that's where it's most powerful. But over time, it's diluted and altered as it's passed further down the chain, until eventually the information becomes worthless.

Insider trading, in a word, is about secrets – and specifically, not being able to keep one.

Secrets don't stay secret for long

When you were a child and you told your best friend a secret, how long did it stay a secret? Probably not for very long.

Well, it's the same thing when adults share secrets that involve money. The moment somebody hears about an event that is going to make them money, not only are they likely to act upon it, but they're also likely to pass on that information to somebody close to them. That could be a husband or wife, a parent, a friend, a neighbour, a work colleague or somebody else. For most people, it's hard to keep a secret at the best of times and if there is money to be made for lots of people, why not help your loved ones, right?

However, this mentality is reserved only for those further down the food chain, the retail investors. This isn't how the professionals think.

Professionals recognise the very severe consequences of insider trading, which is why they keep this information a very tightly guarded secret. They understand that they will go to jail if they get caught. That's why they operate within very small circles of highly connected individuals, with each person playing a pivotal part of the crime and being financially rewarded according to the size of the role that he or she plays.

Of course, information will still find its way down the chain because it's inevitable that data is leaked. It's very difficult to stop information disseminating because people like to talk.

That's why secrets don't stay secrets for long. As soon as the information leaks through that first level of intelligence, i.e., the company boardroom and corporate advisors, it typically spreads at a faster rate.

That's because people are less scared to use information that has already been passed to them by a third party. They assume they can't be held accountable because there are many more people above them who have also already used this information.

That's different to the professionals who have been directly warned that if they either use the price-sensitive information themselves or pass it to somebody else, they are committing a serious financial crime punishable by a fine and potentially prison. They sign documents accepting their responsibilities. They know they could lose their job, be kicked out of the industry and it could even end their career. That may lead to them losing their home, their marriage, their kids... You get the picture.

The retail investors further down the chain don't bear that responsibility and so information freely flows from their lips to the ears of the next willing listener, of which there is no shortage. An 'insider stock tip' heard down the pub spreads like wildfire.

That can result in the share price jumping up. Therefore, the retail investor is not completely blameless when it comes to insider trading.

They might only make a very tiny fraction of what the guys at the top are making - they're almost certainly ignorant as to the severity of crime they're committing - but even so, their intention is still to make money.

However, the professionals are still the ones to blame. They know the value of the data they hold; they recognise the importance of it, and they understand the responsibility that comes from their profession. Without their greed, insider trading wouldn't exist. It only happens because it is leaked from the top. It never leaks from the bottom.

Price-sensitivity equals massive opportunity

Insider trading all begins with senior professionals at the top of the food chain. This includes boardroom directors, senior accountants, auditors, and corporate finance advisors.

The information can be anything from a record earnings report or share buy-back event, to the announcement of a hostile takeover for a new CEO. It could be a significant contract win, a massive legal compensation pay-out; it could even be a change in government legislation or tax.

Whilst all unannounced price-sensitive information qualifies as being 'inside', the most price-sensitive data is where the big money is made. If a company is about to announce earnings broadly in line with what the market is already expecting, this information is not nearly as valuable to an insider trader as a record earnings report which the market was not expecting. They're both pieces of inside information but one will make you nothing whilst the other could make you very rich.

That's because for information to be valuable, the price of the stock must move, and least expected inside information, will have a greater impact on a stock price that's moving. There's a direct correlation between the level of shock factor and the price movement.

Therefore, some inside traders are selective in when they choose their moment to pull the trigger. They feel it's better to trade illegally once a year on that 'big, unexpected news' for a potential massive pay day than take the higher risk of trading illegally several times a year on 'small news' with less money being made. The regulators don't discriminate on how big the pay day is; all insider trades are illegal.

However, the frequency of trading on inside information also depends on who's committing the crime and what information they have access to.

If you have access to the unpublished accounts of a single FTSE100 firm, who make two announcements each year, then you have just two chances in that year to hit the jackpot. If you have access to dozens of FTSE100 accounts, you can pick and choose your trades.

Your position and also your financial position are important to consider, too.

If you're the CEO of a firm and you're already earning several million pounds a year, you probably won't be tempted to trade on your firm's own inside information. Not only would it be quite obvious and harder to disguise. There is also the risk of losing your job, which is too great; you already earn big money after all.

But if you're an accountant earning £50,000 a year and you've got a low-risk way to make another £50,000 on inside information that you have access to well, that's probably more tempting. You can potentially double your salary, thank you very much.

There are certain jobs where individuals are constantly 'inside'. Their whole life is built around not telling secrets. It's like being James Bond and working for MI5; your sworn to secrecy.

For example, if you work in the corporate finance team at Goldman Sachs, or in the mergers and acquisitions department for JP Morgan, you probably have mountains of high-quality, price sensitive information at your fingertips. Even if you're not a seasoned 'criminal' yourself, that's worth a lot of money to somebody who is.

Of course, these individuals are strictly monitored and there are many safeguards in place, but it's impossible to stop information flowing to other people.

Accountants, advisors, bookkeepers, traders, account executives, corporate financiers, investment strategists, directors, bank managers, compliance officers, tax consultants... quite frankly, anybody could be authorized to hold inside information at any time.

There's a big pool of people for professional insider traders to target. Because those people aren't doing any trades themselves, they feel disconnected from the process and therefore are less likely to be caught. Their job is to just simply provide the data and get paid for it.

Most professionals who have access to all this dynamite information don't really want to get their hands dirty trying to trade on it. They'd rather leave that to the professionals, and that's where the network gangs come into play.

Network operations

To pull off a mastermind insider trading scam operation requires multiple layers to work.

Firstly, the person with the information has to be as far removed from the actual trades as possible, which is why multiple accomplices working in a chain are required. A higher number of layers and greater distances between the information provider and the person executing the insider trade makes the crime more difficult to uncover.

The person providing the information should also have no idea what trades are being executed and when. He just receives a fixed price for his information based on how valuable it is, i.e., how 'shocking' it is to the market.

This is a risk to the buyer of that information. He's gambling there is enough money to be made from the information and that the market reacts in a certain way. That's why speed is important. It's also why there has to be absolute trust between the insider and the scammer executing the trade.

The insider can't sell the same information multiple times because that diminishes the value to the person buying the information. It also increases the risk of getting caught as the price starts to move in a certain direction long before the announcement is made, which will attract eyeballs from the authorities.

That's why a big premium is paid by the insider traders to people who have exclusive access to information. If there are ten people who have a certain piece of inside information, this means it can be potentially sold on at least ten times and those people can sell it on another ten times, and so on.

As we know, to stop information leaking is impossible.

Even if it's not sold on multiple times, it will still find its way by trickling down to other people connected with the company. For example, that could be stockbrokers, investment managers, portfolio analysts, researchers, and so on. Or it might be financial advisors, tax advisors and pension consultants. There might also be connections with other suppliers, competitor firms, or business associates.

It's like trying to stop water from leaving a flimsy, paper cup. It'll hold for a while but at some point, it just bursts and spills everywhere, right the way down to Joe, the black cab driver.

As it goes further and further out, the information loses its value. That's why the professional scammers are right at the top. They want information as soon as it's known and they don't want anybody else to have it until they've used it themselves. They want the water whilst it's in the cup and before it spills out.

They also want information they can act on quickly. There's little value in knowing about an event that's going to happen in three months' time, because by that time, the information would have been dissipated into the market and factored into the price.

They want to know information that's being released tomorrow or next week. That gives them the best chance of keeping the information to themselves before others can act on it; before the price starts to move and before the opportunity is gone.

It's all about the timing. The value of the information reduces from the moment it starts to feed down from the original source; the clock starts ticking.

As it trickles down that slippery pole of corruption, from the financial professionals to the rest of society, the value of that inside information is eroding away. It can even become a negative value in some cases.

By the time the retail investor gets the information, two things have happened. Firstly, through Chinese Whispers, the real information is so distorted from the truth that it bears no resemblance to the facts.

Secondly, even if the data is accurate, there are so many people who have already acted on that information, that the price has already moved. In the case of, let's say, a positive trading announcement, the market price has already moved up by so much that it's actually ready for a correction (price reversal). The retail investor is so late to the party that he's buying at such a massive premium that when the 'positive' announcement is made, the price goes down and not up!

Ironically, the inside information puts the retail investors in a worse position than they would have been without it.

Small accounts

The alternative to executing massive million-pound deals is to distribute the information more thinly. This is where hundreds of individuals, usually from less affluent, developing countries have share dealing accounts set up in their names. Relatively small trades are then executed on their account, amounting to a few thousand pounds. The individual gets a % profit and the deal is so small that it is unlikely to get any attention.

It's also set up in overseas jurisdictions where regulations are more relaxed. I mean, will the regulatory authority in the Philippines really care about investigating if one of their citizen's buys £5,000 of shares in a British listed company?

Even if they did, where's the proof of insider trading?

The insider rules of the UK don't extend to other countries and the UK regulatory body isn't going to chase somebody 7,000 miles away for a £5,000 trade.

Even if the person was investigated, which is highly unlikely, they couldn't give any names because they have no clue about what's going on. Their contact would simply be a local recruiter. They'd have no idea of who was pulling the strings. Their role is simply to allow somebody to trade in their name. It's like a drug smuggler using a drug mule. That person gets paid a fraction of the real money that is made and if things ever go wrong, they become the sacrificial lamb.

There's a lot more organisation involved but the payday can still be quite big because although the deal size is small, it involves hundreds of people across different continents. The small deal size also reduces the risk, and means the scam can go undetected for many years. Deals of that size fly straight under the radar. Individuals can open not one but five, ten or even twenty trading accounts and trade them all simultaneously. Even if a share dealing account is shut down for any reason, it can be reopened with another brokerage firm online in a few minutes, which makes it very difficult to stop.

If there are any investigations, it's the small guy who takes the rap, while the big bosses who masterminded the operation just disappear.

Trying to uncover insider trading crimes in places like Pakistan,

Kenya, Nigeria, Mexico, Belize or Ukraine is never going to be easy. In these countries, and many more just like them, there is a distinct lack of corporate governance and plenty of scope for corruption and financial bribery. There is very little the UK authorities can do.

Loose lips sink ships

Insider trading is more prevalent today than at any point in history because information is more freely available than ever before. It's a perfect breeding ground for insider traders as more and more City professionals have access to classified information, which they can send to the other side of the world in just a few seconds, with no chance of being traced.

There have been many times over the years where I have had access to sensitive inside information as part of my work. So, if I can get quick and easy access to inside information, so, too, can thousands of other people who work in my profession.

Whether it's a stockbroker, like me, who has classified information on a company about to dilute its price by issuing more shares, or an accountant who is preparing the end of year accounts for a company listed on the Nasdaq, the result is the same.

The single, most valuable commodity in the world today is not cash, gold or Bitcoin; it's information.

There are literally hundreds of people walking around the City of London right now who have access to information worth millions of pounds. It's insane. The money is not in the briefcase they're holding in their hand but in the numbers, they're holding in their head.

The total sum of that information runs into hundreds of millions of pounds. It just needs to be monetized.

And it's not just in the City of London.

Take a moment to consider how many accountants there are right now who are preparing the accounts for thousands of listed companies on stock markets all over the world. Now consider all the legal firms preparing to defend libel cases for companies who have not yet announced their troubles to the marketplace. Let's think about all the employees who are aware that the company they work for has just landed a massive contract, soon to be announced to the public.

How about the hundreds of government officials, politicians, and thinktanks who are either directly responsible, or are just aware of, major policy changes which will significantly impact the profitability of companies; even entire industries.

Now we need to think about all the people who are in some way connected to those accountants, lawyers, company directors, policy makers, regulators, politicians, and advisors. Think about their spouses, their family members, their children, their parents, their friends.

And what about all the people who regulate the oil and gas industry, or the utility sector, manufacturing, land and property, technology, telecoms and pharmaceuticals. How about all the staff responsible for overseeing high level policies and procedures?

What about the advertising regulators, or the massive media companies who get the news before everybody else does? Think of all the companies they are planning to investigate, or fine, or suspend or even shut down. What would happen to their share price after those announcements were made?

Think about the travel industry, retail, hospitality, medicine and healthcare. Consider what happened during Covid with the lockdowns and vaccines. If you knew that the entire restaurant industry was about to be shut down, could you make money by shorting that industry? Yes, a lot of money.

If you knew that Pfizer had been awarded the mandate to administer 20 million Covid vaccine jabs, do you think you could make a lot of money? Hell, yeah – a life changing amount of money; and some people did.

How about the directors of billion-pound Premiership football clubs who know about player transfers before they take place? Think about how that information could be used with spread-betting and sports betting companies.

What about the entire sports industry where billions of pounds are gambled each year... horse racing, cricket, athletics, boxing? People on the inside have information worth a lot of money. Players who are injured, for example; or maybe players who are implicit in rigging the result.

Think about all of these industries, all of their regulators, all the companies that work within these sectors and all the employees who work in those companies. Just add them all up in your mind. >ï you see in your mind a massive spider web of people all inter-connected by valuable pieces of information and data? It's a matrix worth many tens of billions of pounds.

And we're not finished yet.

What about the ratings agencies? Massively influential firms, like Standard & Poor's and Moody's, are responsible for assigning the risk ratings of some of the biggest corporations, and even governments, in the world.

What would happen to the share price of a company that is about to be downgraded?

How many millions of pounds could that wipe off an investment? What if you knew that was going to happen before anybody else?

How about knowing a decision by the Russian government to restrict the supply of gas to Western Europe before anybody else? Or the US government's decision to place sanctions on Iran? Or perhaps a decision by OPEC to increase the production of oil? Or it could be North Korea's decision to declare war on South Korea and start firing nuclear tests on its border?

Whatever the news is and wherever it has emanated from, it's priceless to an insider trader.

The amount of money that can be made on big economic data points, like Non-Farm Payroll data showing the employment figures from the United States, GDP figures, and a whole host of other macroeconomic numbers, is almost unfathomable.

How about the Monetary Policy Committee (MPC) who decide

on interest rate decisions, which not only move share prices but can literally move every financial asset, including entire stock indices. They move the bond markets, the currency markets, the swaps market, the derivative markets, mortgages, bank interest deposit and loan rates. They change the price of just about everything.

How about the Federal Reserve, the European Central Bank (ECB) and all other central banks around the world?

Of course, interest rate information is just one piece of economic data. What about the dozens of other pieces of economic data released every day in pretty much every developed country in the world?

The list goes on and on...and on.

I think you're getting the picture. It's quite a task to solve.

Information is power

Controlling information and accessing price-sensitive data is the easiest way to get rich.

Whoever has access to information becomes rich. Whoever has information before everybody else becomes very, very rich.

That's why social media platforms, like Google and Facebook (Meta), are so powerful; it's because they have access to your information. It's a different type of information to the price-sensitive trading data that's used in insider trading, but it's just as useful for marketing purposes.

The amount of money, and the final number is so big that, quite frankly, it's too large to comprehend.

That's because the money can be hidden in investment machines, like the foreign exchange market which supports not billions but trillions of dollars of transactions per day. It's easy to hide a few million pounds when the market is so large.

It's impossible to police completely.

This may all seem like a faraway place that you're completely disconnected from, but insider trading secrets affect you more than you may think.

It's not a victimless crime because for every winner in the financial markets, including the stock market, there has to be a loser. Those combined losers are the millions of average investors who are oblivious to what going on. They don't have the information that others have so their decisions are based on what they do know, which is not a lot.

The professionals are making better informed decisions because they know things that you don't long before you have a chance to find out the information.

You're playing the investment game without really knowing the game at all. Even if you do know the game, they're cheating. How do you possibly win against somebody like that?

Imagine playing a game of poker against somebody who knows what the dealer's next card will be. That's what's happening on a mass scale and it's costing you money every year.

As the scammers make their money, you're losing yours. You just don't notice it because they're taking it out of your pension pot a few pounds at a time. Collectively, it's costing millions of pounds, but you never get to see that.

90% of takeovers involve insider trading

In January 2018, *The Independent* reported that the FCA's own figures showed almost 20% of all takeovers were preceded by "suspicious share price movement". That's staggering.

It means that at least one in every five take overs leaked information to a sufficiently large number of professionals scammers, who then purchased a large enough number of shares to move the share price by an acceptable amount, such that the price movement could be detected as suspicious.

Here's the worrying thing. If 20% is actually detected, it means the real number must be much, much higher.

Professional insider scammers are very smart in covering their tracks. They can disguise their buy orders amongst all the sell orders without pushing the price up. If the price does go up, they will usually stop buying to avoid attracting suspicion.

This means that should as many as one in five be found to be suspicious, the real number is probably 80% or even 90% of the time. Nobody knows the real numbers.

If there isn't a 'suspicious' price movement, it doesn't mean insider trading isn't happening; it just means it's being hidden very well, or amateur scammers are using the information ineffectively so the price is not moving.

An amateur scammer (a retail insider) might make, say, a £500 bet on some inside information, but a professional insider might make a £5 million bet on the same information.

Obviously, £500 won't show up on any price charts and so it goes undetected. But that's not to say insider trading didn't happen. It did happen, just not very effectively.

The authorities also don't want to concern the public with what's really going on. It's hardly good for investor confidence if we're told there are people making loads of money before any takeover is announced; which means that everybody else is at a disadvantage because they're acting on old information.

Most insider scams are very discrete.

Professional insider trading scams are run like business operation where trades are executed in a way which doesn't create unusual price action. This requires discipline because it means the scammers can't be too greedy. It's very tempting to put all of your chips on number five at the roulette table but if your number keeps coming in, the casino will eventually figure out that you've somehow rigged the system and you'll be kicked out.

So, the professionals have to place a few chips on the losing numbers, too, to avoid their account being flagged. Should their trading account be looked into, it will show some losses and therefore help to avoid suspicion.

Scammers also need to think about playing the long game and not putting their valuable 'information mole' at risk. Once they have a reliable insider, they can trust to release regular information, they can't jeopardize him or her. They can't put their mole at risk. It's like killing the golden goose laying all those wonderful eggs.

Therefore, price movement has to be controlled so it stays within the realms of usual market volatility; meaning the authorities are none the wiser. If the price doesn't move, there is nothing 'suspicious' or unusual.

To avoid detection, the trades are also evenly spread and executed across multiple platforms, over different time zones, in varying geographical jurisdictions and through different products, including CFDs, options, spread bets, futures contracts and so on.

There are even less obvious trades that can be placed, which are not as profitable for the scammer but are attractive because they are impossible to detect.

For example, if Shell, the oil company, is set to announce record profits, there's a good chance that BP stock will also go up in price that same day. If Shell goes up by, say, 8%, BP might go up by, say, 3% because of its association, i.e., it's in the same sector.

A 3% move doesn't sound like much, but you can multiply 3% to make 30%, or even 300% using derivatives. Even the tiniest of price movement can result in massive profits for scammers.

Best of all, it goes completely undetected because BP didn't make an announcement, so there can be no accusation of insider trading.

Bad news equals maximum profits

There are, of course many different statistics; some more honest than others.

The Times, for example, found that in 67% of cases where a FTSE100 company had issued a major profit warning, its share price fell significantly one day before the warning was made public. That's a staggering figure because, once again, if 67% of cases showed unusual price action, that must suggest the real number is much higher.

Insider trading on a profit warning is also more detectable than, say, a big contract win, because anything that results in a price going down, which will potentially cost people money, evokes a stronger investor reaction; a more desperate reaction.

If somebody knows a company is about to announce something which is going to cause their shares to drop 20%, they're far more likely to sell the shares quickly. They're not going to hang around and try to be too clever about how to disguise their tracks. if they don't act quickly, they know they could lose thousands of pounds. They're less worried about getting caught and so are more likely to act because the risk of not doing anything will impact them negatively. That's the emotion of fear.

Compare that to investing in a company in which somebody doesn't already hold stock. Then it becomes an emotion of greed, which is not as strong as fear. If they don't act, they won't make any money but at least they won't lose anything either. Therefore, they're going to be more sensible and measured with their trades.

That's why the statistics for insider trading on profit warnings is more obvious.

Downward pressure on price is also more visible because share prices always fall faster than they go up. That's just the mechanics of how share trading works; meaning there is always more money to be made with bad news than good news, if you know what you're doing.

It's not just people who want to sell shares that hold shares. There will be many insider traders who will short stocks using CFDs, spread bets, financial futures and options.

This may all still seem slightly innocuous but there is a darker, sinister side to this. Money is never far from real crime and insider trading is no different.

The City of London currently run several independent groups of very well-connected financial professionals who act as moles for some of the world's biggest gangs. They are drug warlords, terrorist organizations and criminals of the highest order. We're talking syndicated crime networks, gangster families, the ruling elite, oil oligarchs and even entire corrupt states.

It's an odd relationship that, on paper, shouldn't exist but not only does it exist, it flourishes.

Insider moles who disseminate insider information are respectable, pin-striped, middle-aged gentlemen who live in large, detached houses in the leafy Surrey suburbs. They have access to a few seemingly harmless numbers from a company's balance sheet, or information on the government's statistics; you wouldn't look twice at them if you saw them walking down the street. Yet they're responsible for fueling gangs, murder, international crime, drug cartels, terrorism and much more.

From doners to dollars

The story I'm about to tell you could have been taken straight out of that brilliant film, The Goodfellas.

It was called 'Operation Tabernula' and it took the authorities more than eight years to crack this case; involving 320 hours of secretly recorded telephone conversations and forty-six full binders of evidence. It also cost the taxpayer an estimated $20million! That just shows how hard it is to pin down these crimes.

The ringleader was an Iranian man by the name of Parvizi, known his friends as 'Fatty'. He came to the UK with nothing after the Iranian Revolution in the late 1970s. Like most immigrants, he did what he could, working in labour-intensive jobs to make ends meet. He first worked in a doner kebab shop and other fast-food outlets as a pizza delivery boy.

However, he had a problem; he enjoyed gambling too much, but he knew that selling kebabs wasn't going to be enough to support his love of the poker table. During one of his frequent casino trips, he bumped into a guy called Maxwell-Brown who went on to introduce him to some very wealthy people, including Nigerian and Saudi Arabian princes.

It wasn't long before Fatty was mingling with the elite and super high net worth individuals. His network grew and he soon connected with an investment banker on the inside who had access to corporate information.

Fatty saw the opportunity and put both of his grubby hands on it. He became the middleman and retrieved price-sensitive information from the banker and passed it onto his new wealthy friends.

As the poor son of an immigrant, it was everything he had dreamed of.

Over a few years in his new messenger mole role, he amassed a reported personal net fortune of more than £70million! That's staggering.

By that time, he had recruited numerous accomplices to help him with the scam. They all had colourful names, like, 'The Fixer', 'The Banker', 'The Mad Mathematician', 'The Fruit', and 'The Uncle'.

The senior investment banker feeding the inside information was a guy called Martyn Dodgso. He worked closely with a chartered accountant by the name of Andrew Hind.

These two unassuming, suit-wearing, silver haired, educated, highly intelligent men are the kind of people you would trust with your life savings. You would never have guessed what they were up to, knee-deep in the gangster world. When it was time for the judge to give his summation at court, they were both handed heavy custodial sentences.

Dodgson had worked for Morgan Stanley, Lehman Brothers and Deutsche Bank; he always had regular access to insider information. What he didn't have was an outlet to monetize it. After meeting Fatty, he was able to sell the information on to very wealthy royal individuals for a lot of money.

The encrypted information was passed through unregistered mobile phones; payments were either in cash or as 'payments in kind' to avoid detection. But despite their efforts to hide their tracks, the gang was eventually caught thanks to the National Crime Agency (NCA), which supported the FCA by providing surveillance.

It was reported in the press as a highly sophisticated gang of criminal masterminds, but I'm not sure if that was true. It was really just a bloke who worked in a kebab shop, who connected some people together. There are many more sophisticated gangs who know the game better than Fatty who are operating today, flying under the radar, without raising suspicion.

There are many more very wealthy princes, Arabs, royal elites, corrupt politicians, oligarchs, oil tycoons, wealthy entrepreneurs, crypto investors, terrorists, gangs, drug dealers and warlords, just looking for somebody on the inside who can give their cash a home.

So, the next time you see a big news announcement, and think 'wow', just think of all the people who said 'wow' before you.

TIP 12 –
NOBODY REALLY KNOWS

The zero game

When I found out about this insider trading tip, I didn't really believe what I was hearing. I was in denial for quite a few months until I was able to come to terms with it. That's because it completely turned what I thought to be true about the financial markets, upside down and inside out.

What I'm talking about is the 'zero-sum game' and it works like this.

The investment ecosystem of shares, bonds, currency etc. has a finite amount of money. In other words, there is only so much money in the world. A good comparative for money is energy - it's not created, and it's not lost - it simply passes from one person to another.

That's not to say that over time, wealth can't be created. Wealth can increase through improved efficiencies, better technologies, greater labour output and better allocation of capital, but that all takes time. It takes months, even years, for countries to grow their economic output.

This means that in the very short term, i.e., a few days, very little economic output takes place. There might be a small increase in Gross Domestic Product (GDP) per company, but nothing significant. If you think about the stock market as a collection of companies, each producing a small piece of national economic output, you can see why the stock market, at any given moment in time, has a static level of growth and therefore, a finite amount of cash tied up within it.

It follows, therefore, that if somebody makes money in the stock market, this can only happen because there has been a transfer of wealth. In other words, money is being passed from one person to the next, which means that if you're becoming richer in the stock market, somebody must be becoming poorer.

You can see this in action in the foreign exchange market every day. Trillions of dollars moving daily back and forth, from one investment bank to another, and then onto another, and then back to the original bank again. Over and over again. Nothing of economic value is being created but yet, every day, somebody or some firm is becoming richer by several million pounds. The next day, they're also becoming poorer by several million pounds.

It's the same for stocks and shares.

That's where the zero-sum concept comes into play. If you add up all of the losses and profits from all the people trading in the stock market on any given day, the sum should be zero.

Of course, in reality it's not quite as simple as that and there are some other factors to consider. However, this is not a technical book and for the sake of keeping things simple, let's work on the premise that for every winner there is a loser;

which, in the short term at least, is largely true.

So, if I'm making £1,000, and unless that money is coming out of thin air, presumably somebody must be losing £1,000.

The problem is that when you dive a little deeper, this also uncovers a horrible truth you weren't expecting.

The devastating truth

If the market has finite resources and value, which, in the short term, it does; the zero-sum game means that somebody can only win when somebody loses. Or, put another way, professionals have more chance of winning when retail investors lose.

Or you could rephrase that to professionals become rich when retail investors become poor.

Clearly the professionals are always going to win because they have access to better pricing, more reliable data and faster systems. They also have a much higher level of knowledge, finely tuned skills and experience. They know all the secrets of the game, the little shortcuts, and they also have those useful contacts to tip the balance in their favour when they need to.

If they were playing poker, they wouldn't just know what cards were coming next, they'd actually be responsible for dealing their own cards; that's how heavily stacked the cards are in their favour. They hold so many advantages and they have the ability to extract money from the vast majority of retail investors; those who have worse pricing, less reliable data and slower systems - basically anybody who isn't a professional.

The quickest way for them to win is to find the weakest links and identify investors, who have the least knowledge, the least finely tuned skills and the least experience. Their job is to go out hunting for those injured gazelles.

If you think of it another way, the professionals want you to lose.

Now you can see why the zero-sum game is a problem.

But there's another problem - it's not obvious that the professionals are out to get you and that's because of the anonymous nature of trading. You never know who you're trading against. So, when you lose money there's no transparency about the other side of the trade – how much did they lose? Who are they?

It's also quite possible that the person you lost money to, also lost money to somebody else. That means somebody further down the line made money from both of us, complicating things even further.

Therefore, we don't think of it in the way that we should; we don't view it in the "I win-you lose" sort of way. But that's exactly how we should view it because that's how the game is being played.

You win small, I win big

There's another big problem in uncovering the truth. Over the long term, the stock market always goes up. Boy, does that make things even more confusing. It allows the professionals to cover up their dirty tracks; they can still rip you off and you can still make money.

It's really hard to accuse somebody of ripping you off when you make money.

But what if you were only receiving 50% of what you deserve, for the risk you are taking? That's how the zero-sum game works.

The market goes up by 10% but you only make 5%. What happened to the other 5%?

That my friends, went to the professionals. The 5% is lost through inefficiency, a lack of market knowledge, an inferior investment strategy, bad pricing and poor timing. It's gone, it doesn't really matter where, it's just gone, and it definitely didn't go to you.

But because you still make 5%, you don't complain.

Nobody told you that for the risk you were taking, you should have been paid twice as much. You didn't know that you should have earned 10%.

To put it bluntly, you're being cheated.

You're taking on a disproportionate amount of risk for a relatively small return. But nobody is telling you that. The average investor has no clue how to calculate risk. Think about it for a second, do you know how to calculate the risk of your portfolio?

No, you probably don't; that's not your fault. But you can see the problem.

A trade can only be assessed as good or bad. There are two components; how much money you make and how much risk you take. But if the risk is missing, the assessment can be manipulated. A stockbroker, investment manager or financial advisor can easily tell you to be happy with the 7% you earned last year, but conveniently hide the fact that the risk justified a return of at least 15%.

Even in poor market conditions, you can still make money and you almost certainly will, certainly over the long term, but that's not the point.

The fact you make it to the other side of the road doesn't negate the fact that you very nearly got knocked over by a double decker bus. It doesn't matter whether or not you saw the bus coming or even knew that it existed, you still took on that risk. The professionals pushed you into that road, hoping you wouldn't get hit, but they knew full well what they were doing.

Retail investors are always the guinea pigs; they take the risks. It's the professionals who gamble with their money. They take their commission, fees and other charges but when it comes to the risk, they take none of it. That's always on the investor, the end client and that's on you.

They stand behind you while you face the barrage of bullets and enemy fire.

When the market is generous then great, you both get to eat, and that makes you feel good. But what you don't realise is that you're still eating less than the professionals, even though you're paying the whole bill. But worse still, when the market is not generous, and rations are small, somebody has to go hungry and unfortunately, that person is always going to be you.

Professional investors 1 – retail investors 0

Think about it for long enough and slowly it begins to make perfect sense.

If your football teamed up against another team which had ten players, each resembling Lionel Messi, but the eleventh player was an out-of-shape couch potato, very slow, with zero talent, what might be the best strategy to win that game?

It won't surprise you that the financial world works in the same way.

The professionals want to trade against that out of shape, slow, clueless investor. The one that takes his stock picks from the Daily Mail or leaves his portfolio to his financial advisor and looks at it once a year.

Retail investors are easy money; they're easy prey.

A professional doesn't want to compete with a fellow professional who has access to the same information, knowledge and resources. They want the easy pickings - the retail investor who doesn't understand the game, is the low-hanging fruit of the money tree.

That's not to say professionals only compete with retail

investors. The professionals also trade amongst themselves too. They have no choice.

Quite frankly, they don't care who they take money from. It's just that the investors who know the least will be the ones who lose the most.

In certain markets, like the foreign exchange market and the bond market, most of the players are the big investment banks. So, professionals have no option but to compete with each other against the best of the best.

Apart from the odd retail investor who usually gets wiped out in the first six months of trading, 99% of the foreign exchange volume goes through the professionals.

It may seem unfair that professionals target retail investors but actually it's completely rational. Their goal is to make as much money as possible in the easiest and fastest way possible, with the least amount of risk. It's usually not even a conscious decision.

By default, the worst poker player will be the first one to leave the table as he hands over his chips to the best poker player.

People are anonymous. This isn't personal; besides, capitalism doesn't care about your feelings.

If somebody spends every working hour of every day, for many years, developing a skill then they're going to win. If they are rewarded and get paid more money, and bonuses, for perfecting their craft and becoming better at their job, if it's how they put food on the table for their family; well, they're going to be good at it; better than anybody who does it part-time or for fun.

By default, the better they become, the more money they make, and the more you end up losing.

Ripping off retail investors

If it all came down to just skill and knowledge, you could argue let the best person win. But it's much more than that because there are lies, deception, and deceit.

The game is rigged, it's heavily fixed in favour of the professionals.

It's much more than just a higher skill, greater knowledge, better prices, or faster trading platforms. There's one thing that changes everything – manipulation of the rules.

Professionals know the game so well they can even change the rules of the game. They can present the game inaccurately to their retail investor clients.

Take CFD firms, for example. For well over a decade, there were dozens of CFD firms in the City of London. They all knew that every one of their clients had a less than 20% chance of making money. That's right – less than a one in five chances.

Imagine if your doctor said you needed an operation but didn't disclose the fact that you have a less than 20% chance of survival. He pushes you to have the operation because he gets paid a lot of commission, even though he knows that you're probably going to die. Well, that's the scenario that happened with CFDs for more than a decade.

There were literally hundreds of CFD brokers collectively making tens of thousands of calls a day, pitching their services to unsuspecting individuals.

They talked about all of the glorious benefits of CFDs, like the ability to go short, no stamp duty and lower deposits, but they never disclosed the most important thing - the client had an 80% chance of losing all of their money.

Or at least not until many years later when the FCA made it compulsory for all firms to disclose this fact.

It's just another example of an insider City secret; a scam that the professionals used to manipulate the retail investor.

Just think about the odds again for a second.

Would you ever go into any sort of bet, let alone one which jeopardized your pension, where you had an 80% chance of losing and only a 20% chance of winning? That would be crazy, and you'd never do it.

But yet hundreds of new, unsuspecting clients signed up with CFD firms every month. Thousands of investors flooded the CFD market, and every day, week, month and year, there was a mass transfer of wealth from retail investors to the professional CFD firms, and their advisors.

Whilst the CFD loop has now been closed, there are many more which remain open.

Brokers and fund managers regularly rip off retail investors through non-transparent charges, excessive fees and unfair costs, including exit penalties. It's all possible because the professionals hold the knowledge. They know the game.

It's a different way of extracting money but the end result is the same. The professionals either take money by beating you in the stock market, or they take money from you before you even get to the stock market.

They're constantly taking chips out of your pocket before you even sit at the table. Then they take a big chunk of chips when you're sitting at the table through manipulation, deceit and trickery. They take another chunk by being more knowledgeable and skilled than you. When you've had enough, and you leave the table, they'll steal a few more chips just for good measure.

None of it is illegal.

It's not even hidden. It can't be hidden anymore because the regulators have made a big thing in recent years about 'full disclosure', so the professionals have no option but to tell the truth.

But they still have full autonomy on how they present the truth.

When you're an expert in your field and have superior knowledge, you can present anything in a very favourable light. Any professional in their field can pull the wool over the eyes of the average Joe.

A trusting patient will believe anything that an experienced doctor will tell them.

Play a different game

So, here's my advice. First, don't try and play any game until you know the rules really well. Second, don't make a habit of playing against people better than you in any industry, especially not the financial world or the zero-sum game.

You're going to lose every time.

It's the same for me. If I'm going to play chess, my first choice for an opponent probably wouldn't be the reigning World Chess Grandmaster champion.

The problem with the financial game is that everybody has to play it. We don't have a choice. We all use money.

We all receive money; we all save money and we all spend money. That means we are all affected by interest rates, inflation and tax. We all have pensions or investments. We all have savings or debt. We all have mortgages or rent to pay. We all have bills to pay.

We are surrounded by money, 24-7. Everywhere we turn, everywhere we look, we are reminded of money. We can't get away from it, not for a minute, even if we wanted to.

Therefore, we need to know the game. Period.

It doesn't matter whether it's on the stock market, in bonds, foreign exchange, cash deposits, credit card debt, mortgages, property investments, taxes or anything else, you need to know what's going on. Each of these markets has its nuances and you need to know them.

The less you know, the greater the risk of losing your money, and eventually, over time, little by little, you'll get wiped out. At the very least, you'll end up with a pension pot that doesn't reflect your fifty years of hard work.

It's like the lion hunting the injured gazelle. The lion attacks the weak, the easy kill.

That's what the professionals are doing now. They're weighing you up, seeing how much you don't know.

Then, at the perfect moment and with a smile on their face, they'll crush you.

A master of disguise

Investors who have superior knowledge and experience will make more good decisions and fewer poor ones. This will help them move up the ladder to financial freedom; one good decision at a time. Those who leave it to chance, gamble or just don't want to learn, will make more bad decisions than good, quickly accelerating them down the road towards eternal poverty.

That's just life. A series of good and bad decisions.

The problem is that the stock market, because of its long-term bullish trend, is a master of disguise. It won't allow you to see your bad decisions. In fact, it will disguise them so well it will trick you into believing you know what you're doing.

That's dangerous.

The increase in your portfolio over time makes you feel like you're winning, that you're doing something right. But you're not. That's just the stock market going up with the passage of time.

Being ignorant and blissful at the same time is a lethal Combination for any investor.

It's the same with property investing.

It's impossible not to make money from buying a house if you hold onto it for long enough. Over a ten, fifth teen or twenty-year time horizon, you probably have a 99% chance of making money. But that doesn't mean you weren't ripped off.

Your estate agent pushed up the price by a few thousand pounds because he knew you loved the property so much. Sour mortgage advisor went to the lender that gave him the biggest commission. Your solicitor charged you extra because he knew you weren't going anywhere else. The architect doubled his price because he knew you were desperate to do the loft conversion. The builder fixed a roof that was never leaking. The gas company put you on the higher variable energy rate instead of the cheaper fixed rate, and the gardener laid the cheap artificial grass, but charged you for the more expensive one. Even the cleaner stole a tenner from your desk drawer when you weren't looking.

Despite all of that, you still made money on that house.

Along the way, for many, many years, you were continually screwed by one professional after another; each one an expert in their field - and you still made money.

It's the same with the stock market; you can get screwed every year and because you don't know about it, and you're still making some money, you feel okay about it.

The worst thing is that each poor decision is so well disguised, you can't learn from its lesson. It means the same mistakes are repeated over and over again. Unfortunately, none of us know what we don't know.

If I put my hand over a burning match, I'm going to learn my lesson pretty damn quickly not to do it again. But the stock market burns people every day without them realising.

Stock market mistakes are not just hard to spot, they're impossible to uncover. To the untrained eye, to the retail investor, they're completely missed.

In contrast, to the trained eye of a professional, there is a clear distinction between good and bad trades, between good and bad investment decisions.

Knowing how the game is played is integral to your success.

You may have heard of the zero-sum game before you read this chapter, but I doubt you ever thought it's responsible for putting a great big 'X' on your back for the professionals to shoot at.

Regulation is your friend

So, what's the solution?

First, don't overload yourself with too much information.

You're not going to become an expert so don't even try to become one. It's no fun, a lot of hard work and completely unnecessary. Just focus on the core fundamentals, the basic rules of the game. That's it.

Second, learn about the regulations and compliance. Investing is not just about the trade. It's the mechanics of the trade, too, including how it is executed and settled.

It's understanding the protections you have as a retail investor. One of the benefits of being a retail investor over a professional investor, is that the regulations will protect you more.

The problem is that most retail investors don't understand what that protection looks like. They don't really understand the complaints process or how to maximise their chances of earning financial redress. Many investors don't even know they can claim, or how to claim effectively.

That's a big problem because you need to learn how to defend yourself effectively. Hopefully your professional advisor is genuine and sincere. But, if you end up with a firm that cares more about their profit than your performance, then at least you know your stuff.

Make them aware you know your stuff. They won't mess with somebody who knows the game. If they know that you are prepared, they will leave you alone. They'll take the easy target frst; the one that won't complain, that doesn't know the system, that doesn't ask any questions, that isn't prepared. That's who they want to win against.

That doesn't mean you should antagonise your advisor or

make life difficult for him by questioning everything that he says. There has to be mutual respect between you both.

There's always a happy middle ground between bending over with your trousers around your ankles and being that annoying client who inspects every single clause in the terms of business with a magnifying glass.

Over the years, countless policies have been introduced by the regulators to ensure financial firms treat retail investors more fairly. They're all designed to protect you.

But despite all of the regulation in the world, without understanding how you can use them to protect yourself, they have limited value. They'll still protect you but not nearly as much.

A life skill you need to learn

Investing is like riding a bicycle and regulatory protection is like giving the cyclist a helmet, knee guards, elbow pads, and protective gloves. That's all great, but the person still needs to learn how to ride the bike. No amount of padding is going to help him.

Even with padding, falling off still hurts.

That's why if he falls down enough, he might just get fed up and one day throw the bloody bike in the bin.

Except he can't. Because this bike doesn't disappear.

That bicycle is with him for life. It's the money machine bike

– stocks, bonds, property, cash, gold, crypto... it's the world of finance and investing.

He's going to need to learn how to ride that bike eventually and if he doesn't (many people never do), he just ends up living a life of discomfort and pain because he keeps falling over. He stays poor. If he was born rich, over time he becomes poor.

Of course, he doesn't realise he's falling over. He just knows that he never seems to make any real financial progress in life. He may not even be 'poor' in financial terms; he might have a nice house, and a nice car, be middle-class, but if he's worried about money, then he's still poor. It's a mindset.

A lot of middle-England and middle-America and middle- any other country you can think of, are in a middle-class poverty trap. They're not poor, they have money. But they don't have freedom in the truest sense.

They're tied to that job because of the pension. They're tied to having those two or three holidays a year. They're tied to thinking carefully about how much money they can draw down this year. They're not in a bad place and better off than the poorest, for sure, but it's not real financial freedom.

They still think about, and even worry about, their money, about their finances.

How is that possible? If somebody works for fifty years of their life in a decent job, how is it possible that öåäü still worryabout money?

It's because they didn't learn that life-skill.

They worked hard to earn their money but unfortunately, nobody told them what to do with it.

Instead of learning how to multiply money through investing, öåâü left that to the professionals and paid a heavy price. They should have just learned , but never took the time.

Earning money is the hardest and least effective way to create wealth. You have to trade your time for money and you only have so much time.

If you're reading this and you're not 'financially free', it's not because you didn't work hard enough, or you weren't intelligent enough, or because you were unlucky.

Anybody even with a modest income can become financially free and some can even become a millionaire several times over, if they make sensible investment decisions.

We all just need to gain the financial intelligence necessary to ride that bike.

Once you learn about investing, you will never forget it, just like riding a bicycle. It is about understanding how to invest money, how it flows, and more importantly, how you can make it flow to you.

We all know how to make money in our own way, but very few of us know how to keep it and fewer still know how to multiply it. It's as if all that hard-earned money, which took so much work and sweat to earn, suddenly dissipates into thin air.

If you feel that your money comes slowly but it always seems to leave you quickly, then you haven't mastered the art of money management yet. That's okay; there is always time to learn.

If you really want to get the tools, then I suggest you get a copy of my investment book www.dividendincomeplus.co.uk Kick your expensive advisors into touch and take back control.

Otherwise, you'll be constantly on that hamster wheel of making money, spending money and going back to work to make more money to replace what you've lost. If you're retired, it's even worse because there's no replacement money coming in.

It's that leaky bucket scenario. No matter how much water we pour into it, that damn bucket keeps emptying out and we don't know why.

We all need to work smarter, not harder, me included. Financial intelligence is one of those things that can be taught and we can always be better.

Everybody can improve. Even the professionals can become better, and the best ones do exactly that, year after year. So, don't worry about climbing the mountain in a day, just put one foot in front of the other and begin to learn.

Otherwise, you'll either keep falling off that bike or you will be so scared that you'll refuse to ride it. That's what so many people do, when they sit on lots of cash.

There's no way they can fall off, but it also means they'll never reach the finishing line. Every year, people who started investing later than them will whizz straight past.

Inflation catches up with you and if you're not moving forward, you must be moving backwards.

It's not a life that you either want or deserve.

The problem is that the professional investors derive great pleasure from watching you fall off your bike. It's how they make their money. That's why they're happy to provide you with misinformation and put obstacles in your way. Sometimes, they'll just blatantly push you over.

That's how they make their living. There is a finishing line ahead, and they don't want you to cross it.

But don't worry, because when you get good at riding that bicycle, well, that's when the magic happens. Just hang around and keep reading; you will be doing wheelies in no time.

Remember, the professionals are not out to get you personally, it's just business to them. They don't even want you to lose necessarily, but they do want to win. Their desire to win is much greater than their desire for you not to lose.

Unfortunately, one of you has to get crushed, and it can't be the professional.

It's an unfair match because you are competing with some serious people; you're up against the big boys – the hedge funds, investment banks and professional day-traders. You're competing against stockbrokers, wealth managers, and financial advisors. They all have better information, knowledge, and experience than you. They have clever lawyers, compliance and support networks to catch them if they fall.

You don't. You're on your own.

They'll hide those investment products and strategies which are designed to help you, but will hinder them. Instead, they'll sell you the highest profit margin item on their shopping list, which is usually the one which you least require.

They'll guide you effortlessly to the products which you don't need but you've now been brainwashed into thinking that you do. This is mind warfare, control and manipulation.

In a capitalist world, money is constantly being passed around from one country to another, from one business to another, and ultimately from one person to another. It's a constant flow of money.

One person's income is another person's expenditure.

Every single pound you earn is because somebody must have spent it.

Yes my friend, in this world, it is very unfortunate that in order for you to become richer, somebody must become poorer.

TIP 11 –
DIRTY LAUNDRY NEVER GOES OUT ON THE WASHING LINE

The zero-sum game is not illegal, and depending on who you're speaking to, it may not even be immoral. But it's nasty and horrible.

But something that is both illegal and immoral is money laundering.

Money laundering is where it starts to become very serious.

You see, money laundering involves crime; serious crime. Forget about petty crimes, like shoplifting or stealing car radios. That sort of low-level crime in comparison to what I'm about to expose is child's play.

Money laundering is where the big boys come and play. It involves drug smuggling, international cartels, prostitution, human trafficking, kidnapping, torture, and murder.

Sound like a movie? It's much worse. In real-life, there's no hero to save the day.

It is estimated that £100 billion of dirty money is cleaned through the City of London every year, making it the money laundering capital of the world. But nobody really knows what the real figure is because nobody knows the true extent of the problem.

It happens everywhere, from the biggest international banks laundering billions of dollars down to the small, one- man currency exchange dealer sitting in his booth on Oxford Street dealing in a few thousand pounds.

Many millions of pounds are laundered every single day through the financial markets, in property and land transactions, in drugs, in cash, in over-the-counter deals and in the underground, black market.

It happens everywhere in the City, and it's impossible to stop. I know this only too well because it very nearly happened to me. This is a true story and for the purposes of anonymity, I'm going to be using fictitious names.

The Russian billionaire who didn't care

I set up my stockbroking firm back in 2008 and over the years, I've had many different people, from many different walks of life, in and out of my office doors. I've also had many University interns join my firm during their placement years to gain work experience.

Interns generally work on projects through one of my team members and because of their short time with us, I usually don't remember them. However, one notable intern that I'm unlikely to forget in a hurry is a chap called Daniel. He worked with me for a few weeks during his work placement from the University of College London (UCL).

He was born in Hungary, a very likeable person, always very keen and willing, as most interns are. He was also particularly interested in learning about trading and so spent more time on my desk than most other interns.

About two weeks into his internship, he approached me and told me that he had a friend, Nikolas, who worked as an agent for a high-net-worth client in Dubai. Apparently, this rich client was unhappy because he was being unfairly treated on his foreign exchange trades by his local bank and his agent wanted to know if I could help.

I said 'Yes, *sure, I would be happy to look into it*', thinking nothing of it.

I know about foreign exchange because that was my first experience in the City when I began trading. I also know people in that space and I knew that I could make a connection to help. I also knew that whomever I referred the business to would be thankful and would return the favour in the future. It was a win-win. This type of word-of-mouth recommendation is commonplace in the City; there was nothing extraordinary here.

Shortly afterwards, Daniel told Nikolas that I would be happy to help and Nikolas passed on the message that he very much appreciated my offer and wanted to meet me. He was going to be in London on business for a few days and was hoping to meet me for a coffee. Under normal circumstances, I would have declined this offer. I don't typically see any value in meeting somebody for a simple FX deal; even less value in meeting an 'agent' of somebody.

At the back of my mind, I had also assumed the deal would

be quite small. I never imagined for even a second that our little student, Daniel, would be moving with any major players. However, he was keen to impress, very willing and incredibly persistent. So, after a bit of persuasion, I agreed to have the meeting. I also invited Daniel so he could learn something from the process.

A week later, Daniel, the agent, Nikolas, and I all met at the Hilton Hotel, just a few minutes' walk from my City offices. I met many   of my clients there because at the time, I had a serviced office of about twenty-five people in a lovely Grade II-listed building, but there was no separate boardroom.

The meeting began and Nikolas explained his client's problem. He didn't disclose his client's name, stating that he wished to remain anonymous. That was fine by me, although it sounded unusual, given that we weren't actually doing any business.

After about thirty minutes of talking, it became clear that the client had several successful companies and was turning over a lot of money – in fact, hundreds of millions of pounds a year. I was shocked; I wasn't expecting to hear that kind of number. I thought that it could have been maybe a few hundred thousand pounds, or perhaps two or three million at the most.

This guy was a very serious player. I looked at Daniel but he didn't appear fazed at all. I assumed he'd already known about the money involved, which would also explain why he was so insistent that I agreed to the meeting.

Suddenly, the whole business deal became very interesting.

If I could strike an attractive deal, undercut his current FX provider and offer a genuine alternative, then we could all win. Daniel would also get a referral fee from Nikolas, I assumed, for brokering the deal.

I continued to listen, now more intently than before, and what I learned intrigued me.

Nikolas explained that his client was originally from Russia and had taken over the family empire after his father passed away in the 1990s. Unlike the oil oligarchs who had made their fortune from the fire-sale of Russian state assets, his family was a big player in the retail clothing market. I scribbled notes on my pad, as I always do for my client meetings. I would have all of this checked out in due course but on the face of it, it was a very plausible and detailed story. His family history would be easy to track down through his company, and Nikolas assured me that he had all of the relevant documentation. It all seemed very much above board.

When dealing with international clients, there is something called 'Enhanced Due Diligence' (EDD) which means I have to conduct more checks than I would typically carry out for UK investors. However, in this case I didn't personally need the information as I was simply making a referral. I wasn't doing the transaction, so I wasn't taking on the compliance risk.

However, at the same time, I had to make sure that the guy was legitimate before making the introduction. Otherwise, I would just be wasting everybody's time.

It's like inviting a stranger to somebody else's party who end up drinking too much alcohol, acts inappropriately with the female guests, and punches the party host in the nose, before throwing up on the carpet and passing out. Nobody likes those types of referrals.

Nikolas continued with his story. He explained in vivid detail about the corruption in Russia. In particular, he told stories about kidnappings in Russia of people that he knew. That's why his client had no choice but to get out and Dubai was the obvious choice for business and political reasons. It was a safe haven for him and his family.

Now based in Dubai, he was safe, but he was being held to ransom in a different way; by the banks charging extortionate FX rates of up to 5% on currency exchanges for $1 million deals.

When he told me that number, I nearly fell off my chair. That's $50,000 for a single deal! – It should have cost 0.1%, i.e., £500! No wonder the guy was desperate to find a new firm to deal with – he was being seriously abused. Nikolas told me that he had spoken to various other FX houses in Dubai and had tried to negotiate a better rate but couldn't find anything.

I found it hard to believe that another bank couldn't offer a more competitive rate than 5% and questioned him hard about this. But his story was polished and seemed genuine. Nikolas told me that he had tried but because his client was not a citizen of Dubai, he was being marginalised. Apparently, it was common for Russians to pay much higher rates to use the same banking services in Dubai because of the higher political risk in dealing with Russian nationals.

Also, there were only a handful of banks in Dubai that could handle that kind of flow. The smaller operators didn't have the compliant structure to settle daily transactions worth millions of pounds. Even if they did, the risks were too high and it was all too easy for them to disappear. Regulations are not the same in Dubai and there's even less protection for non- residents.

This all made sense to me. My memory immediately recalled a story a client of mine once told me. He had lost over a million pounds in a property deal that went wrong because his business partner had ripped him off. When he fought it through Dubai's courts, his lawyer told him that because his partner was a local citizen, he had no chance of winning. My client had done everything correctly and had all of the legal paperwork, but after two years of bitter fighting in the courts, he finally came back to the UK having lost his entire life savings in that single crooked deal. He told me I should never do business in Dubai and that sent a shudder down my spine because just the year before, I was thinking of doing exactly that.

A wealthy Russian being ripped off by local Dubai banks therefore sounded feasible. It all seemed reasonable, I thought, but I would check it all out later anyway.

We terminated the meeting and I agreed that I would try and help, subject to having the right paperwork and due diligence in place. Over the next few weeks, Nikolas maintained regular lines of communication with me and we spoke several times. He also sent me various documentation, which all seemed to check out. But it was made clear to me that no documentation would be sent on the client himself until after another meeting. He wanted to keep his details anonymous until a plan had been finalised and we were definitely doing business together.

We built up a solid rapport and a relationship quickly developed over those weeks until one day, Nikolas announced that Mr Petrov wanted to meet me personally. It seemed he had done his due diligence on the firm. Mr Petrov was a shrewd businessman and so, of course, it made sense that he would want to meet me if he was going to do any deals through my contacts. Similarly, I needed to meet him for my own due diligence purposes. So, a date and time was set for the following week and we all agreed to meet again at the Hilton Hotel.

The big day with Mr Big

So, there we all were; me, Daniel, agent Nikolas, and Mr Big himself, Russian billionaire Mr Petrov. It seemed odd addressing somebody as 'Mister' Petrov and during the meeting, I did ask for his frst name, but he didn't respond. I wasn't sure if he didn't understand my question or he just chose to ignore it. Nikolas didn't follow up either so, that was that. I figured I would find out his first name soon enough once I had his identification documents.

At no point did I smell a rat. It was all legitimate business.

Nikolas did most of the talking as Mr Petrov's English was not great. He reiterated much of what I already knew, placing particular emphasis on the problems that his client was facing in detail whilst Mr Petrov stared at me intensely, nodding his head every so often. Occasionally, Mr Petrov would abruptly interrupt Nikolas with his broken English and without warning, if he felt his point was not being put across with sufficient robustness. Nikolas didn't seem fazed by this at all, he was clearly used to it.

I remember thinking that the conversation was all very specific, very detailed, with exact dates and times, actual names of firms, and pin-point locations. I didn't see it at the time, but I can see now that it was very well rehearsed. Nikolas and Mr Petrov were in perfect harmony, just with different levels of intensity – they repeated the same story without missing a beat. There were no discrepancies.

Nikolas explained which banks they used in Dubai, from which dates, what rate they were receiving, how much it was costing them and so on. He also gave a detailed history of the business empire in Russia and even went into some softer detail about Mr Petrov's family, many of whom were still there.

All of my questions had been answered except one.

I still didn't understand why Mr Petrov and Nikolas had chosen me. Why they hadn't gone directly with an FX House?; There are dozens of them in the City, they just had to pick one.

The answer was as polished as all of the ones that had preceded it.

Mr Petrov didn't trust any of the big banks. In fact he detested the big firms because of how they treated him. He also had 'unresolved' issues in Russia so, ultimate discretion and anonymity was important to him. He didn't want to use any of his own contacts because they knew the people that he knew, so word would get out. He was a very secretive person and wanted to conduct his business quietly, with the least amount of fanfare and noise.

That's why he preferred to use a small, independent firm like mine that could make anonymous enquiries on his behalf. An intermediary would be the perfect vehicle to ensure that his name would remain protected.

It wasn't long before we started talking about the numbers. I already knew that even a tiny percentage on the volume would be very worthwhile of my time. I was nervous and apprehensive as to what their response might be, but when it came, I was left speechless.

He would give me 1%! Wow, that was huge. That means if he exchanged £100 million of currency over a year, it would give me a million pounds! £1 million pounds for doing nothing. If his business transacted £200 million of currency exchange, I would make £2 million!

Okay, now this was sending alarm bells ringing. This doesn't make any sense, I thought.

At that precise moment I just realised that my life was potentially about to change forever.

The deal of the century

I looked across at Daniel who had sat quietly throughout the whole meeting. I thought about this little, unassuming kid who I hadn't previously given a second thought to and tried to take in what had just happened. I couldn't.

If my calculations were correct, I was going to make a million pounds from this single deal. It wasn't just a one-off either. This would be for recurring fees, and it could be for years, for decades even. I couldn't get my head around the numbers.

I put on my best poker face, but I could feel my mouth becoming dry. I wasn't sure what to say. Should I play it calm and say that I'd think about it?, Should I thank him for his generosity, or should I just drink some more water to try and cool the f*ck down.

I played it all back in my head to make sure I hadn't missed anything. I realised that none of this was going to involve any real work on my part. It was just to do an introduction.

How was that even possible?

Millions of pounds for doing literally nothing except make a phone call and a bit of compliance.

The stuff that I had to do for Mr Petrov was easy, I could do it standing on my head, I could do it in my sleep; damn, I could do it standing on my head whilst I was asleep. I had connected people together so many times before and I wasn't even paid for it, nor did I expect to be paid. They were just small favours, putting people in touch with each other. We all did it in the City. That's how the City works.

Now I was about to be paid a million pounds to do the exact same thing.

We mapped out again what he wanted.

Sure, there was some work involved but it was insignificant. I had to do some running around for him, a little bit of legwork. I had to make a few phone calls, set up some meetings, do the due diligence on the FX firm, and of course, negotiate the best terms for his FX exchange rate all with minimal fuss.

I also had to do some checks on Petrov and his businesses to make sure that it was all legitimate; that would take a bit of time as an overseas client.

Most importantly, I had to do it all covertly without the City or the FX firm, knowing his identity or his business. I had to broker a deal only with the CEO of the FX firm and set up a separate trading account away from the prying eyes of other FX traders working there. Secrecy is what he was willing to pay a big premium for and it was my job to find him that shelter.

Nikolas knew Daniel, and Daniel knew me. That's why Mr Petrov wanted me. He could trust me. I also wasn't trading FX myself so there was no conflict of interest – he could rely on me, knowing that I would work hard to get the FX rate down for him. It was in both of our interests for me to negotiate the best possible rate.

We concluded the meeting.

I was left exhausted and overloaded, but my adrenalin was pumping. I was euphoric. It had felt as if I had won the lottery. I had read and heard about this type of thing happening to other people, but this never happened to me.

Apart from winning the Sports Day 200m 'marathon' race as a seven-year-old kid, I can't recall winning anything in my life. I've always had to work hard and fight for anything that came to me. But today I had just won the jackpot.

It's not every day that you sit across the table from a billionaire. I was in a daydream for the rest of the day. I really thought I'd wake up at any moment to the alarm clock ringing.

Back in the office, I immediately got to work and began to ring some of my FX contacts. As soon as they heard the size of the numbers that were being talked about, of course they all wanted the business.

I set up meetings with two FX firms that I knew well and a third to make a fair comparison. I knew the game so I could negotiate a deal without putting myself or my new client at risk.

But there was one risk I was still exposed to, and it was huge. After setting everything up, I could easily be cut out of the deal. Once Petrov had his contract in place, I would be surplus to requirements and the FX firm would also be incentivised to conveniently push me out of the way. Petrov and the FX firm only needed me now, at this moment in time.

I tried to figure out how to mitigate this risk, and a legal agreement would be the best way to do that. But it wouldn't count for much. I wasn't about to sue a Russian billionaire if he decided not to honour the deal.

But I figured that he wouldn't screw me. I was small-fry; his time, and his reputation was worth far more to him than the few crumbs he was planning to throw to me. Besides, I would be his trusted London partner and there would be other deals that could develop from this one. I was sure that was worth a lot to him. He wanted professional friends in London that he could trust. I was happy to be one of them.

The next few days were very hectic time for me. I cancelled meetings for my own business, I changed my schedules, I had people fill in for me, I did nothing but think about how to execute this one deal transaction. I was working on the deal of a lifetime, and I couldn't mess it up.

We all get one massive life-changing opportunity at some point, and this was mine.

The bomb just went off

Two weeks later and finally, everything was set up. I had chosen the FX house and agreed terms for the transactional flow. I had all the paperwork ready, and everything logistically in place. I even had my lawyers draw up terms of business to protect my interests in the deal. It was worth less than the paper it was written on, but I had to at least offer some form of deterrent, even if he knew that I was bluffing. Now I just needed the final part, the compliance and due diligence.

This would be done in part by me but mainly by the FX firm. Petrov would be their client after all. So now my work was almost complete.

Another meeting was arranged with Petrov and Nikolas.

That's when the bomb went off.

Suddenly, and totally unexpectedly, the deal of a lifetime I had been working on for the past fortnight quickly turned into a nightmare.

I never expected what would happen next.

After all of the terms and commissions had been agreed, Nikolas dropped the final piece. It wasn't a coincidence; it was deliberate and timed to perfection. They had left it to the very end because now I was already invested in the deal, I was already committed, not financially invested but invested with my time, resources and energy. I had also committed other people, so now their time and effort were also invested.

We had already agreed that I would be paid 1% of the deal and I had assumed that this fee would be added to the FX rate, then rebated back to me. That's how it usually works.

So, if the FX firm charges 0.1% on the deal, Petrov would pay 1.1% to the FX firm and I would be rebated 1% by the FX firm.

Now Nikolas was moving away from this agreement and saying that Petrov's firm would pay me a 'consultancy' fee, rather than a rebate. That was the first alarm bell that went off for me, but I didn't say anything; I just listened carefully.

He explained in detail the proposed structure, including the payment trails.

Petrov's firm in Dubai would transfer between $3 million and $5 million every day to the FX house. The FX house would convert those dollars into Euros and send half back to Petrov's firm, and the other half to a different firm also owned by a business contact of Petrov's in Russia.

That was the second alarm bell that rang in as many minutes. The funds would be leaving one business and going into a completely new business, an unconnected third party. The funds would go from Petrov's company into a new company. That new company would effectively be receiving at least half of the total funds as 'clean' money from an FCA regulated foreign exchange firm.

That means the company could take that clean money, making it more difficult to trace where it originally came from.

Then came the third alarm bell and it was the biggest of them all. He dropped a bombshell about the FX fees. Petrov didn't want to be charged the standard commercial rate, which is typically around 0.1%. Instead he wanted to be charged 4%! In other words, he wanted to be overcharged.

The 4% would be split in two payments, 0.1% would stay with the FX firm and 3.9% rebated back to me. However, it was agreed that I would receive 1% and so the remaining 2.9% would then be sent back to yet another different company, which was also held in somebody else's name.

The deal structured in this way means that two unrelated companies receive completely clean money. The first one from the FX firm and the second one from me. In total it costs Petrov 1.1% to clean his money.

It was a smart move on his part.

He figured that if the FX firm didn't agree to having a third party payment, he could at least do a back-door deal with me.

The clean money is then free to be used to buy property, land, stocks, shares, crypto or anything else. The money is clean because the new companies receiving the money have no connection to Petrov or his firm – therefore, it has no connection to the original illegal source of funds.

If the 'source of funds' is ever questioned by another bank, it's easy to show that the funds came directly from an FCA regulated stock broking firm or from an FCA regulated FX house.

The money that gets funneled back into Petrov's firm from the FX firm is also cleaner because even though it's been returned to the original firm, it's gone through an FX deal and so now it's sitting in Euros with a different bank, in a different geographical jurisdiction with a different regulator. If those Euros are subsequently converted again, this time into Yen and sent to Nomura Bank in Tokyo, and then the same process is repeated again, converted to US Dollars and sent to Singapore, and then to Africa, the Middle East and South America, it won't take long before the trail becomes so complex and impossible to follow, that the money itself becomes clean.

The funds can still remain in the original company but with every transaction, it's one step further away from the original crime.

This is called 'layering' where layers of transaction are placed on top of each other until the initial source of where the money came from is lost in the complexity of it all.

When money travels across different country borders and

continents, with different laws and jurisdictions, it becomes very difficult indeed to keep track of everything. The original drug deal which happened thousands of miles away, which generated all of this cash, is now all but a distant memory. The cash is in the system and the drugs are on the streets.

My head was starting to spin, and I felt my mouth go dry again.

Just days before we were about to go live, the whole game had changed. Suddenly, all the alarm bells started to ring simultaneously, and my head was pounding.

The million-pound dream had just become a million-pound nightmare.

Cleaning dirty laundry

One of the challenges of working in the City, especially holding any senior position means you're always going to be targeted. There are always people who want to work with you for the wrong reasons.

You hold the key to something they want – money. But it's not your money that want, it's their money and you have the key to unlock their safe.

That key is your good name, your reputation, your regulated business, and your contacts. That key is your FCA licence, access to a trading platform, compliance advisors, market makers, FX custodians, your ability to open dealing accounts for them and to transact.

That's worth infinitely more to them than any money they

might try to steal from you. They already have money, that's not their problem.

In fact, they have the opposite problem – they have too much money, but all of it is dirty.

Their problem is that their dirty money connects them to the original crimes that led to the money being made in the first place. It's derived from illegitimate sources, whether that's tax evasion, drug smuggling, bank robbery, terrorism, blackmail, or something else.

If they try to spend their dirty money, they can be directly linked to the crime.

As you read this, there are literally tens of billions of pounds in the hands of gangsters, and crooked businessmen, that can't be spent. Yes, tens of billions.

It's all just sitting in bags of cash in warehouses, or in offshore untraceable bank accounts, in gold bars, in properties that can't be sold, in crypto accounts that can't be accessed, or on memory chips that are password encrypted.

Wherever it is, that money is worthless without the key. Not a single pound, Dollar or Euro can be spent without raising suspicion.

What finance professionals can offer gangsters, terrorists and organised crime is that key. They have the ability to unlock those riches and get paid a lot of money in the process.

That's why I'm always a potential target. Anybody who runs

their own regulated firm in the City is a target and that's what Petrov saw in me.

It turns out, of course, that Mr Petrov wasn't Mr Petrov at all. He was just a little minion.

He was just a front for the real Mr Big. The whole thing turned out to be one big theatre show, a Punch and Judy performance, an elaborate charade. Or perhaps more accurately it was the Nativity, and I was playing the lead role of the donkey.

The real criminals never show their faces. They have a dozen Petrov's and a hundred Nikolas's working for them. At this very moment, there's another Petrov talking to another Ranjeet Singh, somewhere in the world, and that Ranjeet Singh may not be so lucky. He might take the bait.

In the end, I'd like to think it wouldn't have mattered because any FX firm worth its salt would not have agreed to that deal. They have to abide by the rule of 'third party' payments which means funds must be sent back to the same account from which they were received. They also couldn't charge 4%, that would be ridiculous and would raise a red flag.

But I'm also sure there would be some firms who would have been tempted to take that deal. Some will even have gone one step further and advised Petrov how to structure the deal so there was less chance of it being raised as suspicious. In other words, if they're going to do the deal, they'd want to do it with the least amount of risk for them. Now they're complicit in the crime themselves.

This makes the money laundering scam even harder to spot.

The very firm that's supposed to be highlighting dodgy deals to the National Crime Agency (NCA) is instead actively working to bury those deals amongst the thousands of trades that it executes every month.

Smelling a rat

FX firms simply can't charge a client 0.1% and pay their agent a rebate of 3.9%. That would be non-compliant.

But what if Petrov hadn't been so greedy? What if he had made it more interesting for the FX firm and cleaned his money less aggressively?. He could have given 0.3% to the FX firm and paid a consultancy fee of say 0.5%. That might have worked.

He could also have just had the money wired back to his own business name but in a different geographical jurisdiction rather than asking for money going to a new business. That might have worked, too.

It was just a little too obvious. He was too greedy, and there were just too many red flags.

Money paid to consultants or introducers, money transferred to different bank accounts in different names or to different countries, money moved via multiple transactions (layers), money moved back and forth, trades being executed with little regard to fees; all of these things have the hallmarks of money laundering.

So, the deal had to fall apart.

Shortly afterwards, Nikolas' left the firm and his telephone number also stopped working. As for Petrov, I never saw him again. It was like neither of them ever existed.

I still have no idea how much Daniel knew. My guess is not very much.

The whole thing had been an elaborate con.

Daniel was just the innocent kid who had the misfortune of knowing somebody who knew somebody who knew somebody that had a lot of money; he was just a pawn. I don't think he actually had a clue.

His internship was completed, as normal and he went on his merry way, none the wiser. Of course, he asked me if a deal had been done, and I told him that we couldn't agree terms. He smiled and that was the end of that.

But you know the crazy thing?

What I found myself entangled with was a mere drop of water in a vast ocean. It was a huge thing for me to see something so close up and personal, but it was actually nothing in the grand scheme of things.

The biggest money launderers are not individuals or small FX brokers. They are the massive international banks.

These banks willingly let money flow through their systems. They regularly launder not a few million but billions of dollars. They take money from royal families, from Russian oligarchs, from Saudi oil barons, and from billionaire businessmen and they do it intentionally.

HSBC was fined a staggering £1.2 billion for supplying banking services to Saudi Arabia, Iran and North Korea. I'm not going to pass comment on this particular case, but I just want to draw your attention to the £ 1.2 billion fine. How much money must have been laundered if the fine was more than a billion pounds?

I'm not a lawyer, but my guess is that HSBC might have done something just a teeny, weeny bit wrong.

If it happened to one of the biggest and most reputable banks in the world, it could literally happen anywhere.

TIP 10 –
HOW REALLY INDEPENDENT ARE IFAs?

What is the first thing that comes to mind when you hear the three immortal words 'Independent Financial Advisor' (IFA)? Do you think of somebody you might call a friend, somebody who pops around to your house once or twice a year for a cup of tea to chat about your investments? Could it be somebody who you play a round of golf with from time to time, or maybe it's someone you might send a Christmas card to?

Most importantly, is it somebody you trust, and you believe acts in the best interest of you and your family?

If what I have described above resonates with you, read this chapter once, make notes, and then read it again. Oh, and just in case you are standing up in the train while you are reading this, ask somebody to kindly give up their seat.

I don't care if she's pregnant, in a moment you're going to need that seat more than she does.

Financial advisors are rotten

To avoid the risk of being ambiguous, allow me to be clear from the outset. I don't have anything against financial advisors. I don't have anything against any profession, and I know many honest, hard-working advisors who do a great job for their clients. However, and like any industry, there are some who abuse their position, and these are the people I want you to watch out for.

These are the professional conmen who take money out of your pocket and deliver no value. These are the slick, educated professionals who befriend you. These are the people who sell you the sizzle rather than the sausage. In fact, there's no sausage at all.

The irony is that many financial advisors don't actually provide any *advice*.

They essentially act as intermediaries who connect you to somebody else who provides advice. In other words, they charge you an annual commission for simply pushing your money around from one wealth manager to another. Although that's terrible, that's not even the worst thing – when you dig a little deeper, you find out their motivation to recommend a particular wealth manager is based on just one factor – their commission.

Of course, there are certain financial advisors who provide specialist services, from financial planning to tax advice, and for those tailored tasks they should be paid. I understand and agree to that. Any advisor who provides solid advice, information and support to somebody should be paid.

But advisors who generate income from 'referral' commissions when they move their clients to a particular wealth management firm, do not add any value. This fee 'kickback' typically amounts to 0.5% - 1% per annum for doing absolutely diddly squat.

What makes it even worse is that IFAs have a word in their

title which is entirely misleading - 'independent' - they are anything but independent. In fact, you couldn't find somebody less independent if you tried.

I can say this because over the years, I have probably met at least a hundred financial advisors, and I can tell you that the vast majority of them want the same thing – lots of commission. It doesn't matter about your product or service, or the risk of your firm defaulting, or the investments failing, or even whether the investments are suitable for their client.

It's all about the monies.

I'm regularly approached by IFAs, and not once have I been asked about my performance or track-record, or what strategy I might employ, or how safe their clients' assets might be if they invested with me, or anything like that.

Yet these are the most important questions their clients would expect them to ask.

The only question they want answered is, "How much commission can I make?"

That's why IFAs move clients from firm to firm when it suits them, which is usually when their commission kickback is reduced. Then they're very quick to tell their client they have found a 'better firm'.

"Hmmm.... Better how, exactly?" I wonder.

Unfortunately, there are plenty of people out there who are naïve enough to think their advisor has carefully chosen the investment firm because of its track record – I don't wish to appear harsh, but I sometimes wonder which is worse - the cunning of the IFA or the stupidity of the client.

If you have an IFA that you see as a personal friend and you find yourself shaking your head in silent protest, thinking 'that's not my IFA', then you either are one of the few people who has found a genuine financial advisor, or you are in self-denial.

I'm sorry but you are owed my honesty. If it means I have to ruffle your feathers to save you tens of thousands of pounds and a lifetime of being ripped off, then that's what I'm prepared to do.

Besides, next year you'll thank for me it.

Don't give up that seat just yet, we're not finished.

Getting paid for 'not a lot'

What happens after your IFA introduces your portfolio to his preferred, high commission paying, wealth management firm?

Well, usually nothing; and that's the point.

The IFA usually does absolutely bloody nothing.

All the portfolio management, the strategies, the buying and selling, the analysis, research, the trades executed, and all of the hard work is carried out by the fund manager. The IFA might make the occasional switch from one fund to another (with the same firm of course) just so that he appears busy.

He'll also happily come and see you at your house twice a year and 'discuss' your portfolio, but that's also just another con. He'll have your portfolio printed out ready with all those lovely, coloured pie-charts and tables but he did none of the work, none of the hard graft. He's just the mouthpiece.

No doubt he will be scanning your facial expression searching for clues. Under the pretence of this meeting, he is secretly wishing, longing, that you will be happy with the numbers so he can get his sweaty, fat ass off your sofa and get the hell out of your house. He doesn't want this to be a drawn-out afternoon. He just wants you to sign off another twelve months of free commission for him.

"Just sign the bloody papers!", the little voice in his head is screaming, as he smiles sweetly at you.

The whole thing is a farce because the IFA wasn't responsible for any of the performance. Somebody else was managing your portfolio. He was just sitting back either twiddling his thumbs or playing with his testicles, perhaps both, if he could multi- task.

Of course, if the performance is good, he'll be quick to take the credit. After all, was it not he who recommended the fund?

"Surely, Mr Client, with a sterling performance like that this year, for which I take full credit of course, is another double-chocolate digestive not in order?" I can see the smugness on his face, just thinking about it.

Most importantly that's his hook to entice you to transfer more money into your portfolio. That's the only useful purpose of the meeting, if there ever was one; to try and convince you to move your other execution only portfolio from Hargreaves Lansdowne so that he can manage it with Fisher Investments, St James' Place or ABC, or whoever's paying him the most commission.

But it gets worse.

Let's say the performance is not good and you're not happy. Now, the IFA quickly transforms into his new role of a white knight in shining armour.

Now the fund performance suddenly has nothing to do with him and everything to do with the fund's investment manager. He expertly distances himself away from the portfolio whilst convincing you to stay with the same firm. He suggests a different fund, maybe a different sector. The fund manager has let you both down and that's unforgivable.

'We need to find somebody better' he tells you, reassuringly.

Interesting how he takes all of the credit in the good years but none of the responsibility in the bad years. That's a highly sought-after mis-direction sales skill in the IFA world.

Of course, the performance is neither in his control nor at the forefront of his mind. He has no idea about how one fund manager might perform over another; he just spins the wheel like everybody else. Even the fund manager doesn't know if he's worth backing.

Then, of course, are the little 'sleight of hand' tricks. Even if you are happy with the performance, he still needs to recommend a couple of small 'strategic changes' because otherwise you'll quickly realise that each year, he does absolutely nothing for you.

Just a few tweaks here and there, maybe a switch from one fund to another, maybe a little money moved from fixed income into equities, or a little shift from the UK to the US, or whatever it is. The changes are meaningless; they're just decorative and aesthetically pleasing.

He will say that it's time for some changes. It's all nonsense. It's just his little magic show and you're his number one fan, sitting wide-eyed and mesmerised in the front row with a box of popcorn in your lap.

If your IFA really believes that he's adding value by suggesting those pointless changes, then he's more delusional than conspiratorial, which is even more dangerous.

The truth is that your IFA has no control over your portfolio and has zero control over its performance. He has no power over how your money is managed unless he manages it himself, which he isn't qualified to do.

Your IFA has never met or even spoken to the fund manager responsible for your investments. He knows nothing about him. In fact, you probably know more about the fund manager than he does because hopefully you took the time to do some research.

You should also consider that despite having another 'average' year, your IFA didn't have an average year. He had a great year. He got paid a few thousand pounds for eating chocolate biscuits at your house.

In fact, your IFA had a great year this year, and last year and the year before that, and he had ten great years before that. Your fund manager also had a great year, and the wealth management firm also had a great year. Because they get paid the same money, regardless of what they do or don't do, irrespective of their performance.

They keep rolling up to your house each year to collect their cheques and you keep writing them. In fact, everybody gets paid the same money year in, year out, except for one person- you.

And when you lose money, it's funny how nobody else loses money; not your IFA, not the investment firm, and not the fund manager.

Even in those loss-making years you still have to pay for the chocolate biscuits.

The pointless questionnaire

Then there's one final act to the show. For good measure and just in case you're still unconvinced that your IFA is worth every penny you pay him, out comes the most ridiculous, irrelevant piece of paper known to man.

Step forward the pointless annual questionnaire.

This is – wait for it - your golden opportunity to let your IFA know if you've experienced a 'change in circumstances'. Of course, your circumstances haven't changed. They haven't changed for ten years but every year you still fill in one of those stupid forms. Do you know why?

Well firstly, it's because the IFA can then demonstrate to you once again, he's working for his money.

Secondly, it makes you think you really are at the top of his list. It's comforting when people take an interest in you, isn't it? You assume the IFA can only be asking these questions if he genuinely cares about you.

Thirdly, he's covering his behind again with more paperwork which stops you complaining if and when the penny finally drops that you've been paying him to play with his balls for the past decade.

Of course, the form looks oh so formal and official with the IFA's pretty little logo at the top. Isn't that cute.

Surely such an important looking form, printed on high- quality embossed paper, can't just be a box-ticking exercise.

"No, this must be really, really important and my IFA is doing such a good job. He's really interested in me and taking such an interest in what I want. What a lovely chap he is".

Look, it's time to burst the bubble - let me tell you something.

Let's get real

Your IFA just wants the meeting to be over.

He wants you to stop boring him about the big speech that

you're so proud of when you gave your daughter away at her wedding last year. You know, the one that you invited him to, but he never turned up, because he conveniently got sick with a mysterious stomach bug just twenty-four hours beforehand.

He also wants you to put your Mediterranean Cruise photo album back into the cabinet and never, ever show him any of your holiday pics for as long as you both shall live.

He's also begging under his breath and silently praying for your wife, Margaret, to stop filling his cup with more tea.

But, most importantly, he wants you to STOP talking and wasting his time so that he can carry on with his day and make some money!

In fact, he really just wants one thing from you.

He wants you to shut up and then say the following seven words ... "Great work John, see you next year".

That means he can get the hell out of your house, miss the rush hour traffic, and not have to worry about you or your ridiculous investments, that he has no control over, until the next meeting. The End.

I'm sorry but that's what he wants.

I know these are harsh words, but I make no apology in going out of my way to make them feel slightly painful. Remember, I'm your friend, even if I sense you becoming slightly annoyed with me. That's okay. You can be annoyed with me.

More than any other chapter, this is the one which really needs the point driven home.

I don't get the opportunity to sit down and eat biscuits with you, let alone milk chocolate digestives. I have only one chance of saving you and all that I have are my words. These words need to be strong enough to penetrate your complacency and pierce your denial.

I'm asking you to listen to me, somebody that you've never met in person, over your IFA who is somebody you've known for years. I want my words to stoke enough emotion for you to get pis*ed off.

Whether that anger is directed at me or at the IFA I genuinely don't mind.

I just need to knock you off the "it couldn't happen to me" pedestal that you're currently perched on.

Remember, I have nothing to lose or gain, whether you stick with your IFA or kick him into touch. If nothing else, you have a much better perspective now.

Money, money, money

I'm not suggesting for a moment that IFAs want you to lose money. They don't.

IFAs don't want your funds to lose money, of course not. Thankfully that's quite a hard thing to do because as you know, the stock market is a master of disguise, and it always goes up in the long run.

The IFA just wants to take their fee. They want you to make as much money as you can (without it affecting their fee), and they want you to be as happy as possible and stay with them forever. They want to do that with the least amount of work and fuss.

Finally, I just want to remind you that I'm not suggesting every IFA works like this.

Every financial professional has the capacity to do good or bad for his or her clients. The IFA world is the same. That's life.

I personally know of some very good, honest, and sincere financial advisors. I can vouch for them because I have had the pleasure of working alongside some of the very best IFAs, and they have always treated their clients well and charged a fair fee for their service. They have gone out of their way to put their clients first. I absolutely don't think that it's wrong for a financial advisor to earn money when that kind of value is being provided.

But it is also not true that every IFA in the country is looking after the interest of their clients before their own, being honest about their motivation and providing value for money.

Whilst this seems to be an obvious statement, nobody will accept that it's their IFA who is the bad apple. It's always the other person's IFA; their neighbour's IFA, their brother's IFA, their work colleague's IFA. It's never *their* IFA.

That's because they have allowed their IFA to become a friend, they've become too close to them and now it's hard to be truly objective. After a year of working with the same person, how do you begin to question them?. After ten years, it becomes ten times harder.

Remember I'm not suggesting they're going out of their way to rip you off. They're not.

It would be financial suicide for an advisor to deliberately find a wealth management firm that performed so poorly, it consistently lost money for its clients. Clearly the client would quickly sack the firm and the advisor.

But because that rarely happens it's really quite difficult to annoy a client to the point where the IFA is sacked. The fund manager on the other hand is never in the client's living room to defend himself. That's why it's so easy for the IFA to deflect all of the blame on to the fund manager.

The IFA is like the cat with nine lives. He can just keep jumping from one fund to another.

Eliminating the itch to switch

There's another problem to be aware of.

We all suffer from *inertia*; nobody likes to change, and barriers to exit is a real thing which an experienced advisor can use to their advantage.

The cost of moving from one firm to another takes time, effort, and money. It means forms have to be completed, and more headache. This makes the original deal 'sticky', which means the client generally won't change firm unless he is deeply upset.

The IFA may even have his own terms that make it costly for the client to leave him.

Whilst the regulators over the years have done a good job in curbing this practice it still exists.

Some firms also impose hefty penalties on exiting funds, which makes it even more difficult. The penalties can be directed either against the client, the IFA or both.

The end client doesn't usually know the full terms of the agreement between the wealth management firm and the IFA. Typically, IFAs will lose at least some commission if their client leaves prematurely, usually within a certain timeframe from opening the account.

For example, some firms have a minimum three year window. If the client leaves within this period the IFA has to return some or even all of his commission.

Imagine that for a moment; now think about this.

If the firm performs terribly in year one and two, and the best option is for the client to use another firm, what do you think the IFA might say to him? Will he encourage him to leave?

Or will he encourage his client to stay so that he doesn't lose his commission?

You can see the obvious conflict of interest here; your IFA is going to defend that fund to the hilt, even if you're losing money. He's going to make it as difficult as possible for you to leave.

He'll discourage you with whatever he can which strikes a chord. That could be financial costs, the time and inconvenience of filling in paperwork, the risks of leaving, or the opportunity to recover your portfolio if you stay. He may even drop his own fee for that third year.

He will do everything he can to keep you with that fund for the third year because the financial cost to him, if you leave, is too great to bear. Because you don't realise that he is going to suffer a massive commission refund, you trust what he's saying. Your IFA will be more passionate and animated than usual, so, he must be right. You feel obliged to take his advice.

But the truth is, he doesn't care about what the risk is to you. He doesn't care that the fund manager has lost his way or that your funds are falling like a stone. He's looking at himself. Just one more year of loss for you, and the IFA collects his final pay cheque; then he's free to move you.

That's how they all look at the game.

IFA's are never looking for a great performance for the client and mediocre fees for them; they're looking for a mediocre performance for the client and great fees for them. As long as you don't get the itch to switch, your IFA is happy.

The game is simple for your IFA; to find the worst performing wealth management firm you will tolerate that gives him the *highest fee*. If there are two firms and one performs better than the other but pays less commission to the advisor, there's a good chance the lesser performing firm will win the business.

In other words, if two funds give him the same fee, the IFA will choose the best performer. But when there are two dogs in the race, and you're happy with both, your IFA is always going to back the one that pays him the most and you the least.

Because 90% of portfolios perform okay, it's a massive problem.

The problem with 'okay'

When you have a portfolio that does 'okay' you're really up the creek without a paddle. That's because 'okay' stops you from taking any action. At least a terrible performing portfolio gives you a reason to change but okay keeps you dormant, inactive and subdued.

'Okay' is also almost impossible to assess. It's such a subjective term. There is nothing to compare 'okay' to other than the benchmark index. Even that has multiple variables, such as different risk levels and investment objectives.

The truth is that IFAs can get away with so much because they are experts in their game. It's like trying to debate physics with a scientist.

I've even seen some IFAs compare the performance of their clients' portfolios with the interest on their clients' cash savings. What a ridiculous comparison, given that one has zero risk, and another has significant risk - but their clients still believe it. Incredible.

St James' Place

I am wary of naming and shaming companies because I could end up upsetting a lot of people and getting sued in the process.

But I will mention one name with caution.

It's one of the largest wealth management firms in the UK, St James' Place, or SJP. As you may already know, this is a huge firm that's grown incredibly quickly in recent years. It's very profitable, has billions of pounds under management and is even listed on the London Stock Exchange.

Now, to be clear, what SJP does is not illegal in any way. Their business practices, how they run their operations, how they recruit, the financial advisors that work with them, their commission system – none of this is illegal, and no rules are being broken.

I'm not even going to pass a moral judgement. I don't want to be sued so I'm going to give you the facts with no bias or subjectivity.

The only reason I'm using SJP as an example is because it's one of the best commission payers for IFAs in the country. There are many other firms that operate in exactly the same way, but I'm just using SJP because it's one you are probably familiar with.

Unsurprisingly, firms like SJP who pay some of the highest fees will naturally attract the most financial advisors, all other things being equal. Those financial introducers, in turn, will refer the greatest number of clients. Now we need to think about how SJP and other similar firms can afford to pay their financial advisors so handsomely.

Well, the money has to come from somewhere and it comes from the fees that SJP charge its clients through their funds.

In other words, it comes from the investor, the client.

If the IFAs are being paid high commissions, that cost must be passed onto somebody, and that somebody is you.

It's no coincidence that as one of the best commission payers in the marketplace, SJP also has more financial advisors than any other firm in the UK; roughly a whopping 5,000 qualified advisors at the time of writing, according to their website.

So, the question has to be, is this right?

I mean, should financial advisors refer their clients to a firm because of how much commission they earn? Surely the job of a financial advisor is to ensure their client's share portfolio is managed by the best possible wealth management firm? Shouldn't their objective be to seek the best performance for their clients with the lowest fees?

You can see the potential conflict of interest.

Think about this rationally. Are all the financial advisors flocking to SJP because of the quality of SJP's funds or is it because SJP pays the most commission in the marketplace?

Let's also consider this – this year the performance of SJP's funds improves by 50% but at the same time SJP slashed the commission paid to its financial advisors by 50%.

So, clients would make 50% more but financial advisors would make 50% less.

What do you think might happen to the number of financial

advisors referring clients to SJP? What would happen to the total number of SJP clients? What might happen to the total funds under management?

Would it go up or down? I'm sure it would go down.

A few individual investors who independently review the SJP performance might invest their funds directly into SJP moving from a different fund manager. But the vast majority of funds under management and the vast majority of clients are controlled by the IFAs. If the IFA says 'move' then their clients will move. Even if performance has gone up, the IFAs can bend the truth and change the narrative to suit their needs.

They could say that SJP's fees are too expensive and that they've found an alternative advisor who will perform even better, and for lower fees.

My point is, how much of a factor is the IFA's commission in their decision-making process? Is that a healthy formula for achieving a positive outcome for clients?

If it's the main contributing factor that drives the IFA's decision to either invest or not invest their client's portfolio with a particular investment firm, then I think it's a problem.

Fees and a conflict of interest

We all agree the financial advisor must be paid and it's reasonable that their fee should be part of any conversation about where a client's funds should be invested. Clearly an IFA won't recommend a wealth management firm that doesn't pay the IFA anything.

Therefore, my point is how big a part should the fee play?

Is it the main leading part or should it be a small cameo part?

If there are no strict rules around this, which usually there aren't apart from some flimsy 'best practice' guidelines, then really, you're trusting another human being to act in your best interest above their own. I'm not convinced that's a sensible way to approach something as important as your life savings.

If you're an IFA, and both you as well as your client is winning, but you're winning more, could you live with yourself? Probably yes. Most people won't feel too bad about that.

If you're an IFA and you know you're not really doing anything, although you are still being paid, but your client's making money and is happy, could you live with yourself? Probably yes, again.

Sure, there will be a few, morally upstanding financial advisors who will genuinely choose the best firm with the best performance for their clients, even if that means a lower fee for them, but they're in the minority. Everybody else chases the money.

The problem is that without accountability and monitoring, the temptation is too great for most advisors to not focus on the commission. We're asking too much from the human spirit.

It's like leaving a big juicy T-bone steak in front of your hungry German Shepherd, and then popping out to the shops for a few hours, trusting him not to eat it. It's not realistic. When I was a young kid, I had a German Shepherd called Rocky who

I loved to bits, but I wouldn't put a bowl of meat in front of him unless I wanted him to eat it.

The system has to change, it's broken. Over the years, improvements have been made with better rules and regulations on how advisors are paid, to avoid this obvious conflict of interest but there's still a long way to go. It's far from perfect.

You need to protect yourself.

You need to know exactly what your advisor is charging you and what the wealth management firm is paying him. Then do the maths. Is your advisor choosing a firm that is expensive?

How much is he earning? What's the justification for that?

If the performance of SJP (or any of the more expensive wealth managers) is justified because it consistently produces better results and higher profits for its clients, then that's great and there is no argument. But to my knowledge SJP doesn't do any better than any other firm.

One could argue about reputation and brand, or the size of funds under management or the quality of the fund managers. Whilst I'm sure this is all very helpful for the advisor in presenting a glowing case to his client as to why he should use SJP, it's not the true motivation of the financial advisor.

But he can hardly say *"Listen John, here's the deal. SJP will pay me twice as much as the next firm so I think you should put your money with them".*

So instead, *he'll say "SJP is the biggest and best wealth*

management firm in the UK. They're well established and have a great reputation. There are a few different firms out there that I'd be happy to recommend but SJP would definitely be my top choice. Yes, they're a bit more expensive but you get what you pay for, and I recommend all of my clients to use them. "

This comes back to *'presentation'* of facts. What does your IFA want you to focus on? Misdirection is a real thing in the financial world.

Business is business and your responsibility first and foremost is to take care of your family. If your IFA is putting your hard- earned life savings with the firm that gives the biggest commission, not to the firm they believe will give you the best service, then you are allowing that person to put your financial security at risk.

That's your future, and your children's future – it's not a joke or a game.

The numbers don't lie. There is a clear correlation between firms that offer the highest fees and the number of financial advisors they have on their books.

I'm just here to make you think. That's all I'm asking you to do. You're smart and intelligent, you can join the dots as well as anybody else.

You are now more than equipped to protect yourself from being ripped off by your financial advisor. But if you allow yourself to remain ignorant after what you've learned, then I'm afraid you and your family will pay the price.

At the very least it might be time to re-visit your Christmas card list.

TIP 9 –
PUMP & DUMP

The 'pump and dump' is a horrible name for a horrible dirty secret that costs investors millions of pounds every year. But this insider secret is quite unique because unlike most of the others, it's not monopolised by the professionals. There are groups on both sides of the fence that play this game; the retail and professional investors.

It works like this. First comes the pump.

Step 1 – the pump

A small group of investors work together and circulate false information on the internet, usually via share forums, to drive up the price of a particular share. This is called 'talking up a stock'. It is where individuals post positive comments in an investor chat room regarding soon to be released news about company ABC.

In all cases, company ABC has to be a penny stock because it's only the illiquid shares (assets not easily converted into cash) that can be manipulated enough in this way to generate sufficient returns.

Let's say the company is a small oil and gas company drilling in some remote part of the world, trading at 1p a share. If an investor posts a comment saying that the company has just struck a massive oil field, or that it's about to be taken over, then one of two things will happen.

If the person making the comment has no credibility, he is usually ignored. However, if the person has credibility within the trading floor chatroom, their view will be listened to, and, in many cases, acted upon.

Credibility comes from belonging to an investor group for at least a few months, and have previous engagement by, making comments, discussing topics, and being part of the collective gathering. Conversations help to build trust and the online world is a fickle one. It doesn't take long before online investors can be trusted, and very quickly they can accumulate numerous trading 'friends' as well as people who share their views.

Credibility also builds from getting 'good calls'; so, if you say that a particular stock is going up or down, and it subsequently does, that gives you the reputation of being a 'player', or 'in the know'. It means that what you are saying is worth listening to.

When credible players post, their online friends and friends' friends will start chatting about the rumour that has just circulated. Like Chinese Whispers, it's not long before the original source of the information is lost in the mayhem and the whispers take on a life of their own.

The forum chat hots up while the whispers develop and grow. Some investors will try and dig up for research to corroborate the story but the fact that nothing turns up doesn't dissuade them. After all the fact the information *isn't* yet public, is what makes it so exciting.

They know this is inside information, and they shouldn't

be acting on it. The irony is, of course that it's not inside information at all. It's just a pack of lies. But nobody knows that, and everybody is scrambling to buy shares in the company before the news is released.

As the information moves from one investor's keyboard to another, the story gathers momentum. And it does so, it creates confusion and uncertainty, an air of not knowing what is going to happen next, and that only serves to attract even more interest; this is where human greed becomes insatiable. The fear of missing out on an opportunity, especially when everybody seems to be talking about it, encourages poor decision making.

It's dressed up as insider trading except with one big difference.

Genuine insiders go to great lengths *not* to reveal their information to the marketplace, but the pump and dumpers do the opposite; they're telling everybody the information they have. They want everybody to believe what they have is valuable and worth a lot of money, but the information they hold is worthless; in fact, it's less than worthless – it will actually cost you money if you follow it.

The only reason the price moves at all is because it's a 'self-fulfilling prophecy'. If enough people believe it, then it actually happens. If enough people believe a share price is going to jump up, they buy shares in that company and hey presto, as if by magic, the share price really does jump up. Those who bought the shares are left feeling very pleased with themselves, not understanding what even happened.

It's called FOMO - Fear of Missing Out - drives all investors to act; to either buy or sell. But in order for it to work, the price needs to move, and the only way to do that, is to convince enough people; just one credible person can't do it on his own. He might be able to convince a few people, but he needs more than just a few.

So, in the middle of all these whispers, commotion, and buzz, another 'respected investor', another credible source, who is sat in a completely different chat room, spreads *the same rumour* as the first investor. In other words, another ripple somewhere in a different part of the pond has been created.

Simultaneously another anonymous investor in yet another chatroom says something similar.

Each of these individuals are apparently completely unconnected. They have different online names, avatars, online profiles etc. But they're all saying the same thing.

Next, we'll see more investors in the *same* chatrooms, verifying the initial rumour to be true. The information may not match exactly (that would be too obvious), but it's broadly the same and it corroborates the first story. Therefore, you now have multiple people in the same chatroom talking up a stock, plus you have other people in other trading chatrooms also talking about the same stock.

So, now you have multiple, seemingly unrelated individuals holding valuable, inside information about a company that is soon to be released. With a few clicks of the button, a hot insider trading tip can spread like wildfire, just like a video of a funny cat can go viral on social media.

With the internet moving information at the speed of light, it doesn't take much for one rumour to become major news in the online investment community. It doesn't take long before investors from different places, become excited enough to take action and start buying shares in the company.

Very quickly people are not only trading to take advantage of what is about to happen, they also start *writing* about their trades. People are sociable animals, and in the online world, they are more sociable than in person. They are happy to share their stories; their experiences, and they will post comments. By doing so, they are seeking validation and finding comfort in the actions of others who copy them.

They want others to know they're buying, to encourage them to do the same, and they don't want to be alone. It makes them feel good if others are doing the same; it gives them that seal of approval and that they're not being stupid.

They're already in their trade so they're not worried about pushing the price up if others start to buy, too. They *want* the price to go up. They *want* others to buy, too.

It's the classic 'safety in numbers' psychology at play here with a community of like-minded people. They all want to get rich together and they all think they're doing something clever and sneaky. But it's not clever; it's the opposite of clever.

Now, everybody is posting comments, such as "It looks good to me; I've just bought a small stake of £2k – let's see what happens". Or "Yes, all aboard the money train...choo choo..." Or whatever it is, you get the idea.

With each comment, each post, each positive affirmation, it's enough to send one more unsure person across the line. He gets involved and buys a few thousand pounds. The price goes even higher, and that pushes another cautious investor over the edge. He's watching the price go up and up and he's kicking himself for not buying an hour ago when the price was 1p; now the stock is at 3p, and he's worried he's going to miss out on the deal of a lifetime.

The chatroom is going crazy at this point, and predictions of 10p, 15p, even 25p are being thrown into the air with no rhyme or reason to it. Crazy prices that make people believe 3p is cheap.

It's like one clueless sheep after another jumping off a cliff.

As more and more people invest, the self-fulfilling prophecy goes into fifth gear, and the price starts to skyrocket. This means yet more and more investors, bigger and bigger deal sizes and even the earlier buyers start adding more to their original positions. It's just a car crash waiting to happen, full of greedy punters.

It's at this point the conversation quickly moves from being a rumour to a real, share price movement that people start patting each other on the back.

One chap feeling particularly pleased with himself might write, "*Have you just seen the price move? It's just jumped up 25% - ... I'm buying more.*"

Before you know it, there is a mad rush to buy this rumoured stock from all over the country, across multiple chatrooms, which just an hour ago, nobody had even heard of.

The share price gets out of control as investors pile in.

Logic and rationale go out of the window now because it's all about the two emotions of investing – fear and greed. People are fearful about missing out, and greedy because they want some action. It plays on human nature in the same way that all scams do.

Think about taking a punt and throwing £2,000 into a 1p stock. By the end of the day that company is trading at 2p; well, you just got back £2,000, a £1,000 profit – a 100% return – what other investments can you think of that pays that kind of return?

If you kept the same £2,000 in the bank earning 1% interest, it would take 100 years to make the same return!

Now, imagine that the stock doesn't move just from 1p to 2p, but to 5p, or even 10p. Depending on how much money you invest, that could be life changing.

But the price can only continue to move upwards if there are more buyers than sellers. As long as there are enough people in the chatrooms fueling the fire of speculation, there is nothing to stop the company accelerating into the stratosphere....at least for a while.

Then 'the dump' happens.

Step 2 – The dump

Fraudsters know that the absolute best time to sell their shares is when the market is flying high. Everybody is still buying, and the stock appears to be unstoppable. That's because when this happens, it eliminates the biggest problem of penny shares, which is illiquidity.

This allows the fraudsters to sell thousands, even tens of thousands of pounds, of shares which they could not have sold before.

They can then exit their position with a handsome profit, having already bought the shares BEFORE the pump.

So, if the scammers bought, let's say, £50,000 of company XYZ at 2p and pumped up the stock to, say, 10p, through internet trading chat rooms and social media posts, that would be a whopping 5x gain worth £200,000!

Initial purchase = 50,000/2p = £50,000 x 5 = 2.5m shares
Sale proceeds = 2.5m x 10p = £250,000

That's a pretty big move even for a penny stock and so that may not happen in just one day. That may take place over a number of days or even weeks.

The charade lasts for as long as there are enough gullible punters willing to believe the story. It's all about how many people can be convinced that a particular company is worth buying, how illiquid it is, how long that story can be perpetuated for, how gullible investors are, how strong the scammers are in terms of the size of their team, and how far below the radar they can fly without alerting the authorities.

Once the first cracks appear and investors realise this so called 'record gold discovery' announcement doesn't appear to be forthcoming, the doubt creeps in and the whole thing unravels very quickly.

However, most scammers don't want to play the long game because they know that while they can potentially make more money, the risks are greater when they hold for too long. The pump is often explosive and short term, and usually the biggest move is within the first few hours.

After that, it's hard to maintain that same level of price movement and interest in the false narrative. It's also difficult to keep positive momentum because investors who got in early are going to start taking profits.

Even if the scammers want to play the long game, they are handicapped by the other early-bird investors who had nothing to do with the scam, but just reacted quickly, and buying in at a very low price. When they see a decent profit, they may start selling which will cause the price momentum to wane and could even drop all the way back down again.

Ironically, there's a risk the scammers actually end up making *less* money than those who had nothing to do with the scam!

They are only too aware that a share price which jumps up quickly can also fall just as quickly. So they need to find that right balance between selling too early and selling too late. They want to sell just as the price peaks, but they have no idea when that is.

There are other risks to holding on for too long. It increases the possibility the company sees their price going up and feels obliged to make a market announcement to deny the rumours being told. If it's a huge contract win or a take-over rumour, the whole bubble can be popped with a single RNS (Regulatory News Service) from the company itself.

At some point, the pump and dump scam is exposed, the price collapses back to where it started, and if the scammers haven't sold their stock, they'll be sitting on £50,000 of shares they can't sell. So, timing is everything,

You might think the directors of a company would be happy if their share price was rising. However, that's not the case. If the share price has gone up on the back of false rumours, then it's actually hugely damaging for them. Investors buy on facts that can be trusted and if a stock has been manipulated it will detract investors in the future.

The scammers have to pump and dump quickly before their price jump attracts any serious media attention that might alert the company. Directors will be typically quick to quash any false claims to ensure their credibility isn't damaged; (unless, of course they are part of the scam, which sometimes they are).

High speed as well as getting in and out of a trade in the same day, also has another big advantage – in fact it's one of the *quickest* ways to make money in the City. There aren't many scams where an uneducated, unskilled, 18-year-old college dropout, can make a thousand pounds from his laptop, sat in his living room.

It's also highly replicable; you can play this game every day of the week, literally Monday to Friday. You can even play the game multiple times on any single day.

In fact, most professional scammers will do exactly that; they will operate multiple scams *simultaneously*. Not all of them will work but the ones that do could net a scammer several tens of thousands of pounds in profit.

The business model

Scamming is a profession; it's a full-time business and the pump and dump scam has business costs like any other. But the costs are low.

In a worst case scenario, the scammers end up investing £50,000 in a penny stock. It's not the end of the world. If there are five scammers in the operation, that's a modest £10,000 investment each. They still hold the asset, and they could still make money in the future if the company does well.

It also has a very low barrier to entry which is why you find it so popular with retail investors rather than financial professionals. In fact, there are more retail scammers in this space than professionals and that's because anybody can do it.

It doesn't require an in-depth knowledge of trading or exclusive access to contacts or any investment qualifications. You don't need a PhD or a scholarship.

You just need a group of friends, a few brokerage accounts set up, a little bit of start-up capital, a laptop, and some free time. That pretty much sums up a lot of young people who are either studying, working part time, or are unemployed.

It's actually a pretty amazing job. You wake up at whatever time you want, there's no commute to work, there are flexible hours, no previous experience necessary and you earn loads of money. That's not a bad job offer for a lot of 18–25-year-olds who don't want an office job.

Plus it comes with a great remuneration package, especially for the most effective scammers who are able to build the strongest teams and really spend time learning their trade.

There are hundreds of penny stocks in the UK but there are some which can be manipulated more than others because they are less liquid. There are also some where the directors don't care too much about what happens to their share price and are unlikely to make any announcements. Also, some companies don't get a lot of press coverage. This knowing type of information is important because it helps the scammers make more money.

Most stocks can only be successfully pumped and dumped once or twice before people realise what's happening. After that, the scammers need to be creative and look at new opportunities.

Scammers also continually need to reinvent themselves because after a few pump and dumps, their online profile may become exposed. They won't necessarily be ousted as a pump and dump scammer, but they'll be remembered as the guy who spread the rumour that turned out to be false. In that moment they lose credibility.

That's why scammers don't have one online profile, but several. In fact, an individual scammer might have as many as ten or twenty aliases operating at the same time in a dozen or more chat rooms. That's because they know that eventually one of those aliases will get 'blown up' and won't be usable again.

The other aliases won't be involved in the pump and dump schemes at all, they will be submitting regular posts to build up credibility over time. Their job is to create trust in the community, but not to support the stock that's being pumped. In fact, they might post something like "I'm not sure about this one. I'm going to see how it goes. Good luck to everybody else!"

When that rumour is exposed false, this alias suddenly becomes a hero. Now his trust and credibility increases.

Little do the other investors know that it's the same person operating under different guises. In this way the scammer can have a ready pile of trusted aliases to operate the next scam. For every trader that gets blown up, two new traders come in to take their place.

Another good business strategy is for the scammers to underplay the rumours.

If they can make small but consistent profits without raising suspicion and without compromising their scam, they can use the same set of aliases for years. Rather than pump up the stock through big claims of, say, a massive takeover rumour, their approach is more subtle.

Their goal is to push up a stock from, say, 2p to 4p, rather than 2p to 20p and that's possible without making outlandish claims like takeovers. They can just say something like, *"This looks good on the charts; I think this stock is going higher...would be worth taking a punt and seeing what happens..."*

There are no false promises or claims, which means the trader doesn't get called out. He's not creating a huge level of momentum but he's hoping he can pump the stock up just enough to make a bit of profit.

The 2p to 20p payday is much bigger and more attractive, but it also attracts a lot more heat. Whereas the 2p to 4p is still a 100% profit, but with a fraction of the risk.

Penny stocks often go up from 2p to 4p and then back down to 2p, then back up to 5p and back down to 1p and so on. So that's not going to raise any eyebrows, which means the scammers can simply repeat the process. The price never moves enough to interest the media, the regulators, or the companies involved.

Even the investors who bought at 4p watch the stock fall to 2p and, are none the wiser. They're not going to complain and, they're not going to think that they were scammed; in their mind they just got unlucky.

That's because it's a perfect scam; it's rarely identified and, much less, reported.

Market makers

One of the main differences between penny stocks and blue-chip stocks is the lack of liquidity and transparency. That's because when you buy a large, blue chip share you are usually buying directly from another seller, via a system called 'Direct Market Access' (DMA). There's no middle person in between you and the seller and you can see the price before you agree to the trade.

With penny stocks it works differently. Because there is not a high volume of shares being traded, a market maker typically sits between the buyer and seller to create the liquidity. Their job is to make a two-way price for those stocks, a *bid* price for the seller and an *offer* (or *ask*) price for the buyer.

The market maker makes money from the difference between the two prices, i.e., the spread. That's because he buys at the lower bid price and sells at the higher offer price.

The problem is that sometimes the market maker might end up with too many sellers and not enough buyers. This means he has to drop his price, as he begins to accumulate shares he doesn't really want to hold.

From all of the people selling their share to him, he might end up holding a few hundred thousand pounds on his trading book, which now exposes him to significant risk. That's the opposite of what he wants, which is to have a *balanced* book with a relatively small amount of stock and a good cash-float at any one time.

He wants stock that flows in *and out* of his book *quickly* so that he can keep things turning over while he makes his money. He's not bothered if the price drops as long as he's not holding any of the stock he paid a higher price for. He has a bit of a safety net because the stock has to drop by more than the spread before he can lose any money but he's still at risk.

If he ends up holding a lot of stock and there are no buyers, even at a lower price, he's now exposed to any negative company announcements. Other market makers will drop their price if that happens, and he'll have no choice but to drop his price too. Therefore, he's inflicting upon himself real financial pain.

It's like a greengrocer who holds a hundred bags of potatoes worth £10 each (£1,000). If the price of each bag falls to just £5, this means his inventory has lost 50% of its value (£500). He needs to get rid of those potatoes quickly.

If the price continues to fall, the greengrocer eventually gets wiped out. The market marker gets wiped out, too.

That's why the market maker is incentivised to *pump* up the stock price.

The only way for him to remove his risk is to sell his inventory. The only way he can do that profitably is if he can convince enough people to buy his potatoes for at least what it cost him i.e., £10, ideally at £15 per bag so he can make a profit.

The problem is, how the hell is he going to sell the potatoes for £15 if the price has already started to fall?

Well, in the same way the retail scammers are doing it; by manipulating the price via circulating false rumours in the marketplace. A modest price increase helps to reduce the loss incurred and a big price move can turn a loss into a decent sized profit.

But of course, market makers are known in the City, and they're busy at work, so they can't sit at home all day posting lies and false rumours on internet chat rooms.

That's where *their teams* come into play. Professional market maker scammers employ and pay a trusted group of people to do their dirty work for them.

Indeed, that's how many of the retail investors enter the marketplace for the first time. Professional market makers teach the inside game to groups of trusted retail investors who in turn, are used to scam other retail investors.

They teach them the game and they share in the profits.

A few well-worded comments in a timely fashion by a group of internet traders can push a stock up by 30%, 50% or even 100% or more, which is enough for the market maker to start offloading (dumping) his position to unsuspecting new buyers.

When there's no interest and no excitement, prices don't move, and the market maker's trading book just sits there becoming stale. The best way to encourage people to trade is to make stocks look interesting, even when they're not. A little rumour here or there can do wonders to spark interest and rejuvenate a stock that everybody had previously forgotten about.

In the absence of corporate announcements, which typically only happen a few times a year, most companies just don't get very much interest.

Market makers have to *create* interest. If that means 'fake news', so be it.

Money on the way down

The market maker scammers hold one big advantage over retail scammers; they can just as easily make money on the way down as they can on the way up.

If they don't hold a lot of stock and there are a lot of investors who want to buy, then it's difficult for them to make a lot of money. That's because their stock is quickly purchased and investors buy stock from other market makers.

In this case, the market maker scammer needs to find a way to *buy* stock and they can do this by creating negative rumours in the marketplace. This helps to drop the price and it panics investors to start selling. It also puts a brake on those investors who were keen to buy.

However, after the price has fallen and the market maker scammers have bought loads of stock, that's when the rumours are quashed, and the price suddenly jumps back up. The market makers can now push up their own price and make a killing.

Whilst the goal of market markers is always to run a balanced book without too much stock or cash, that's only when they are not manipulating the price. If a market maker knows the likely direction of price travel, he will want to have a very *unbalanced* book. Either he will want to be massively overweight in a stock (if he knows the price is going up) or massively underweight (if he knows the price is going down).

Whenever a market maker's inventory-cash 'balance' is disrupted, they can counter the risk by shifting their price accordingly. However, price manipulation isn't always easy or straight forward because market makers don't work in isolation. Other market makers will make their own price and so the *best* bid and *best* offer by any market maker will be the one offered to the marketplace.

In the UK there is always a minimum of two market makers on any penny stock company but typically, there are at least three or four.

Because market makers can't just move their price up or down on their own, it's helpful for them to have other tools in their toolbox they can use including the pump and dump strategy.

I'm not suggesting that all market makers do this all of the time, but some do at least some of the time. Market makers won't screw their fellow market makers because it's such a small club. They all know each other and they have to work together. They also know that if they do a favour for somebody today, they can call in a favour tomorrow.

There is plenty of collusion between market makers because they play for one team. You and the rest of society, the retail investors, play for another team. It's you against them once again.

Remember it's nothing personal, just business.

Of course, there are different degrees of collusion and varying levels of corruptness. Some market makers might just skirt around price manipulation whilst others are neck-deep in dirty tricks and market abuse. Where they sit and the stocks they manage also have an impact.

There's more chance of collusion when there are just two market makers rather than five. So the stocks with a smaller number of market makers are more likely to be manipulated. It feeds back into the cycle of illiquidity which is why you have to be so careful with penny stocks.

Money on the way up

Market makers can set the price at whatever level (within reason) that they want to. If the market maker's team of scammers post positive comments the market maker can *shift up the price* to validate those rumours. For example, he can push the stock up from say, 7p to 7.5p, and a few minutes later from 7.5p to 8p. That sends a very powerful message to the marketplace. It gives the impression the rumours are real.

Even though no trades have been executed, investors won't necessarily know that. Even if they looked at the publicly available information on executed trades, the fact that no trades were executed isn't necessarily a bad thing. It appears the market maker is verifying this rumour by moving up his price even with no new buyers.

That's a powerful statement. Now the rumour has been indirectly verified by a professional maker. It must be true!

Now imagine if you're in that chatroom and the price is going up. Is it going to encourage you to buy or not? Of course, you will want to buy.

Whilst being a very clever and highly deceptive ploy it's not without risk for the market maker.

Because a rising price whilst designed to attract more buyers could also inadvertently attract more sellers, (those who are not in the chatrooms) and that would be terrible. The upward price move itself doesn't impact the market makers provided nobody acts on the new price. The market makers don't lose anything and if nothing actually happens the price, it can be returned to its original starting point at any time.

But the majority of investors who are oblivious to all of the chatroom noise, will just see the price go up. Some might use it as an opportunity to sell their own stock. That's bad news for the market makers.

However, the market maker is betting the small number of sales at the higher price will be more than offset by the increasing buying activity that would come from within the chat rooms. The market maker is hoping that a well-timed, modest price increase when coupled with positive chat room comments, can be the perfect catalyst to generate a fantastic, buying frenzy.

The increased price means that the market maker can now dump his old stock at a better price and make a decent return. He's been able to turn his 'dead stock' that was sat on his trading books, gathering dust, into cash.

He has done the magician's equivalent of pulling another rabbit out of the hat. From a paper-loss, dead weight investment that was going nowhere, he's been able to magically turn it into money. This gives him the ability to buy new stock that he can hopefully turn into a profit.

Those dodgy potatoes that nobody wanted yesterday for £5 a bag, have flown out of the door today at £15 a bag. Not only has he managed to get rid of that unwanted stock, but he's also raised a load of cash which he can now use to buy some bags of apples with. Old stock that was making no money out, new stock in.

I'd love to tell you that's where the pump and dump ends, but of course, it always gets worse.

The directors

In most cases, companies targeted by the pump and dump scam are completely oblivious to it. However, there are some companies who are not just aware of it, but are complicit in its operation.

Picture this.

You're the director of an AIM company which you have spent the last thirty years working to nurture and grow. Your entire life's work and the security of your family's future rests on the success of this company. Pretty much every last pound of your total wealth is tied up in shares of your company. The problem is, business has not been doing so well recently.

New competitors have joined the marketplace and you can see the cracks appearing. The company had a decent year last year; you had an opportunity to exit the business at a great price and take early retirement, but you didn't. Now you regret that decision.

Over the past few months things have changed dramatically and every day it's becoming worse.

You've tried everything possible to turn the business around, but nothing seems to work. You're two years away from retirement and you're sitting on the edge of the abyss. What was an amazing business just six months ago, is now a nightmare. It's got no more than a few months left in it before the cash dries up, the bills can't be paid, and the whole thing goes 'pop'.

Thankfully for you, the market hasn't picked up on your troubles because you haven't announced them yet; but it's only a matter of time. Another few short months, and the marketplace will know the truth because you have to post your company results.

You know what happens next; the share price collapses, and your retirement goes down the swanny.

You are dreading it. Everything you have worked so hard for is about to blow up in your face. You need to find a way to exit and get your money out quickly. Your family have no idea. They're enjoying the big house, the nice cars, and the villa in the South of France, but it's all on credit and being supported by the business. If the business goes, it all goes.

The company share price is trading at 10p, but you know that once the bad news gets into the public domain, the shares are likely to fall to 5p, 3p, maybe even down to a penny. You will lose everything. Your life savings tied up in the business are about to disappear. You should have taken your money out as you went along but you thought it was the right thing to keep it invested. Now it's too late. There are no buyers for your business and there's no exit strategy.

It's a nightmare situation. What do you do?

What you've just read is not made up. That's the real-life situation many business owners find themselves in.

Step forward the solution – the pump and dump scam.

Having read the above, you might feel that faced with such a nightmare, helpless situation, directors could be forgiven for doing whatever it takes to get their money out. That means pumping up their share price, if necessary, so they can sell.

But I'll remind you this is not a victimless crime.

For the company director to keep his life savings, it means somebody else has to lose theirs.

If you're the company director of an AIM company, you've already done better than 99% of companies because the vast majority private companies never float on the stock exchange. The directors of those companies work just as hard and probably earn a lot less.

Directors of privately held companies can't play this game of trickery with their shareholders because *they're* the only shareholders. They can't cheat themselves.

They can't play games with their share price because it wouldn't impact anybody but them.

So, it's not fair that the directors of listed companies can play these games and mislead the market.

The AIM directors owe a duty of care to their shareholders, the existing ones and the future ones. Those shareholders are investing their ISAs and pensions into their business. They're relying on and trusting those directors to keep their promises, to be honest and trustworthy.

These are everyday small investors; many of them are pensioners. The guy who invests a few thousand pounds in an AIM company is almost certainly less well-off than the director of a company listed on the stock exchange. He can't afford to lose.

If somebody has to lose money, that loss should be shared equally according to the share ownership of the business (in the same way that profits are shared equally).

Accurate information needs to be freely available. As a director, you can't hold back data just because it suits you, especially if it seriously disadvantages somebody else. You can't lie and deceive.

Besides, if a business is failing, whose fault is that? It has to be the board of directors, the people in charge.

If a director is going to make loads of money when his business does well, then he must accept that he can lose loads of money when his business doesn't do well. That's the life of an entrepreneur; that's what he signed up for.

The owner of a limited company has to take the whack himself, so he feels the full force of all decisions, good and bad. When things get really bad, he can lose everything. He can't fiddle the books or make false announcements or mislead his investors or manipulate the share price to his favour. Because he's the only shareholder. It's all on him.

But the director of a Public Limited Company (PLC) can play skullduggery if he wants, even if he knows it's wrong and illegal.

The PLC director should not be able to exonerate himself from risk, especially when he was responsible for it. He can't pick and choose when he wants to be in charge. That's why there is no excuse.

I'm sorry for the AIM director who invested thirty years of his life and now the business is failing but it's the same for every business owner; you take your chances in this game.

He's the captain. If his ship sinks, he sinks with it.

Greed over fear

Whilst the pump and dump scam is used by some AIM directors when they're desperate and fearful of losing their life savings, it's actually worse than this because there are many times when they use this scam because they're just plain greedy.

They might already have millions of pounds stashed away in their bank accounts. But they know they can make even more with the pump and dump scam.

This is especially true when company directors are remunerated according to 'shareholder value'. In other words, their pay is linked to the *share price* of their company.

Imagine a director who is running a company that is failing but nobody yet knows about it. Let's say the share price of the company is 10p and the director has a million pounds worth of stock options which are exercisable if the share price goes above 12p. In other words, he can only sell his shares at a profit if the price goes above 12p.

Clearly, there is now a massive financial incentive for him to push the share price up. He's sitting on a million pounds that is literally worthless unless he can somehow convince the marketplace that his company is worth more than it really is.

The only way to do this is to create 'good news' – that's where the pump and dump comes in.

It's like the captain of a sinking ship, making a passenger announcement that the destination will be reached shortly. The captain gives the illusion that everything is okay before he jumps into a little rescue dinghy with his pals. A few moments later the ship crashes into a massive iceberg and all the passengers drown.

It's pure greed and manipulation.

The mechanics of a pump and dump 'team' work in the same way.

A group of stay-at-home mums, some college dropouts and a whole online community of pot-smoking teenagers get paid to post comments to push up the price of the stock. In this case they're not trading their own account. Their job is to push up the price and for that they earn a salary, a fixed wage.

The price increase gives the directors an opportunity to exercise at least some, if not all of their share options. It also gives them the opportunity to dump their existing shares at an overly inflated price.

As the stakes increase so too does the sophistication of the scam.

Fake investor websites

When the potential pay-out is several million pounds, company directors don't just use bored housewives sat at their kitchen tables in between breastfeeds, to push up their stock price. They recruit and pay very well and assemble a professional team for the job.

This includes dodgy research analysts, shoddy newspaper columnists and corrupt investor websites. Any publication, post or article that paints the company in a positive light is one step towards tricking people into buying shares in the failing business.

The City is full of 'independent analysts' who are more than willing to write whatever you want them to, for the right price. I know because I've been approached many times myself.

In fact, every year since I opened my business in 2008, I'm approached and asked if I would like to be nominated for the 'Top Stockbroker of the Year' award or the 'Best Trader of the Season'. How do I win that prize? Well, that's easy, I just need to sponsor the biggest and most expensive table at their annual black-tie do. Sometimes there's a 'vote' which, of course is also rigged. But, usually, it literally comes down to who's willing to donate the most to that particular company.

That's it. I pay for my award if I want it. That's what many wealth management firms do. It's a complete con, which is why I refuse to entertain them. Yet I see many of my competitors doing exactly that; literally buying up all the awards that they can.

When you see these 'Best Stockbroker of the Year' or 'Best Trading Platform' or 'Best Research Analyst' or whatever the hell it is, just remember that it's all bull*hit.

I've even had newspaper editors and columnists say they will do a full, front page spread about me and my business in 'long interview form'. But here's the catch; there is no interview! I'm supposed to write what I want them to print as if I'm being interviewed. What a farce.

That's it and, they will print it. I can say I have a 99% trading success ratio, that all of my clients always make loads of money and never ever lose, and that I'm the best trader to have walked on this planet.

It's all about money. Who's willing to pay the most wins this game.

The AIM directors know this. They can have anything written about their companies by any number of independent researchers and analysts. The more they pay, the more glowing will be their report. The more 'credible' websites which have a greater online footfall, more subscribers, and more engaged followers, will charge more.

So, as an investor, if you Google a particular penny share, you don't know which research report is genuine and which is false. With enough money, directors of AIM companies can flood the market with positive research reports and comments. They have a monopoly on trading chatrooms, investor forums, magazines and, investor awards.

In recent years there has even been a big push for celebrity endorsements. You've got some Z-listed has-been celebrity, bimbo who came third in Big Brother a few years ago, that everybody has forgotten about. Now she's promoting a foreign exchange course, even though she doesn't know how to spell foreign, let alone trade FX.

Companies also pay for advertising and sponsorship deals with golf clubs or partner up with private member clubs, where wealthy and affluent people congregate. This is all advertising and marketing, and nothing to do with the company itself.

I could have one of my analysts write a report today about penny share company ABC and why it's the best thing since sliced bread. The director of ABC pays me say £10,000 in a brown paper envelope, and I distribute the article to my database of investors, which currently sits at approximately 9,000.

Think about that. I have access to 9,000 financially qualified, potential investors who I could encourage to buy shares in company ABC. Even if only 100 of them bought a few thousand pounds worth, the share price would skyrocket. That would give the company director the opportunity to sell his shares, exercise his options, make a million quid and disappear.

There are many other companies out there which have a bigger audience and reach than me. This is why you have to be so careful and understand that a lot of the research and data you are reading, and basing your investment decisions on, is not independent.

Of course, there are rules governing what directors can and can't do. For example, directors are not allowed to buy or sell shares within a certain 'closed' period which is a set time before a company announcement is made.

But that doesn't stop the pump and dump happening *before* the closed period. Company directors know months, even years in advance what their exit strategy is, so it's an easy thing to prepare for. Besides, they don't want to exercise all their options in a single day. That would be too obvious, especially after a price has been pumped. Small but often is the secret.

There are also restrictions about how many share options can be exercised. But, again, this is open to manipulation and is generally controlled internally by the firm itself.

Directors mustn't raise suspicion because that would lead to an investigation, so, they're unlikely to take silly risks. The pump and dump must be subtle and unassuming, so it can be explained away with natural market volatility. If the price goes up and then down again, well that doesn't mean anything. Shares go up and down all of the time.

The actions of company directors have to appear natural and in line with business practices.

But sometimes, dodgy analysts, researchers and investor

website reports are not enough. The directors want more...
much more.

Falsified accounts

There are many examples where companies have gone one
step further and have completely fabricated, and falsified
their own company accounts. Forget spreading that false
rumour about a takeover or massive contract win, or having
a false analyst report, or buying a fake 'best company of the
year' award; why not go the full nine yards, and blatantly lie
on the end of year accounts?.

Why leave anything to chance? If you want to make serious
money, like Jeff Bezos, founder of Amazon, but your company
more closely resembles Mr Patel's discounted 24-hour corner
shop, (yes, I can say that, I'm Asian), then don't worry about
it, you have a solution.

Just fudge your accounts to show better profits, more assets,
higher cashflow, and lower costs so your business appears to
be much better than it really is. Just like Mr Patel does when he
polishes his out of date tomatoes and hopes nobody notices.

That's a sure-fire way to get the price of your stock moving up.
Plus, you don't need to mess around with paying internet keyboard
warriors and stay at home mums to pump up your stock.

Sounds crazy but this happens, much more than you might
think.

The situation is now so bad and out of control, there are
even several self-styled 'financial vigilante' firms that investigate

company accounts to check they're genuine. They highlight the liars on the internet to make investors aware that their accounts don't stack up.

For example, Quintessential Capital Management, a US hedge fund warned investors for several months that a technology company, Globo, was falsifying its accounts. At the time, the regulators hadn't spotted it, but it turns out that Quintessential was right.

The firm was making false announcements clearly designed to push up the share price. At the same time, the Chief Executive of the company, Costis Papadimitrakopoulous, (yes, I'm not making that up, that really is his surname), offloaded more than a staggering 42 *million shares* at an over-inflated price.

Investors heard the announcements and realised the share price had to go up, so, they started buying. Little did they know that it was all lies. This wasn't a small penny company which goes to show that lies and deceit can happen anywhere in the financial markets.

At its peak Globo was worth more than £300 million and it had raised more than £100 million in sales of stock and debt. Where did all of that money go to? Of course, to Costis and the other directors.

It's hard when you're on the outside to think that this could happen.

You might wonder how it's even possible that a company can blatantly lie? How can it publish wildly inaccurate numbers? Are there no checks and balances? What about the accountants and the auditors, - didn't they check?

Money talks. It's as simple as that. With enough of it, you can buy anybody out. When you're set to make £10 million or £50 million, you can easily throw a couple of million pounds to a friendly accountant or auditor who's paid to conveniently 'miss' a few things. I don't know about Globo and I'm not suggesting their auditors did anything wrong.

I'm simply making the broader point that auditors can and are bought out.

Look, as I've said before; the financial system is corrupt because it is all about money and where there is money, there is corruption. None of this should shock you. I know it does because when I first found out, it shocked me, too. But it shouldn't.

Nobody wants to be in the heart of the lies and deceit, and they don't need to be. They just need to turn a blind eye. They might get charged with incompetence but it's a lesser charge that's worth the extra million pounds of revenue.

Besides, they'll cover their own asses by getting the companies to sign off documentation to say the accountant is not responsible for the validity of the data.

The company itself can then go and cover its own ass by taking out Professional Indemnity Insurance (PII) so its liability is limited in case it gets sued by any of its shareholders or investors. From there, the insurance company goes out and covers its ass by hedging its risk with a larger insurance firm in case the claims are too significant for them to handle, and so, the merry-go-round, goes around and around.

If one accountant or even an auditor senses something dodgy is happening, and raises it, the company simply terminates their contract and calls in a new firm of auditors. Remember that auditors are *self-appointed* by the firm, and the firm pays the auditors' salary. This is very different to an independent audit which form part of a financial investigation. The majority of auditors who pick up on something 'dodgy' prefer not to be involved rather than report it to the regulator; it's much easier to just walk away. So, if they discover some minor financial irregularities, they prefer to pretend not to see it.

That's not always possible because auditors have an obligation to disclose irregularities. And if the fraud is so obvious and serious that it must be reported, then the auditor has no choice. That's why company directors are very careful what they disclose to 'untested' auditors. They start off with a little bit of information and then add more as the trust builds.

It's a weird set-up. It's like a lawyer defending his client who he knows has committed first degree murder. That's the sort of thing the lawyer really *doesn't* need to know. He just needs to defend his client and if his client is so indefensible, the lawyer walks away rather than go to the Judge with an audio recording of his client's confession.

Neither the company nor the auditor want to get caught up in an investigation. That takes time and money, and there's no upside for either the company or the auditor. It can also create huge reputational damage for the auditor because it earns the highly *unsought* reputation of being a whistle-blower.

That's hardly great PR for the auditor to win new contracts from other businesses in the same industry, even if those firms are doing things correctly.

It's not just small penny stocks either.

Let's not forget the oil giant, Enron which defrauded its shareholders out of a staggering $70 billion. This wasn't over a few weeks or a couple of months. It was over eight long years.

How is that even possible? How can that have been missed? We're talking about one of the biggest oil companies in the world at that time.

Did anybody not know anything? Really?

Just a pack of lies, false accounts and complete price manipulation.

Crypto pump and dump

Pump and dump scandals occur not just with stocks and shares, but also with cryptocurrencies and other illiquid investments where the price can be more readily manipulated. In some cases, it's not even disguised but openly marketed as a pump and dump scheme.

Social media and communication networks like WhatsApp and Telegram are used to send messages to hundreds, even thousands of subscribers in particular groups.

Participants are aware that an announcement will be made by the group administrator at a specific time, on a specific day. At that precise moment, the administrator announces the name of the crypto currency that is to be bought. Immediately a crazy frenzy of buying takes place as thousands of people rush to buy. Everybody knows it's a pump and dump, but they don't care because they expect to be in and out before the next person.

The buying frenzy sends the price rocketing for a couple of minutes, then back down again after investors take their profits and start selling. If you're not a part of this group you will have no idea what's going on, except that a tiny crypto stock has gone up 300% in the past ten minutes and now its back down again!

You're left scratching your head while a whole underground movement of speculators are controlling the price.

The administrators are the only ones who are guaranteed to win because they buy the crypto *before* they make their announcement. Some even charge subscribers to be a part of their group, but the subscribers don't care. They figure that if they can get in and out quick enough, they can make a quick killing.

Everybody knows what they're getting into, but it's still not good because this doesn't promote sensible investing. It just makes a mockery of price discovery, of free capital markets. The idea that you can make money in this way is typical of the new young group of 'get-rich' schemers.

Even gambling is better than this, at least it can be fun. There's nothing wrong with the occasional flutter on the horses or a spin at the roulette wheel, because for most people they understand it's just a game. The problem with these official pump and dump set-ups is that some people really believe that they are 'working'. It's become a job for them.

Instead of getting off their sweaty behinds and building a product or offering a service, even if it's just cutting a lawn or serving sandwiches in a deli, where your existence has meaning and societal value, we now have a growing generation of lazy, internet-induced zombies who think they're professional crypto traders.

Price manipulation

Pump and dump is an evil cancer in the stock market because it threatens and destabilises the very basis upon which investing is built, i.e., the ability to fairly value a company so you can have the confidence to decide on when to buy and when to sell. If you take away that fundamental foundation, you are left with nothing. That's why it's so damaging.

It removes certainty, and in the absence of certainty, there can only be chaos. Investors don't know when to buy or sell and investing becomes gambling. That's when people step away from the market and the whole system is at risk of collapsing. When enough people lose faith in the system, it will disappear.

Trust and confidence are the foundations upon which governments and democracies are built.

It's also the foundation upon which financial markets operate.

In its simplest form, the way any investor makes money is to buy something which he believes is underpriced or sell something which he believes is over-priced.

This principal doesn't just apply to equities, but to every product in the world. It applies to houses, cars, computers, fruit and vegetables, as well as a gazillion other goods and services in a free market economy.

Therefore, the *integrity* of price is not just important, it's critical.

That's why the pump and dump is so dangerous – it has the potential to destroy all that is good about the markets; then we'd all be in a big heap of trouble.

TIP 8 –
MARKET MANIPULATION –
THE HOUND OF HOUNSLOW

Price manipulation is one of the secrets to how dodgy professionals become very rich and with penny shares, you can see it's relatively easy because of the lack of liquidity. With a little bit of financial clout, and a few friends banded together working in unison, you can manipulate prices and make a lot of money.

But it's not possible to play that game with the larger, blue chip companies. That takes millions of pounds, even tens of millions to move the share price sufficiently to make a profit.

Nobody has that kind of money, except for one institution.... the banks.

Price, confidence and trust

When the price is *controlled*, the market is being abused, hence the term 'market abuse'.

The market is being abused because it's not being allowed to operate freely. It means the current trading price is not based on freely made decisions, but is being artificially pushed in one direction or another.

Just imagine a situation where the price of everything is wrong. Think about walking into a shop and knowing that every single item is mis-priced. What would you do?

Well, you wouldn't buy anything and if you did buy something, you'd spend a long time before you made that decision. You'd have to try and work out for yourself whether something was fairly priced. You would go to other shops, you would speak to friends for their advice, you would look online for alternatives, you would basically spend more time thinking and less time spending.

When that happens and is multiplied by eight billion people in the world, there is market mayhem. Nobody buys anything.

Buying anything from anybody stops – economic activity grinds to an immediate halt.

The market collapses, and eventually, there is no more market. We go back to the dark ages of local bartering with rice, goats and camels. We go back a thousand years.

The entire financial market is based on trust. Our currencies, our money, our savings, our deposits, all of our assets, the way we transact – it's all based on trust. It all involves either pushing pieces of paper around that have the Queen's head on it or pushing digital numbers around electronically.

There's no gold to back up those pieces of paper like there once was; so now there is just hope – across entire nations, across billions of people. That hope is misplaced because the system is broken.

However, the illusion still works because only a few people know they're in the middle of a massive scam. Billions of people have no idea their pound notes and dollars are worthless, not even worth the paper they're written on.

They don't know they're in the world's biggest Ponzi scheme.

But when enough people wake up and realise that the money in their pockets is worth less than the Monopoly board money their kids play with, then we all have a big problem.

That's why the people, society as a whole, can't lose trust in the system - not ever.

Eventually it will happen, the lies will be exposed, and the old system will have to be replaced with a new one.

Until then, let's keep playing the charade that it's all still worth something.

That's exactly what Narinder Singh did (no relation of mine, all Sikhs share the same middle name).

He played the game better than anybody. "Who's Narinder", I hear you ask?

You're about to find out.

Investment banks and copycats

If the price moves proportionately to the amount of buying and selling, it follows that the biggest players who do the most buying and selling in the marketplace, can move the price the most. This means that central banks, governments, investment houses, hedge funds, wealth management firms, and pension funds are the biggest price drivers.

Pricing is therefore largely determined by the *volume* of shares being bought and sold, otherwise known as 'size'.

The little guy who buys a thousand pounds worth of shares in a company makes no difference to the share price whatsoever. But the pension fund that buys £10 million worth of shares, can move that price by 1%, 5%, 10% or more.

Therefore, the basis upon which everybody makes money, which is the price, is effectively controlled by a small number of major players, including big investment banks like JP Morgan, Goldman Sachs, Deutsche Bank, UBS and several more.

In fact, there are probably around a dozen major players that control 80% of the price action.

They have the deepest pockets, the biggest credit lines, the largest deal sizes and ultimately, they yield the greatest power and control. That's why when one of the big boys make a play, everybody watches with interest because they know the price is about to move.

It's also why 'copy-cat' trades are commonplace on Wall Street and in the City. That's where investors follow the banks. We've already seen how it happens in the retail investor market, where somebody sees a price move up or down, or hears a rumour,and then copy the trade, without doing any research. They just blindly follow.

It's the same with the professionals.

If Goldman Sachs suddenly starts to pour money into a particular trade and is being overly aggressive, the JP Morgan trade desk is likely to follow suit. They will assume that Goldman Sachs knows something they don't. If JP Morgan doesn't copycat the trade, at the very least it will be wary of going the opposite way, and betting against that trade.

So, if Goldman Sachs is buying aggressively then JP Morgan is either likely to buy or will sit out of the game rather than sell or go short, at least until it's figured out what Goldman Sachs is up to.

The resulting impact is a sharp price move in the direction of the investor who is most bold and confident, and who places the biggest bet.

The same goes for the central banks – if the Federal Reserve (FOMC) or European Central Bank (ECB) suddenly starts buying a particular currency, they have so much liquidity and cash available, it would be silly for other banks and institutions to bet against them. They also hold all the political power and directly control the key factor that impacts currencies the most, which is the ability to change interest rate levels. So, it would be foolish to take the opposite side of that trade.

The same applies to the International Monetary Fund (IMF), and any other global institution that has access to big wads of cash. In some cases, they don't even need cash. Remember, central banks can just print money.

Imagine playing poker against somebody who has a never- ending pile of chips. Even when he loses, he just magics another hundred chips out of thin air. Do you really want to play against that guy?

That's why investors often make a big song and dance about doing their research and analysis when really a big chunk of it is just copying others. As we saw with the pump and dump game, even research isn't truly independent.

Sometimes, it's just blatantly false but even when it's not false, what is it, other than a regurgitation of another person's research? Where did they get their research?. That's right, from somebody else.

Of course, at some point, somebody, somewhere, with a high IQ, very thick glasses and sitting in a windowless office, had to do some research in the first instance. But after that, it's largely copied from one researcher to another. One research desk makes a judgement on a particular sector, or industry or company based on what they research on the internet.

What they find on the internet, is well, to put it bluntly, the research of other people.

Sure, there is some level of subjective analysis that goes on because a researcher can't just plagiarise somebody else's work; they need to watermark their research with their own unique point of view.

But even then, where does their opinion really come from? It's from the opinion of others, it's from reading hundreds of articles, from digesting lots of news, from watching lots of videos, from analysing many balance sheets, from breaking down countless charts.

All of that data and information has been provided by somebody else's research. It's just a merry go round. There are very few critical thinkers in the world and in the financial markets, far fewer than you would imagine. That's why the most successful traders are contrarian and think outside the box.

But researchers are not traders. They get paid a fixed salary in the most part, and they don't want to sail too close to the wind. They would rather just fit in with everybody else, even if they're all spectacularly wrong.

All of the research in the marketplace at any given moment is just a melting pot of other people's ideas and calculations. Very few people venture out there in the cold on their own.

It's not surprising, therefore, that traders copy traders, banks copy banks, researchers copy researchers and investors copy investors.

Despite the trillions of pounds at stake, this just demonstrates how fickle the whole market can be.

You'd never guess that your pension money was being invested through regurgitated research or gambled through copy cat trades, but that's exactly what happens. There's really no meaningful analysis. Even if there is, prices are so often manipulated, there's no guarantee this supposedly meaningful analysis is any more effective than one that is plagiarised from another firm.

Market prices are a function of human buying and selling

decisions; because humans can be manipulated, it follows that the price can be manipulated. The banks are no different; they just have more money. But they are behind glass doors, they are still run by humans.

So, banks can be manipulated. Or at least one or two of them can be.

The rest will simply follow and what happens? Something very interesting happens.

One man; one massive market manipulation

Narinder Singh was described by friends as very intelligent but socially awkward. He lived in an unassuming three-bedroom semi-detached house in a run-down area of Hounslow, West London, and was a trader with a vision of becoming very rich by manipulating price.

The problem for him was that he was a tiny fish in a massive pond and his goal to get rich was ambitious to the point of being ridiculous. It would be the most audacious move that anybody had tried in living history. His goal was not to manipulate a small penny stock to move by a few pence, but to manipulate the price of entire stock market indices.

But he wouldn't just go big, he would go massive. He went after the *biggest* stock market index of them all, the big Daddy exchange, the US S&P500.

As crazy as it sounded, he knew where the big money was, so that's what he set his sights on.

The problem for Narinder was that while the S&P500 index was the most lucrative stock exchange to scam, its sheer size also made it the most impenetrable market of all. It's like breaking into the Tower of London to steal the Crown jewels. The pay-day is life-changing, if you can pull it off, but it's an impossible feat.

Being home to the biggest and most successful companies on the planet, Narinder's plan to bring down the S&P500 stock exchange was completely crazy.

It seemed ridiculous, but actually, it turns out that it wasn't at all. In fact, it was genius.

Narinder understood human psychology and knew that he just had to convince one or two big investment banks that the price was moving in a certain direction. He was hoping that this might be just enough for the other big banks to copycat the trade, causing a massive, domino effect. He could then take the opposite side of the trade, sit back and make millions in the process.

And that's exactly what he did.

Incredibly, he pulled off this heist not in a swanky City of London office, not in majestic Mayfair, not in downtown Manhattan, New York or in Tokyo. He also wasn't hooked up to the most sophisticated trading platform and neither did he have access to the highest quality computer hardware, or the fastest internet connection. He wasn't working with teams of highly qualified PhD mathematicians, Harvard scholars, MIT graduates, or Oxbridge financial experts. He didn't have an

IT team that could help him infiltrate the most secure stock exchange in the world.

No, Narinder had a different approach.

He broke the American stock market with nothing more than a note pad, a cheap laptop from PC World, and an old BT router. Most amazing of all, he tricked the whole world and crashed the stock market, from his little bedroom.

While his parents were downstairs shaking their heads, as they watched the terrifying news about the stock market crashing, little did they know that their little son, Navi, sitting upstairs was responsible for it.

It was headline news all over the BBC, ITV, Channel 4, Bloomberg, CNBC and frontline news in all the newspapers.

I can just see his Mum and Dad worried and confused, before deciding they didn't understand it, and switching over to their favourite programme, Coronation Street.

While the soap they were watching was unravelling in the living room downstairs, the real drama was unfolding in their boy's bedroom upstairs.

A man who lived with his parents in a little house that nobody knew of, in an area that nobody had heard of, and with a computer that nobody wanted, was somehow able to coerce and manipulate not just one but several of the most powerful, multi-billion-dollar investment banks and hedge funds in the world.

Incredibly he had no help, no accomplices, nobody. He did it completely on his own. (Speechless).

Manipulate one, the rest will follow

This is how he did it.

By laying out some clever trading traps, Narinder was able to entice investment banks and their huge amount of volume (flow) to go in the wrong direction. This created the impact he desired as other banks followed suit. It was nothing short of the classic Pied Piper fairy tale with Narinder playing his flute as the greedy banks danced merrily behind him.

He was so brilliant at manipulating the banks, that *he* was directing their buy and sell orders. Without a single spoken word, email or letter, he was able to convince global multi-billion-dollar banks to buy or sell on his command.

He was the maestro of the orchestra, and they all followed him like desperately hungry rats into the sea.

Who would have thought the most powerful banks in the world could so easily transition into puppets, or that little Narinder would be their puppeteer?

He didn't do it once, or twice. He did it every day, for many months, and in the process, he made many tens of millions of pounds.

Spoofing

The technical term to what Narvinder was doing is called

'spoofing'.

While it could be argued that it 'undermines' the stability of the stock market, it's not nearly as bad, in my opinion, as the pump and dump. It doesn't have the vicious undertone, or the same impact on the lives of everyday investors. That's because the only people who end up with egg on their faces are usually the big hedge funds. That's very different to the penny share pump and dump scandal where the private investor gets royally screwed.

In fact, unlike the pump and dump, Narinder didn't lie, he didn't cheat, he didn't even deceive. He certainly didn't pay people to write up false articles. He wasn't passing brown paper envelopes to researchers for positive reviews, and he wasn't paying off market makers to artificially drive-up stock prices.

But yet, what he did was enough for the US authorities to extradite him to the US to face charges which carried a maximum sentence of 380 years in prison! Talk about disproportionate.

The US doesn't like to be messed with and unfortunately for Narinder, he became the poster boy for what happens to people who try and fool around with the US authorities. It was a deterrent, a warning to others.

However, when you look at what he actually did, he simply used a series of buy and sell orders to create the illusion that he was planning to buy or sell something. He had no intention of executing the trade, so orders were simply there to give the *impression* of his intention to other banks. For example, if he wanted the other players to push up the price, he would place massive buy orders so that it looked as if there were other major institutions that wanted to buy.

That would encourage copycat traders, who would start buying. They could see the intent of other people wanting to buy and figured they would get in their first. He was creating the impression that something was going on with that particular stock.

Except, in this case, he wasn't buying a single stock, he was buying the whole index.

Once the price had been pushed up sufficiently by the other banks buying activity, he would simply sell his real position, make a massive profit, and cancel his 'false' buy limit orders.

He never had any intention to buy anything.

In fact, his intention was always to *sell* what he was already holding, what he had already previously bought. He only gave the *impression* that he was buying so that he could convince others to do the hard work and push up the price, which, in turn, would give him the opportunity to exit.

It was such a simple game really.

It's like 'going all in' at the poker table with a Jack high, hoping you're not going to get called. Fortunately for Narvinder he had a big enough stack of chips in front of him, to discourage others to bet against him. It was the size of his orders that convinced other banks he must be a serious player.

They didn't want to bet against him, so, he just needed one or two of the big banks to decide they would bet *with* him. That would move the price enough, create a little urgency which, in turn, would encourage others to follow. Hopefully with a little bit of luck, Narinder figured that things would spiral very quickly into some real momentum.

They often did.

Computer algorithms

The reason it was so effective and had such a big impact is because most trades are based on automated algorithms. It's not a case of a guy sitting at his computer screen pushing buttons. Automated trading means that human judgement and rational thought is removed, and computers take over. That's what is responsible for severe crashes.

Computer trading models will automatically buy or sell when certain conditions are met, including, for example, if there is a certain volume of shares being traded or if the index moves by a certain % within a specific time-period. When there are lots of algorithms all doing the same thing simultaneously, prices don't just move, they jump.

Of course, Narinder never followed through with any of his pretend 'spoof' orders. The orders were so large that having to satisfy them financially would have ruined him. He was also using derivatives which gave him the massive leverage required to provide the illusion that he was a big player. In reality, he didn't have the financial backing to actually execute the trade and he certainly couldn't hold positions overnight.

The margin requirement was just too big.

His trades were also entirely anonymous so the banks had no idea that these huge limit orders were the work of one guy in his little bedroom. Rumours would circulate as to which bank was so bullish or bearish, which only served to fuel the speculation and drove prices up even further. Nobody wanted to miss out and so the speculation and greed fed itself into a frenzy of price anomalies.

Who's to blame?

I'm not condoning any behaviour that affects the integrity of the market, but I do wonder who really is to blame. If the investment banks had focused on their own research and spent less time concerned about what this mystery trader was doing, then nothing would have happened. If banks hadn't put their computer trading systems on autopilot and had instead managed the positions themselves, would they have made the same decisions? Probably not.

Directly or indirectly, the banks allowed themselves to be influenced by Narinder's false orders.

They were either lazy and relying on algorithms to do all of their work for them while they went for lunch at the most expensive restaurants in town, or they were just plain greedy. That's when they threw out their own research and created mass hysteria by copying what others were doing.

Unfortunately, there are no laws against either greed or stupidity, but there probably should be; certainly if somebody is guilty of both simultaneously.

The master and his trade

The banks are always ripping off the small guy with impunity and finally, here we are, where the small guy was able to beat the banks at their own game. It was the classic David versus Goliath battle.

Prices were manipulated, but not directly by Narinder. They were moved by the greed of others, in this case, the banks. Narinder didn't take any direct action himself. He wasn't responsible for the chain reaction and apart from his spoof trades to sell which he didn't even execute, he only did two trades, one to buy and one to sell. The rest of the trades were done by computer algos.

So, he wasn't responsible for the price action.

Narinder's strategy was a very high risk to him. If he wasn't quick enough to cancel his orders, a single bad trade could have blown up his whole account.

There would also have been many times where his spoof trades *didn't* trick the banks into copying him. No doubt there would have been times where he lost money on his trades, too. But that's not talked about.

Paradoxically, if Narinder wasn't as good as he was, his crimes would have gone unnoticed and unpunished. As it turns out, he was very good. He was a victim of his own success. His personal fortune swelled to over £30million in the space of a few short years, which I assume didn't help him to win any popularitycontests either.

The truth is that the US authorities were embarrassed and made him a scape goat. Mainstream media spun a story that made you want to hate this poor guy. Of course, the investment banks and big hedge funds, they're never to blame.

They never do anything wrong, do they? That's the true injustice in this case.

It was an opportunity to hang the small guy out to dry and to make an example of him to anybody else who even thought of doing the same. You only have to look at Julian Assange from Wikileaks to know that the US authorities are not averse to making examples of people.

Narvinder should be applauded because he never gambled with other people's money, it was always his own. He never speculated with the money of pensioners, like the hedge funds do.

He played with his *own* money and beat the professionals. That's quite an achievement.

As to the stock market collapse and instability he caused, they were all temporary crashes that lasted for a brief moment, in some cases, just a few seconds. The market would always quickly return to fair value so nobody was being affected, apart from the big players running their huge intra-day positions.

Nobody was affected from his actions, apart from some bruised egos on the trading desks.

Ironically, Narinder was just too talented. He became too good at the game.

On 6th May 2010, he infamously caused the '*Flash Crash*' which wiped off nearly a billion dollars from Wall Street in just five minutes. Even though the prices immediately recovered there was uproar from the banks and pension funds that had just lost millions of dollars in that trade. They grouped together and pushed for an investigation so that the identity of this anonymous bank causing havoc for them, could be revealed.

Little did they know it wasn't a bank, but an individual.

It was the only way they could beat this trader. The banks were used to winning and now they were losin. So, they cried out loud enough until the authorities did something about it.

The pressure eventually led to an SEC (Securities Exchange Commission) full-blown enquiry which took a full five years of investigation. The party ended abruptly one early morning in April 2015 when armed police (yes, armed) surrounded Narinders's little, unassuming family home.

It was something out of a Rambo movie. Totally over the top, as if there was a big drug lord inside the premises, and armed to the teeth. Instead, they found glazy-eyed Narvinder sitting in his Minion boxer shorts playing FIFA World Cup on his Nintendo.

Narinder was extradited to the US to face trial on twenty-two separate charges, including wire fraud, commodities fraud, and market manipulation. However, after co-operating with the authorities and returning his ill-gotten gains plus disclosing to the regulators how he managed to pull off his incredible heist, he was fortunate to escape from a prison sentence. Personally, I'm happy about that.

We know price manipulation is not good for market confidence and stability, and I'm not suggesting that what Narinder did wasn't wrong. It was wrong and he shouldn't have done it.

But the punishment didn't fit the crime.

When you see prices moving up and down with no logic or reason, there's a good chance there might be algorithms hitting a series of buy or sell stop loss orders. So just take a moment to think before you act, before you buy or sell, and don't follow the noise.

Ask what's really behind the price move?

Could it be the banks or groups of traders colluding together?, Could it be manipulating market makers?, Could it be false reporting?, Could it be directors pumping up their stock?, Could it be insider trading?

Or could it be that Narinder is back to his old tricks again?

TIP 7 –
PIE IN THE SKY EVALUATION

If you remember back to the 1980s, under the reign of the Thatcher government, there was a big shift of power from the state to the private sector. Utility companies, including gas, electricity and water went from state ownership into the hands of private investors as they floated on the stock market in a wave of privatisations. A lot of money was made, and it was the watershed moment when the stock market became truly accessible for the first time to the average person on the street.

Since then, the stock market has become more and more popular. With the internet and cheap trading platforms, it's a market that's now open to everybody. Interest in new flotations has also increased. The added excitement of something 'new' coming to the market attracts more wallets and purses than anything else.

But what most people don't realise is that 'new' is riskier than 'old'. New companies floating on the market may be more exciting, but that excitement comes with a big price tag attached to it, as you are about to discover.

This next insider trading tip is a scam so well-hidden that it affects millions of people across the world and yet incredibly, still goes undetected.

How an IPO works

In simple terms, an Initial Public Offering (IPO) is when a privately-owned company decides to join the stock market and 'Go public'. Provided the company fulfils certain criteria, a corporate finance team can help to list it on to an exchange.

This means the business owners, (the shareholders) can sell shares in their company to new investors at an agreed 'flotation price'. That's the IPO price, which is decided between the company directors and their corporate finance team.

But remember this. We have already established that whoever *controls the price* makes the money. Therefore, it follows that the ultimate control and power is given to the person who actually gets to *choose* their own price.

Think about it. Instead of trying to conjure up different methods to manipulate price using pump and dump schemes, spoofing or other forms of market deception, what could possibly be better than just *picking* whatever price you wanted in the first place?.

Why bother spending so much energy to push the price of a share up (or down) by a few lousy pennies, with all of the risk that comes with it, and even then, no guarantee that it will work?.

Wouldn't it be so much easier if you were able to just **decide and fix** the price at whatever level you wanted? If that was possible, then that would be the definition of ultimate price manipulation and control.

Here's the best bit; it's not only possible but entirely legal. That's right – YOU set your own price.

If a company director can choose the price of his own shares, he basically sets his own exit strategy. He decides on how much his business is worth and how much money he makes. He chooses how much of a windfall payment he receives when he sells to unsuspecting investors.

Once he sets his golden-ticket price, his job is now to convince enough people that his price is not only sensible but the deal of a lifetime.

A few rotten apples

This scam is genius because like all good scams, it's so hard to identify. It's almost impossible to spot dodgy IPOs because they are very well-hidden in between genuine IPOs that are priced correctly.

That's the secret behind all scams. They work because they are interspersed across large numbers of genuine investments, making it difficult to distinguish the good from the bad and the bad from the damn right ugly.

If every IPO was a scam and all new listings came to the market at an overinflated price, they would all collapse very quickly. Investors would see the trend of IPOs and would not invest in them, making it impossible for new companies to float.

That would cause huge disruption to the marketplace because it removes one of the best and most effective tools for companies to raise capital cost-effectively. Businesses would fail, the economy would shrink, and we'd all be very much worse off.

However, because there are plenty of fairly priced IPOs, and indeed, a few very good, underpriced IPOs in the marketplace, there is always a constant flow market of hungry investors. The best scammers are always able to hide their IPOs among those genuine IPOs.

Think of it this way; the amateur scammer goes into the bank with a balaclava and sawn-off shotgun, and steals a million pounds. The professional scammer walks into the bank with a suit and tie and convinces the bank manager to write him a cheque for a million pounds.

It's all about disguise.

Pricing for a favourable exit

Genuine IPOs are designed to raise money for the business; dodgy IPOs are designed to raise money for the business *owners*. That's the main difference.

In genuine cases , the board of directors have usually taken their company as far as they can, and simply want an exit. That's perfectly fine and fair. They've built up a profitable business over, say, twenty years and now they're looking to cash in their chips and sell. Nothing wrong with that.

This means that even genuine IPOs are designed with price in mind. That's not illegal, wrong or immoral.

Business owners will clearly want to sell their shares at the best possible price. That's why companies always float on the stock exchange when stock market conditions are strong. This allows company owners to charge the highest possible price and make the most amount of money for themselves.

The perfect time for company to float is when the stock market is in a strong bull market; that's when new investors won't think twice about paying a premium. Think of how many IPOs came out of nowhere during the technology sector boom in the late 1990s. Every second company that popped up out of nowhere was a new tech start up purporting to be the next big thing. Now consider how many technology companies floated after the bubble crash in 2000. Answer – not very many.

Why? Because the investor appetite was gone. The bubble had burst the silly valuations that made the directors stinking rich had disappeared into thin air.

Companies go to great lengths to list their business when the demand is at its greatest. They offer shares to the public at the best time *for them*, and that means they can make the biggest profit. Their goal is to raise the most amount of cash by selling the *least* number of shares, i.e., they want investors to pay the *highest price.*

I don't have a problem with this per se.

The problem I do have with IPOs is how they are *marketed.* I view it as a form of mis-selling. IPOs are sold as this great opportunity for investors, and sometimes, that may be true, but in most cases, they're just not.

It's really all about what's best for the company directors, for the existing shareholders. It's never about the investor because if it was, companies would float when market conditions were *poor* and where IPO prices were heavily *discounted*. But we know the opposite happens.

IPOs are regularly cancelled during bearish market conditions, when the directors know they can't maximise their share price. We see it all the time.

It's kind of crazy to think that this goes unchallenged.

My view is that a business shouldn't float at the maximum price unless it's being completely sold and there is a full exit. Then it would make sense. If I own a business and I want to sell it, then the buyer knows that I don't give a sh*t about him. He knows that I just want the best price.

I know the buyer doesn't give two hoots about me either and wants my business at the lowest price. We both know where we stand so it's a fair battle.

But an IPO isn't usually a full sale. It's a partial sale for a percentage of the business to raise money to grow the business. The directors still retain shares in the business, and they're still going to be running the business. The sales pitch is one of '*invest with us and let's get rich together*'.

At best, only half of this statement is true.

I win, you lose

IPOs, like investing in general, is a zero-sum game. A business only has so much value; it can only be worth so much. Therefore, somebody has to get a raw deal. Either the directors sell their shares at a bargain price, or they sell them at a premium price.

They can never really be sold at 'fair' value because that's a subjective, fixed price at a single point in time. Besides nobody really knows what a fair price is and that's the problem. If there was one definitive price that people could refer to, then this scam wouldn't exist.

But there isn't. A price is subjective and based on numerous factors, many of which are unknown. This hugely benefits the scammers, and it hugely disadvantages the investors. Price can be once again manipulated under the cloak of uncertainty.

Faced with the possibility of selling shares to an anonymous investor that you never meet, see, or even speak to, at an over-inflated price, and become rich in the process, has to be tempting for some company directors. So, that's what happens.

It's one of the easiest financial scams you can get away with – and it's risk-free. There's no penalty, no crime being committed, but it's still a scam.

If you knowingly rip somebody off by tricking them into paying twice the price for a product and you know it's true worth, and you intentionally mislead the investor into believing that the price is not only fair but a bargain, then what is that, if it's not a scam?

Price is fluid and constantly changing and nobody can decide the price except for the market. But, in this case, there is no market, not yet anyway. By the time it hits the market, it's already too late. The pound notes have already left and gone to the directors.

If faced with two options, either sell your business at a bargain price or sell it a premium price, what do you think the company directors will choose? If you could get £1 million for your shares or £2 million for your shares, what would you choose?

It's human nature.

The scam comes from the deception, the trickery, the smoke and mirrors surrounding the valuation. That's where the lies are, that's where the scam comes in.

Too often company directors will go out of their way to make their IPO a good deal for them, which, by default, must mean it's a bad deal for their investors. It has to be. They can't both win this game.

The directors can get away with this because they hold the advantage of not being forced to sell. They can test investors potential appetite at whatever silly valuation and price they want to. If they don't get any interest, they just pull the whole deal. Investors don't get that choice. If they commit to any investment, they have to follow through with it.

That's why during times of mass market hysteria like a booming stock market, it's easy to create ridiculous valuations which people are willing to pay. That's why so many people lost their life savings at the height of the dot com bubble in the late 1990s.

One could argue that investors were also to blame because they became very greedy. I'm not suggesting that greed isn't a real thing, it's real and it affects us all. But we need to remember that it's the professionals against the non-professionals.

It's Liverpool Football Club's A team against Accrington Stanley's B Team.

"*Accrington Stanley? Who are they?*" To which the little Scouse kid in the milk advert, replies in a devastating, deadpan fashion, "*Exactly*".

There's a big difference between the knowledge and experience of financial professionals and the retail investor. It's an unfair match.

Just because it's easy to sell crack to drug addicts, it doesn't exonerate drug dealers from selling it to them.

The best timing for them is the worst timing for you

RAC, the car breakdown company, planned to float on the stock market for £2 billion in 2014. Just three years earlier, Carlyle, (the private equity firm) had bought RAC from Aviva for just £1 billion. However, after sniffing around for the best deal they found a higher bidder in a Singapore sovereign wealth fund and sold it to them.

There's nothing illegal or maybe even immoral about this, depending on what you think the true definition of capitalism is, or should be. It's just business, that RAC sold to the highest bidder.

I just want you to be under no illusion that a firm's decision to float on the market is *not* for your benefit. The intention is for the full benefit the people floating their business, i.e., the original shareholders. In the case of the RAC IPO deal, the flotation would have given senior management around £300 million but as it turns out they made even more.

Nobody cared about you or me, the investor. They just wanted the highest price.

Here's the kicker. In that same year there were almost one hundred scheduled IPOs cancelled , either because of '*market volatility*', '*waning investor demand*' or '*mismatch on pricing*'. All are Morse code for '*we want to make more money*'

The incentive is for firms to artificially inflate their initial flotation price and see if they can get away with it. It's like putting your house up for sale at a ridiculous valuation hoping you will find enough buyers to say yes.

At the risk of being sued (again), the RAC IPO was, of course, *not* a scam. It was completely legal and executed correctly. It just shows you that if a genuine IPO, like RAC, was able to maximise its price, what do you think the scam IPOs are able to get away with?

It's frightening how much scope they have to impact price, and it all starts with muddying the waters.

Complex valuations

Step 1 - if you want to charge a ridiculous price for a business, make the business ridiculously complicated to value.

Investors are sold a story based on forecasts and next year's trends. Companies also valued using intangible assets such as goodwill, intellectual propertyrights, existing and pending patents, brand awareness, social media presence, online subscribers, and lots of other things that can't be quantified easily, many of which may have zero value.

When you base a valuation on things which can't be measured or predicted, you are able to stretch out an IPO price that sits miles away from the company's true value. If the price was based on cash in the bank, real assets, and profitability, scammers would desert the IPO market like rats from a sinking ship.

But IPOs are designed to reflect the expectation of what might happen in the *future* rather than the reality of what's happening today. It's all about tomorrow's hopes, not today's truth. Even stock prices already listed on an exchange, are based on the future expectation of next year. Income paying stocks are priced largely on the *future* discounted value of expected dividends. It's all about next week, next month, next year, never about right now.

That sounds reasonable.

It would seem fair to value a company on what the future might bring, but that also opens up the potential for serious abuse and price manipulation. Dodgy company directors who want to flog their failing businesses have a passport to become very creative with their valuations. They can make all sorts of optimistic assumptions and use different forecasting models to justify an over-inflated price.

Valuations are a very funny thing.

It's just a number and in its crudest sense, any value is possible. You could put a price on just about anything and if somebody is prepared to pay that price, the that valuation becomes instantly justified. If somebody pays £100 million for an abstract piece of art that looks like it was painted by a five-year-old, then that's the correct market value.

A buyer and seller came together and executed a transaction at an agreed price.

Job done. Mission accomplished.

Aston Martin

Take luxury car manufacturers, Aston Martin, for example. The company floated at an IPO price of £19 per share in October 2018, which valued the company at £4.3 billion. Here was a company which hadn't made a profit for almost a decade, back in 2010, and had filed for bankruptcy not once, but a staggering SEVEN times in its 105-year history!

The question is, who gave that £19 valuation? Who set that price? Who decided that was the correct IPO level?

It's a really important question. In fact, it's the most important question you can ask.

The price determines how much money will be transferred from the bank accounts of new investors to the bank accounts of existing shareholders, i.e., the company directors, and staff members.

Remember, this *isn't* a scam. This is legitimate business.

But as investors in Aston Martin were to find out, it doesn't need to be a scam for you to be screwed.

In less than two years the value of the company dropped to less than 10% of its original IPO value. Or put another way, Aston Martin's directors sold shares to the public at a price **ten times** more than they were really worth!

Of course, things may have happened in those two years, market conditions might have changed, etc. But they didn't change by that much.

Fundamentally, the IPO price was wrong, but not just a little bit wrong, it was wrong by a massive amount. It wasn't wrong in favour of the investors; it was wrong in favour of the people who decided the price. Isn't that a coincidence?

It wasn't just a little bit over-valued; it was **ten times** over-valued. The free market decided that the IPO price of £19 was complete nonsense and called out the directors on their bull*hit. They moved the price to where it should have always been.

The question is whether the mispricing was incompetence, deliberate, or both?

Thousands of people have just become poorer because of it. What was it – sheer incompetence or were they intentionally sold a pack of lies?

The company directors, the corporate finance team, and the professional marketing machine are all responsible. They all play a part in this game.

Imagine you went into a shop, and were told that a particular gold-plated pen was worth £100 but, in fact, it turns out that it really was really only worth £10. You'd ask for your money back.

Well, with IPOs, you can't do that.

It's quite possible that Aston Martin's corporate finance team genuinely believed that a failing car manufacturer with a chequered history, with multiple declared bankruptcies, a weak balance sheet, little cash, falling car sales, facing very difficult trading conditions, in an over-saturated and highly competitive industry, was a really great investment opportunity.

I don't know, maybe I'm just being slightly optimistic.

What I do know is that Aston Martin somehow managed to flog 25% of its business to the public for considerably *more* money than the worth today of the remaining 75%. That doesn't make any sense, no matter how nicely it's dressed up.

Price ranges

One of the ways in which a ridiculous price can gain credibility is through setting a price *range*. That's where the company and their advisors decide on a lower and upper limit. It's clever stuff because it frames investors into a way of thinking.

In the case of Aston Martin, the initial price range was between £17.50 and £22.50.

The range is to test how much interest there is, or, if you have a healthy level of cynicism, how gullible investors are. If there is high interest then great, if there isn't then the board of directors drops the price or just pulls the deal completely.

This clever way of framing the investment opportunity gives a reference point to work from; it helps investors to anchor any future price discussion. If somebody tells you they expect a product to list between £17.50 and £22.50, then two weeks later you are told that it is listing at £19, you're going to think that it's pretty reasonable value.

That's because you've already bought into the concept that £17.50 is really cheap and £22.50 is expensive so anything towards the bottom end of that range has to be good value for money.

But who decided the range? It's clever manipulation again.

By setting a range and then setting the IPO price towards the bottom end of that range, it makes investors think they are getting a good deal.

It doesn't matter if the £22 figure is plucked out of thin air. It allows the marketers to *frame* their investment in the most optimal way.

Two minutes ago, nobody had any clue or conceivable idea about what a fair price for Aston Martin should be. Now, we've all become experts in thinking what is a reasonable price. We ignore the fact the price range is made up by the firm itself. Now a £22 price tag sounds expensive and £17.50 seems exceptional. It's all made up numbers.

What would have happened if the price range for Aston Martin had been set between £8 and £10? Does that change things for you as an investor? Yes of course.

Now, a price tag of £19 sounds crazy, and nobody would invest.

Selling the dream

Sceptics could argue that the board of directors still own the majority of shares after an IPO so it's not in their interest for the share price to fall. Yes, of course directors don't want the share price to fall because it makes their remaining shares worth less.

But that's irrelevant. If they're selling something for much more than it's worth, then the price must fall eventually. It might go up initially, but in the end, it has to fall to what the market deems to be fair value. They already know and accept their shares *have* to fall in price, if they over-price it in the first place.

Hopefully for the directors, it doesn't fall immediately. Hopefully the market and the positive momentum surrounding the IPO will be enough to keep the price supported at least for a few months. That gives the directors some breathing space to slowly shift the blame from themselves and mispricing to 'unfavourable' market conditions.

The greater the time period between when the IPO comes to market and the share price eventually collapsing, the easier it becomes for directors to blame market conditions, rather than face criticism.

Imagine the public uproar if an IPO dropped 90% on its first day of trading. But if that 90% drop was spread over a two-year window, the directors can simply blame the market and not themselves.

The fact is this; 25% of Aston Martin shares were sold at *ten times* more than the firm true price decided by the market just two years later. So, for the directors and employees who cashed in their shares at £19, they've had a massive win.

Their shares were, in reality only worth a tiny fraction of what they sold them for. So, while they don't necessarily want the share price to fall, they recognise that in order for them to make a killing on the IPO, the shares have to be over-valued, and therefore, the price must fall at some point in the future.

Here's another thing to think about.

With the benefit of hindsight and knowing that the IPO price was way too expensive, how many of the directors who benefited from that massive windfall, would be willing to give the money back to investors?

Could they just contact the original shareholders and say *"Listen, we made a mistake with our pricing, so, we'll take back the shares and you can have your money back."* Basically, a share buy-back.

Of course, that would never happen. Logistically, it may not be easy to just undo an IPO, but even if it was straight forward, there's no appetite for that kind of gesture. It would never happen.

The directors know that the remaining 75% of shares they still own can't be manipulated in the same way. The market will decide what they're worth, which means they'll have to sell at the same price as everybody else. There's no advantage, no premium to add, no price manipulation.

That's why the IPO is that small, golden window, it's the one and only time they get to write their own cheques. After that window is closed, the opportunity is lost forever.

After that single parachute payment, that once in lifetime golden handshake deal, they know they can't manipulate the price anymore. The IPO is the first and last time they can control the price, which is why they may well as take the big win now and see what happens.

Once the company floats, the price is determined by the usual market forces of demand and supply so unless they want to start pumping and dumping, which a firm the size of Aston Martin wouldn't be able to get away with, they have zero control over what their shares are worth at any point in the future.

It's simple really - directors and shareholders should not decide what their business is worth, the market should decide. There's clearly a conflict of interest.

The reasons why they can get away with whatever they want to charge is because of two things - clever PR and marketing.

Public relations (PR) and marketing

IPO pricing, at least by some firms is dubious at best and fraudulent at worst. So, the real question is, how can companies get away with it?

Yes, price forecasts can be manipulated, and valuations are overly complex, but there has to be more than that. After all, companies still need to convince investors and that's not an easy task.

Welcome to the murky world of PR and marketing companies.

What's their job? To sell you the dream.

A ridiculous valuation on its own is just that – a ridiculous valuation. But if you have a marketing juggernaut to promote it, it becomes real. If people believe the hype, then a fictitious price turns into a real opportunity, into money.

It all starts with an amazing prospectus filled with high quality, professional photographs, enticing earnings and profit and loss tables, ambitious financial projections, beautifully crafted graphs and pie charts, formidable forecast numbers, and future earnings that look so good, your mouth salivates when you see them.

It means positive analyst reports and newspaper write-ups.

It means huge social media campaigns and influencers promoting the stock.

It means television and newspaper adverts. It means podcasts, columns, videos and webinars.

It means SEO, online presence, Google, YouTube, Facebook and Instagram adverts.

It means websites, landing pages, squeeze pages, click funnels, and traffic conversions.

It means investor presentations, webinars, Zoom conference calls, and countless meetings.

It means teams of salespeople and brokers pitching the stock.

It means sales training programmes, objection handling, introduction emails, numerical calculations, consultancy calls, live pass-overs, more sales, constant pressure, more phone calls, and plenty of closing, closing, closing.

IPOs are just well presented, elaborate, promotional marketing campaigns.

It's brain–washing propaganda.

The PR firm has just one job; to sell you the opportunity.

They want you to feel that warm, fuzzy feeling when you look at the inside cover of the IPO brochure and see a silver-haired chairman smiling back at you, as he welcomes you to join him and his team in this "unique, once in a lifetime opportunity".

It's not about the price anymore, it's about the opportunity. The objective is to distract potential investors far, far away from the financials, far away from the IPO price.

Their goal is to get this company out there into the public domain and generate enough buyer demand willing to buy at the IPO price that has been set. It doesn't matter how ridiculous the price is, somebody, somewhere can and will buy it. They must buy it.

The prospectus must, of course, include all the legal points, the numbers, details of the offer, the potential risks, the potential rewards, and so on. While all factually correct, it's all nonsense really. You can dress up anything well if you give them enough designer clothes.

The clothes are the distraction.

The price, which is the thing discussed the least, is where the money is going to be made or lost for you as an investor. It's the one thing that the marketers will try to stop you from thinking about. There will be plenty of shiny objects thrown in your direction to take your attention away from price.

Here's the litmus test; if you find that a disproportionate amount of time, energy and resources are being spent on brokers selling you an IPO, then run a mile. That tells you all you need to know.

If it was such an amazing opportunity why is the company spending hundreds of thousands of pounds on a marketing machine to sell it to you?

Higher up the food chain

The IPO scam is generally more prevalent towards the bottom end of the food chain. It happens more frequently with the smallest businesses than with the bigger firms. That's because the big IPOs are under a huge amount of scrutiny; they're already under the spotlight.

Giants, like Facebook, can't just go crazy with their IPO price. They can still charge whatever they want based on silly multiples, but it's a different type of manipulation.

But at the other end of the scale, the small IPOs that float for a few pennies, just don't have anywhere near the same accountability or regulation so the manipulation is direct and in your face. There's more dirt and dishonesty.

In my experience, the biggest and most dangerous IPO scammers are, once again, those that float penny share companies on the smaller, listed exchanges, like the AIM market.

That's where dodgy directors can take their failing business and offload to unsuspecting investors before they sail off into their retirement. More about that later.

The IPO team

Think of the IPO team as another professional hit squad; a team of professional bank robbers, organised together to mastermind the biggest haul.

They're on the same page, which is why all team members have the same goal of maximising price. So, if an auditor is asking some difficult questions or the investment advisors are making things a little awkward, they'll quickly be replaced with new, more 'friendly' team players.

No dissenters, no goody-two-shoes, nobody who values their morals more than their pay cheque, that's the selection process to join the IPO A-team.

So, let's meet the criminals.

Industry leaders and key personnel

Before any IPO flotation, the company needs to bring some heavy hitters onto the board who have worked in the same industry. Their reputation and credibility give the illusion the business has some depth and experience. This is just another con. Half of these board members come in for a couple of hours a week, get paid handsomely for doing very little, and are just there to offer some prestige as well as trust. They do absolutely nothing apart from adding a sense of legitimacy to the business.

This is a necessary part of the magic show. When the glossy IPO brochure is published, it contains photographs of highly experienced and very reputable individuals who have decades of experience in the marketplace. It doesn't matter that they've had absolutely nothing to do with the business prior to the IPO and will have nothing to do with it after the IPO. They are the sugar candy poster boys and girls for investors.

It's the same as Coca-Cola paying Elton John to promote its drink. It's just branding. Besides, everybody knows that he prefers Pepsi.

The underwriters

An investment bank will often be appointed to underwrite an IPO. This means that if there is insufficient demand, it will take up the slack and guarantee to buy any surplus shares at the IPO price. You may think this could be a problem if the IPO is overly inflated, and investors don't buy. That would put the underwriter at risk because they have to buy the unplaced shares.

However, it's not quite like that.

For a start, the terms usually include a clause protecting the underwriter by obliging them to only purchase a limited number of shares (not the whole float).

Secondly, the underwriters are not stupid. Before they agree to underwriting the IPO at any price, the market is thoroughly 'tested' for the level of interest from prospective buyers. So they won't agree to a deal unless they are confident that there will be enough demand. If there is any chance the IPO allocation of shares won't be fully covered and purchased in the open market, the company can quickly pull the whole deal off the table.

Remember, the company and the underwriters play for the same team. So, the underwriters will never get screwed over.

The nominated advisors (NOMAD)

The advisors work within the corporate finance team and are responsible for guiding the company through the listing process, conducting their due diligence, getting the paperwork in order, and most critically of all, setting the IPO price.

They work very closely with the firm and make all of the strategic decisions in terms of pricing. They analyse the market, the demand, conduct the price testing and create the perfect conditions for the flotation.

They also get paid a percentage fee from the firm. So, it's in their interest to make the company 'happy' and float the business at the highest possible price.

The lawyers

You will probably already have an opinion about corporate lawyers and their role in protecting the rights of investors. Hmmm, yes, that's what I thought.

The lawyers, like the rest of the team, are on the payroll of the IPO firm so, their actions are designed specifically to help it. Their job description, as detailed in their employment contract, is technically described as, and I quote, "to protect everybody's asses", (including their own).

For the IPO scandal to work, lawyers need to use the right wording and terminology to create documentation, which is so water-tight that the company pushing the flotation can never get into trouble. This isn't a new revelation; this is what lawyers do. Their job is to create legal structures and documents which allow companies to avoid getting sued, even when they do bad things.

They need to protect the firm from the regulators, industry watchdogs, the police and, of course the investors themselves. Their job is to make sure the firm doesn't fall foul of any legal hurdles or future potential claims.

In every glossy prospectus, there are pages and pages of legal jargon that nobody reads, let alone understands. Hidden away within this outrageously voluminous number of backside-covering clauses, you will find protective measures designed to help the firm get away with murder.

The marketing squad

When a company is going to raise a few hundred million pounds on a flotation, it doesn't care about investing a few million pounds on the best marketing and advertising campaign to generate maximum interest and justify the highest possible IPO price. The crème-de-la-crème of marketing teams will be put to work to promote the company.

The bigger the IPO, the bigger the marketing campaign. For smaller IPOs the marketing will be different. Instead of television advertising, it's more likely to be social media led, internet influencers and traditional sales through broker floors. In all cases, however, there has to be marketing to sell the dream.

With greatly inflated IPO prices, the marketing needs to be particularly magical and creative.

Auditors

Everything needs to be audited by an independent firm to ensure the financial statements and numbers are accurate. That's pretty straight forward because nobody is going to lie in these documents. Why lie small with a big risk when you can deceive big with no risk?

Besides, the auditors are being paid by the IPO firm. If the numbers were not quite right, let's just say that with the right 'friendly' auditor, the numbers could be fudged a little. We've seen this before so no surprises here.

If 'creative accounting' happens with supermarket giants like Tesco, then it definitely happens with the smaller firms. Tesco was fined £235 million by the Serious Fraud Office and Financial Conduct Authority in their 2014 accounting scandal. They're not alone either. There are many stories of big firms being more than a little sketchy with their numbers.

Privately held firms don't have their accounts subjected to the same level of scrutiny that public listed companies do. So, there is more scope for 'natural movement'.

IPOs also don't happen overnight, which is why with a future plan, numbers can be easily adjusted to hit certain targets. Companies have a long time to get themselves ready, usually several years. This means they can start to get their books in order and for their numbers to look a certain way ahead of any proposed flotation.

Profits can even be 'enhanced' fraudulently in the couple years before a flotation to give the impression of a thriving business. False contracts, irregular money flowing into the business, artificial new orders, expected repeat business, a spike in the number of clients, and various other metrics can be created, so that a huge IPO tag can be justified later.

As always, it's all about how committed the scammers are and how much money is likely to be raised. The unsophisticated scammers won't bother with this level of groundwork; they just want to get in and out with minimal fuss. But the professional IPO scammers will put in the hard work and effort several years ahead of a big flotation.

Brokerage firms

After the marketing and promotion comes the master stroke. When the firm has exhausted its own marketing through advertising and social media, the next step is to gain access to an immediate group of hungry and willing investors.

There's no better place to find thousands of clients with freely available cash hungry for a deal, than the numerous stockbroker firms in the City. The firms have investors ready to buy; all they need is a 'story'.

The broker will get commission from the deal, known as a 'rip' or a 'turn', which is usually between 3% and 5%. From a marketing perspective it's the real turning point because now the scammers have a direct connection to some of the most powerful financial institutions in the UK.

It's not long before everybody seems to be talking about the IPO. Like a forest fire, the hype around the company builds and spreads quickly. Everybody is now putting in orders so they don't miss out on their chance to participate in the most 'exciting IPO of the year' as the media has decided to describe it.

Different rip rates will be offered to different stockbroker firms depending on their 'placing power' (how much stock they can 'place', i.e., how much money they can raise). Stockbroker firms that don't have a lot of placing power won't go direct to the IPO firm but, instead, must buy on a secondary deal from another larger broker. In this way, the commission is split.

For example, a larger stockbroker firm might place, say, £10 million worth of shares and earn a 5% rip from the IPO firm, which is £500,000. Of the £10 million, maybe they have the capacity to place only £6 million to its own clients. For the remaining £4 million, it will pass this onto other brokers and give them, say, 3%, so they make 2% on the remainder.

In other words, they make 5% of £6 million which is £300,000 and 2% of £4 million which is £80,000 so a total of £380,000. The other broker earns 3% of the £4m which is £120,000.

The company raises £10 million in new investment and pays out £500,000 in total, which they put down as an IPO marketing expense.

Now do you see why the IPO price has to be so high – it's because so much of it has to be paid away to all the middlemen who are promoting it. Of course, there are many more costs that have to be absorbed into the price, too. The auditors, accountants, legal, IT, marketing, advertising, compliance, sales and so on.

It's a typical pyramid scheme with all the gold glistening at the very top, which then slowly trickles down to the bottom. The problem is that you're at the very bottom, which means you don't get to see any of the gold but yet, you take on all of the risk.

At the very top are the directors (the original shareholders) who get their money straight away at the full IPO price, less costs. Next, the advisors and corporate financiers who put the deal together take their share. Then the stock is passed onto investment banks for their cut. Then it's the larger institutions involved in the placing who take their commission. Then the larger brokers take their fee as they place the stock with their clients, followed by the smaller and independent brokers.

Finally, right at the bottom, after everybody has feasted until their tummy is full, is Joe Bloggs, the guy who actually buys the IPO when it comes on to the market. But it's been a full six-months and the professionals have been ravaging the meat off the company, which means that poor Joe is left feeding off an empty carcass.

All the bills, salaries, and invoices come out of the proceeds of the IPO. Which means that whoever buys the IPO pays for these bills.

Somebody needs to feed those hungry tummies, and that person is you, my friend.

The irony is that the people at the bottom of this chain all think they're getting in early. Isn't that what investors say to each other? Things like, *"Guess what John, you missed it, I got in early. I bought Company ABC in the IPO; I was in on its first day of trading."*

At least one part of that statement is true, it was the first day of trading. The rest isn't. It wasn't early at all. It was after a dozen hyenas took their cut out of the investment and passed on the scraps to you.

Now you're left carrying the crying baby while everybody has bailed. Good luck with that!

Secondary placings

Like many of the insider trading secrets in this book, there are always extra degrees and layers to the scams.

That's because scammers realise that if a particular scam works well, it would be a shame for it to be limited to a once only opportunity. A company can only float once on the stock market, which is a problem if you want to scam investors more than once.

That's where the IPO plot thickens and where *secondary* placings come in.

A secondary placing is where a firm that is already listed on the stock exchange raises more capital with another issuance of shares. It makes perfect sense for the directors because a goose that lays a golden egg every six months is infinitely better than a goose that lays just a single golden egg.

It's also a lot easier to raise capital because there is less scrutiny and regulation on secondary placings so less due diligence is required. The company is already listed on the exchange, so it's relatively easy to raise extra cash. The difficult thing is to be admitted to the party in the first place, but once you're in, you're in.

Firms don't need to worry about assembling the A-team of advisors and lawyers as they do with IPOs. Even the marketing is easier and cheaper because the company is already on the market. The quickest and easiest way to raise capital is to simply go back to the existing shareholders and give them an opportunity to buy more shares in the company. They've already bought once before so it's an easier pitch. Regardless of whether the share price has gone up or down, there's always a way to encourage more investment.

Of course, the deal is also open to new investors too.

Issuing more shares and putting them into circulation will dilute the share price for existing shareholders, but the dodgy directors don't care about that. They get another few million pounds in the bank.

Why stop with a second round of fund-raising? How about a third, a fourth or even a fifth? That's actually what happens with a lot of penny shares. It becomes a licence to print money.

But a different approach is required to the scam. Because now, the price can't be manipulated in the same way. The IPO price can come in at just about any price, but the secondary placing price has to bear some resemblance to the current market price; it has to be close to the current market value.

That's a problem for the scammers who want the price to be as high as possible but, as you'd expect, they found a way around this too. Once again, it specifically targets the smaller firms on the smaller exchanges, and, in many ways, it's much worse than the IPO scam.

It's called principal dealing.

TIP 6 –
PRINCIPAL DEALING

In the last chapter, I explained how some IPOs were nothing more than elaborate marketing scams that allow directors to exit their businesses and earn a nice pay packet. I also explained that most of the scams were taking place within the smaller exchanges, like the Alternative Investment Market (AIM).

But it's not just the AIM. There are numerous exchanges which are even smaller than AIM, making them ideal hiding places for dodgy companies. OFEX, PLUS and NEX are all smaller exchanges where the regulations are less stringent, and where unscrupulous company directors will congregate. In fact, there are several exchanges that fall outside the regulatory requirements of a Recognised Investment Exchange (RIE).

These are exchanges that are not recognised by the Financial Conduct Authority . So, they sit outside of the protection afforded by the Financial Services and Markets Act 2000 (FSMA).

But because most investors don't know about the difference between one exchange and another, there is an assumption they all perform the same function. There is an assumption that if a company lists on a stock exchange, *any* stock exchange, then it must be legitimate.

The difficulty to distinguish between the genuine and the

fake is once again used by scam companies to create an illusion and set up the trap. Unwittingly, investors are being moved by the scammers further and further away from the protection they seek. At the same time, the scammers move further and further away from the penalties, restrictions, and legalities they are trying to avoid. . In one big swoop, the scammers have shifted the risk from themselves and placed it squarely on the shoulders of their investor.

This same hierarchical structure of very small, small, medium, and large stock exchanges exists in every developed country all over the world. Not every country has a stock exchange but the ones that do, will all have a range from very big to very small.

The scam will always choose the smallest one they can get away with, and ideally one in an overseas jurisdiction from the people they are scamming. That's why this scam is truly global pandemic.

Penny shares

The term 'penny share' is exactly that, a share with a price that is less than one pound and is therefore priced in pennies. However, not all penny shares are small companies. For example, some huge corporations like Lloyds Bank have a share price which is less than a pound, but it's a multinational, company worth several billion pounds.

That's why you have to be extra careful. The price alone is not enough information to make a judgement. You also need to look at market capitalisation and other relevant factors.

Similarly, there are some companies which may have a share price that trades in pounds yet still operates in that dodgy world, like so many penny stocks do.

As a general rule of thumb, you would be best advised to stay clear of any shares that trade for less than, say 20p, unless you really understand their business.

As always, there are exceptions to this rule and the last thing that I want to do is discourage you from buying into small-cap stocks that are genuine.

I wouldn't even discourage you from buying a company that sat on a small overseas exchange and is not a RIE. There are many companies on these exchanges that are entirely genuine. As an investor, you need to weigh up the risks against the benefits.

One of the benefits of investing in companies which fall outside of direct FCA regulation is that they will have fewer overheads and costs. To list on a UK listed RIE is not cheap and that means less profit for the business, and, in turn, potentially more risk for the investor.

These smaller exchanges certainly perform an important, even critical, service. They shouldn't be shunned or ignored. That would be a mistake.

After all, they allow the smallest firms to gain access to much-needed capital, to grow their business, and to add value to the marketplace. For the most part, and for most companies maybe that is true.

But as you are now finding out, there is also another very dark place that exists, where this is completely untrue.

Black vacuum

This dark place is a black vacuum that attracts foul play. This is where investors are screwed repeatedly and where their muffled screams are never heard because they're so far away from regulated society. They're too far away from help. It's a breeding ground for corruption, a quicksand that effortlessly suffocates thousands of UK investors every year.

At the other end of the stock exchange, we have the bright, glitzy lights of the big companies which employ tens of thousands of people, turn over billions of pounds, and are household names up and down the country. That's what we all see in the papers, on television and on the internet. So there is an assumption that the whole stock market is the same. But that's not the case.

As you move further and further away from those bright shining lights, you eventually enter into a place of darkness. From there, you quickly venture deeper into a financial world of corruption. It's where price transparency and liquidity doesn't exist, where shadows are cast far and wide, and where power is concentrated into the hands of a privileged, rotten few.

With less regulation and fewer restrictions, it's a mysterious world that attracts characters from the underworld. Real gangsters forge the closest of odd relationships with the nerdy suits on the inside.

Very respected mafia families with fearsome reputations use the City of London to solicit their ill-gotten gains. They use regulated and unregulated firms to generate money, to clean dirty cash, and to run their business empires. They also use them to print money, lots of it.

Licence to print money

A company listed on a stock exchange is the closest thing to having your own bank.

The company simply issues shares for cash, and it can issue as many shares as it likes. It's kind of hard to get your head around, it's hard to think this could even happen. It's like having a blank cheque and then filling in the number with however many zeroes takes your fancy.

It's a licence to print unlimited amounts of money and, of course, it naturally attracts criminal activity, from all over the world.

That includes the gangster bosses and heads of mafia families right the way down to little Billy, the small-time, little thief. It lures in otherwise honest and reputable businesspeople who find it too hard to turn away from the spoils in front of them.

Imagine a hard-working businessperson who's been working for twelve hours a day, for the past ten years, but not getting anywhere, is approached and offered an exit out of his business with a substantial pay-off of a million pounds.

It's quite an offer.

The offer is obviously less attractive for somebody who already runs a highly profitable and growing business. They have their focus and attention on growth, expansion, building their reputation and increasing profitability.

But the business owner who is facing bankruptcy in twelve months has nothing to lose. It's the final call at the roulette table so he may as well borrow as many chips as he can from the casino and bet it all on black before closing time. After all, he doesn't have to pay it back.

Private companies regularly go out of business because they run out of cash, which is why Companies House website is littered with bankruptcies. However, when you run a listed company it's a different ball game because you have access to millions, even tens of millions of pounds.

When you're a privately-owned business, you either have to borrow money from the bank or convince venture capitalists and angel investors to help support you. In each case you're dealing with savvy professionals who won't part with any cash until they've checked out your company.

You can't scam them.

But publicly listed companies don't have those restraints because they take money from uninformed, or worse, *mis*informed retail investors who perform no checks – it's as easy as turning on the money tap.

The problem with a one-off big pay day from an IPO is exactly that, it's a one-off. What business owners really want is that big balloon pay-out upfront *plus* regular payments going forward. They want that money tap available to them, all of the time.

'Principal dealing' does exactly that. It's where a stock brokerage firm helps a company that's already listed on the stock market to issue more shares and raise more capital. This is the secondary placing, or 'secondary equity raise'.

By issuing more shares, directors are able to extract more money from the public and put it straight into the business, from which they can now take it out and use for their own personal gain.

The stock brokerage firm, once again, plays a pivotal role because it has access to thousands of clients on its trading book, and dozens of hungry brokers looking to earn commission.

The penny share company wants to raise money and the brokerage firm has access to lots of clients who have cash to invest, so it's the perfect storm.

Now the broker just needs to pick up the telephone and make the connection – to bring the 'opportunity' to the client.

But, of course, there is no such thing as an opportunity, there's simply a transfer of wealth. Investors put their money into a failing business, thinking it's an 'investment' but really, it's just money exchanging hands. There is no opportunity, and there never was.

The brokerage firm is acting as 'principal' because it acquires the shares from the company raising the capital. In other words, the brokerage firm actually buys the shares from the company.

It then has the job of selling those shares on to their clients.

But here's the interesting thing. The brokerage firm never actually pays for the shares because the penny share company gives the brokerage firm an 'extended settlement' date to pay, usually thirty days.

This means that the brokerage firm now has thirty days to sell all of its newly acquired shares. If it can do that, then it doesn't have to ever part with the cash because the client's moneycan be used to pay the company.

So, where's the scam?

Well, as always, the scam takes place within the price.

The brokerage firm buys the shares from the company *discounted* price, then sells them on at an inflated price to their clients. That's the margen.

A big margin is only possible if the share has a 'wide' spread, i.e., a large difference between the buying and selling price. That's why this scam can only work with penny shares, because a 5p stock will typically have a much wider spread than, say, a 500p stock.

Without a wide price spread, neither the company issuing the shares, nor the principal brokerage firm, can make any money.

Big spread, big profit

If a company has a share price trading with a bid offer spread of say, 1p to 2p, then the spread is 50%. This means investors pay 2p if they want to buy, but only receive 1p if they want to sell. In other words, they immediately lose 50% of their investment after purchase.

The company raising the capital wants to get the highest price for its shares and the brokerage firm wants the lowest price, so there is negotiation at this stage.

The brokerage firm's main negotiating tool is the ability to place stock with its clients. If it has access to thousands of clients and can place say £5million of shares, that is very attractive to the company. In return the brokerage firm will expect to pay less for each share. It's a bulk purchase discount. Just like any shopping trip, the more you spend, the less you pay.

However, this increases the risk to the brokerage firm because if it commits to acquiring too many shares and is subsequently not able to place them (i.e., sell them on to its clients), then it must pay for the shares and keep them on its own book. That's bad news for the brokerage firm because they don't want to pay for, less still, keep any of the stock. They already know it's a failing business.

The company issuing the shares doesn't want to discount its price by too much but recognises that it's easy, quick money not available anywhere else. So, in the negotiation, the brokerage firm will usually have the upper hand, unless the company has contacts with multiple principal brokerage firms in the City in which case it can create 'competition' between the brokers.

Delivery Versus Payment DVP

There are variations to the principal dealing model which favour both the company issuing the shares and the brokerage firm. Delivery Versus Payment (DVP) is where the brokerage firm places as many shares as it can but isn't committed to buying them. In other words, the firm doesn't buy the stock 'as principal' onto its own book. Therefore, it doesn't run the risk of not being able to sell them and having to keep the stock.

It sells what it can, takes *delivery* of the stock and makes *payment* accordingly, hence the name DVP.

This reduces the risk to the brokerage firm, which also means the company issuing the shares doesn't have to discount the price as heavily to compensate for that risk.

In addition, the brokerage firm doesn't need a 'principal dealing' licence from the regulator; which is, in itself, a very hard thing to acquire now. The DVP model is open to most brokerage firms without the extra regulations involved so, it's a low barrier to entry to market.

Discounted pricing

After negotiation, let's say the brokerage firm and the penny company jointly agree the broker will buy one hundred million shares at 1p, which is £1 million. The broker's next job is to sell those shares at the highest price it can which will be just under 2p.

The price must be *under* 2p because the broker must be able to demonstrate that its clients are buying at a *'discount'* to the market price. This is necessary to justify from a regulatory standpoint, why clients shouldn't buy in the open market.

The rule is known as 'Best Execution', which means the brokerage firm must guarantee that its clients are getting the best available price in the marketplace.

If the client pays 2p to the broker but can pay 2p in the open marketplace, then the deal doesn't work. The brokerage firm needs to offer the *best* price available.

But a discount can be anything, and it usually is. The discount can literally be 0.1p which means the client pays 1.9p instead of 2p. Hardly a discount.

In fact, typically, the discount is even less. For a 2p penny stock it's usually $1/16^{th}$ of a penny. So, the client would pay one $15/16^{th}$ of a penny (or 1.9375p). The client saves 0.0625p. Amazing.

If it wasn't so sad, it would be funny.

The spread is still a whopping 48%, (0.9375/1.9375), barely down from the original 50%.

But instead of hiding this miniscule discount, it's sold to the client as a big benefit. From a psychological perspective just being able to put in the sales pitch *"Great news, we're able to secure a discount on the share price"* is enough to sway a lot of investors into saying 'yes'.

They also will use the line *"Because it's a principal deal, we can also do this transaction commission-free, saving you another £100"*.

That's enough to get most clients excited. Their attention is turned towards phrases like 'discounts' and 'commission-free', when they should really be focusing on the company and the fact that the brokerage firm acquired the shares at just 1p and is now selling them for nearly 2p.

The more switched-on investors will see that the discount is basically zero and the £100 saving is just a hook, so they won't take the bait.

But as with all scams those investors are bad news anyway; the scammers have a very different target audience. The scammers want the trusting, less inquisitive type of investor who hears the word 'discount' and becomes giddy with excitement.

Now, let's see the profit for the brokerage firm. Get ready to be shocked.

The stock brokerage firm buys the shares for 1p and sells them to their unsuspecting, trusting clients for a whopping 1.9375p. For doing absolutely nothing except sitting in the middle.

Let's say the brokerage firm purchased £1 million of shares (one hundred million shares at 1p) from the company. If they 'place' (aka 'sell') those one hundred million shares at 1.937p, they would receive £1,937,500, giving them a whopping profit of £937,500 or 94%!

If you just found yourself saying the f-word as you read this, don't worry – just move into a quieter room far away from where your grandkids can hear you, because you'll be using more expletives soon.

Clients can't sell - NMS

Buying the stock is bad enough but it gets much worse.

Sure, buying shares in a failing company where you automatically lose 48% of your initial capital, isn't the best way to start the day. However not being able to sell those shares compounds your problem exponentially.

That's because of something called 'Normal Market Size' (NMS). NMS is the minimum number of shares a market maker is obliged to buy or sell at the price that's being quoted.

For example, if the NMS of a company is 50,000 shares, and the price being quoted is 1p to 2p, the market maker is only obliged to buy up to 50,000 shares at 1p from a client who wants to sell.

The client can only sell 50,000 shares at 1p, which is £500. If they want to sell more, let's say 200,000 shares, the market maker will drop his price.

So, if a client buys say one million shares (£19,375), they're never going to be able to sell their shares at 1p. In fact, the market maker might offer as little as 0.25p. For 500,000 shares he might offer 0.5p, and for 250,000 shares he might offer 0.75p. It's completely up to him and outside of the client's control.

The client can't even sell 50,000 shares at 1p, then sneakily try and sell another 50,000 later at the same price. The market maker will drop the price immediately if more than a few people start 'hitting his bid' and selling at 1p. The new price would look something like 0.75p to 1.75p.

If the client is desperate and has no option to sell, the market marker offers the client just 0.25p on the full one million shares, that's only £2,500. The client just lost £16,875 from a £19,375 'investment'.

Investments go up and down, we all understand that, and we know that share prices can fall by 50%, 75% or even 100%. That's also true.

However, the difference here is that the *share price hasn't moved.*

The share price is still 1p to 2p on the trading screen and yet Mr Client has lost 90% of the investment, he made about ten minutes ago. It's instantaneous theft.

Once you agree to the purchase and the deal is done, you're locked in. There's no way out and the loss is entirely attributable to the spread and illiquidity, not because the share price falls.

Let's just go back and so this moment can really sink in.

We all know about boiler room scammers running off with your money, but this isn't a boiler room. This is regulated activity where you are supposed to be protected.

This is dealing with a regulated stock broking firm, a regulated market maker, and a company which is listed on a regulated stock exchange.

If you're still on that train by the way, firstly your commute to work is just too long, and you should really consider changing your job. Secondly, don't give up your seat to anybody, no matter how frail or pregnant they look.

The scams in this book are only just beginning to heat up.

Market makers and price control

There are more facets to this scam, which requires the co-operation of other players, including the market makers.

When the company announces it is issuing more shares, the market makers *should* drop their price immediately. This is because there are now more shares in circulation for the same business. Therefore each share in circulation must be worth less.

However, the brokerage firm that's buying the stock as principal needs a favour from the market maker to *not* drop his price.

The market makers therefore agree (for a fee) to support the price artificially for the duration of the placement. This gives the brokerage firm sufficient time to offload their stock to their clients.

If the market makers drop the price from 1p to 2p to say, 0.75p to 1.5p, the profit margin for the brokerage firm is significantly reduced. Instead of charging 1.9375p it would have to offer the shares at say 1.49p (remember, anything less than 1.5p is acceptable).

Instead of making a 94% profit margin, the brokerage firm must settle for a 49% margin.

So, the market makers have to be onside and in cahoots with

the principal brokerage firm, but this comes at a cost for the market maker.

First, savvy investors who already hold the stock recognise that the price hasn't fallen. They might see an opportunity to start selling their own shares while the price is at 1p, and the market makers have to buy that stock without dropping the price.

Thankfully for the market makers this usually doesn't happen because the spread is already very wide so most investors won't want to sell at 1p.

Technically, the market maker could widen the spread from 1p to 2p to say, 0.5p to 2p, which allows the brokerage firm the opportunity to get rid of the shares with the same profit margin.

However, the spread has to be 'reasonable' and there are limitations as to what the spread can look like.

Second, the dodgy market maker will look suspicious to other market makers if he continues to keep his price artificially high. The price is dictated by *all* of the market makers and so it's not fully controllable by one market maker in any case. That's why this scam works best with company shares that only have a maximum of two market makers rather than four or five.

Third, even if it's the Wild West, there is still a sheriff in town that you don't want to alert to your shenanigans. When a company makes a public announcement that it's just issued shares, then market makers are expected to drop their price. A market maker that doesn't drop their price might raise a red flag with the regulators.

So, the market makers need to tread carefully and work with the brokerage firm. Thankfully for them, this isn't very difficult because the market maker often works in the same company. In other words, the market makers work *for* the brokerage firm, on the same dealing floor!

The market makers however aren't happy to keep the price at 2p for too long because of the financial and regulatory risk they are exposed to. Therefore, the brokerage firm puts pressure on the floor managers who, in turn put pressure on the individual brokers who in turn put pressure on their clients to buy the stock.

High-pressured sales

Because of the time-constraints, it's like a ticking time-bomb, and the brokerage firm needs to place all the stock as quickly as possible.

It's a crazy, frantic time and all hands are to the pump. There are bonuses for the biggest deals, and off-the record financial incentives for the thirty hungry salespeople on the floor. Incentives like "*Do your stock and go down the pub, take the rest of the day off*".

Within a few short days the stock is usually gone, and the mission is accomplished.

The company raises £1 million in cash, the brokerage firm makes a very tidy profit of £937,500, the market makers make their fee for supporting the price, and all of the shares in this failing company have been expertly distributed using a team of twenty brokers, who have sold the stock amongst a hundred unsuspecting clients.

If a stock isn't being pushed out the door quick enough, other incentives will be offered to the dealers to encourage them to work harder. That is either higher commissions and bonuses or financial penalties. Nothing is ruled out in the pursuit of profit for the brokerage firm.

As soon as all of the stock is placed (i.e., the shares are completely sold to clients) the brokerage firm has no equity risk. They have a zero balance in stock and a cash balance on their books of £937,500.

The market makers can now drop their price.

It's like the market makers are holding up this incredibly heavy sofa while the brokers encourage clients to look underneath it for lost pound coins. Once all of the clients are underneath the sofa, and the brokers have crawled out to safety, the market makers let go of it. The clients get crushed.

Further placements

Once a firm raises cash in a secondary placing, it's easy to do a third, fourth and a fifth. In fact, there's technically no limit to the number of placings that you could do in theory. The price continues to slide during that time but that doesn't matter too much. It just means that the placing is executed at a lower price for more shares.

That's why you can see placings at just 0.1p but yet they still raise millions of pounds for the business owners.

Clients who buy a stock at 2p, are likely to buy at 1p and then 0.5p and so on. It's called 'averaging down' and the skilled broker will advise their clients that they should be buying more at the lower price, if they want any chance of getting their money back on the original purchase. It's like a gambler throwing more money down the drain.

As the share price drops the margin generally widens which makes it even better for the brokerage firm. There's even more manipulation and profit to be made.

Of course, there will eventually come a point where the business is literally left with nothing on its balance sheet. Millions of pounds were raised and somehow the business still failed. Fancy that.

You can only squeeze so much juice out of an orange. Eventually you just have to throw it in the bin and that's what happens to these scam companies. They eventually get suspended, delisted from the market, and go into administration.

Sometimes the shares might reverse into another shell company or just float onto an overseas exchange. It doesn't matter, by that time the business is all but gone and your money has gone with it.

It makes you wonder why anybody would even attempt to buy these super high risk, tiny, obscure, companies.

Good question, that's where the analysts come in.

Biased research

So far, we have three firms colluding together against you, the investor – the failing AIM company issuing the shares, the brokerage firm placing the shares, and the market maker manipulating the price. These are all professional firms and experts in their fields. Together their goal is to take money from the public and in return offer worthless shares in failing businesses.

However, there's also a fourth person that is required to join the party – please step forward Mr Research Analyst, or should that be *anal*-yst.

Most companies have a research analyst to assess the trading opportunities for their clients. They analyse and pick what they hope to be the best stocks, thereby helping the firm's clients to make money. That's true when a brokerage firm acts as an agent. But when the firm is acting as 'principal', then it's the exact opposite.

Agency stocks are your traditional, blue-chip companies where clients buy shares in the open marketplace and the firm only gets paid a set commission. In this case the interests of the client and firm are in line so picking good stocks that make a profit is what both the firm and client wants.

However, for principal dealing, the brokerage firm is the seller, and the client is the buyer. As with any transaction, either the buyer or the seller is going to win, they can't both be right. Therefore, the goal of the seller is to buy something as cheap as possible and to sell it for as much as possible.

In order to buy something really cheap, the stock has to be high risk, illiquid, unprofitable and basically a pile of sh*t. The brokerage firm therefore, targets and works with the companies desperate for cash i.e., failing businesses. They are the ones that are happy to issue shares in their business at any price.

Conversely, profitable businesses won't give away their shares for peanuts, they will want a good price. That's why brokerage firms don't want to work with them.

But selling stocks that look and smell like dog poo isn't easy.

That's why the analyst needs to be convincing. Their job is to make the stock look desirable and appealing, even if it has all the hallmarks of your pet's excrement.

The 'independent' analyst isn't independent. There are paid directly by the brokerage firm and commissioned to write a *favourable* report which may appear balanced and unbiased. In fact, it is a subtle two-page sales pitch used by the brokers to pitch the shares. It serves as a sales and compliance function.

Brokerage firms have to justify their actions and are required to act in the best interests of their clients, so, they can only recommend companies which they believe will do well. In other words, they need an anal-yst, sorry analyst, to produce a report stating exactly why a particular company is worth investing in.

So, the researchers and analysts are tasked with finding creative ways of justifying a purchase that any sane investor would run a mile from. They do it very simply with risk ratings.

Risk ratings

There is nothing you can't sell in the investment world, as long as you make the risks clear. That's the job of the analyst. He puts together a report explaining the industry, the business, the risks and the opportunity.

At the end of it, he signs it off with the three magical words 'Highly speculative buy'. That report can now be used by the brokers to sell to their clients, and it safeguards the brokerage firm from any potential complaints.

If they tried to sell the company as a low-risk investment, they would have regulatory problems, complaints and thousands of cases of financial redress that would eventually bankrupt them.

But with those three magic words, they protect themselves.

Of course, the job of the broker selling the investment becomes a little trickier because they now have to sell a high-risk share instead of a low-risk share, but that's not very difficult for a seasoned broker armed to the teeth with sales training and solid objection handling techniques.

As long as their clients are suitable for investing in higher risk shares, (and most are), they can now proceed compliantly with the deal.

The analyst's job is therefore to find whatever positives he possibly can and spin it into a report so that the company is seen in the most positive light. Even negatives like a low share price and a widespread, can be easily manipulated into positive selling points once you understand the game.

Because the research analyst is on the payroll of the brokerage firm, he does what he is told; it doesn't matter how unflattering the investment is, he has to make it look beautiful.

The report can't lie or tell any untruths, because it's in black and white and can be reproduced at a moment's notice if the firm is to ever be sued. But nonetheless there is plenty of grey to operate within.

The analyst will also be commissioned to write an equal number of negative reports for other companies which the firm has no intention of working with. These will be companies also looking to raise capital and are indeed much better investments for the clients, but the margins are too small. The firm wants to give the impression that it considered many companies before choosing to help the one that it did.

They're just useful scapegoats for compliance purposes.

The secret here is that the analyst has to give the impression of being completely independent from the firm making the recommendation. It's a nonsense really because the analyst works for the brokerage firm, is on their payroll, works in their office, and goes out drinking with the brokers every week. How can he possibly be independent?

In any case, with enough research reports, different risk ratings, as well as a mix of 'buys', 'holds' and 'sells' , it's enough of a cover. The goal of giving the impression that the firm has done loads of careful market research has been achieved.

That research is used to justify both the purchase of shares from the company and the sale of those shares to its clients.

'Independent' researchers who do *not* work for the principal brokerage firm are even more valuable. They rubber stamp the initial research conducted by the in-house analyst, which helps to increase the credibility of the report.

Depending on the reach and depth of the broker's pockets, you can even find situations where there are so many positive articles being written by so many independent analysts, that people actually start to buy the stock and push the price up! They don't realise the research is all made-up.

That's brilliant news for the brokerage firm because they simply move up their placing price to just under the new offer price. This increases their profit margins even further.

Long term incestuous relationships

The principal dealing market is very incestuous. It's a small world which means that long term relationships are forged and can remain in place for years. It's a tiny marketplace where everybody knows everybody, so, if you are on the AIM exchange and you want to raise cash, there are just a small, handful of brokerage firms you can approach.

Principal brokerage firms are regularly pitched by companies looking to issue shares and raise capital. After a short while, brokerage firms will know who they can trust and work well with. There's an unwritten agreement about what the goal is; to sell stock in a failing company at the highest price.

That's why you often see principal firms place shares in the same company over and over again. When a burglar robs a house once, he's likely to rob the same house again and again because he got away with it the first time.

So, relationships are built, and the same people work together, firms and brokers, for many years.

It's the same with external researchers and independent analysts. It's not easy to find somebody you can trust so once you've built a team of like-minded crooks, you don't need to look anywhere else.

Give us your worst stocks

You might think that a penny share broker would prefer to have an easy sales pitch to sell to his clients, which would be the best and strongest companies, but in fact he wants the opposite.

That's because he gets paid more commission for offloading the worst companies. It all trickles down from the top. The brokers get a percentage of the money that the brokerage firm makes, typically between 10% and 25% of the 'turn' depending on seniority.

A horrible company that you can buy at 1p and sell at 1.9p gives a 47% turn (0.9/1.9), so a senior broker will get 25% x 90% x the amount invested. If a client invests £10,000, the firm would make £10,000 x 47% = £4,700 and a senior broker would earn £4,700 x 25% = £1,184.

Think about that for a second.

Where can a 20-year-old, school drop-out with no qualifications (apart from a flimsy broker exam), earn more than £1,000 in a single five-minute telephone call?

If the stock was purchased at 1p but was 'only' sold at say 1.1p, the 'turn' would be 0.1/1.1 = 9%. This means that a £10,000 investment nets the firm a gross profit of £909, and a senior broker would earn 25% of that which is £227. Still very good, but not as good as the last one.

Therefore, the commission hungry brokers want the *worst* stocks because they pay the *most* commission.

The best paid brokers are the salespeople who become most proficient in being able to disguise a 'dog' stock as a great investment opportunity.

That's not to say they want the stock to 'bomb' (fall in value). They would love it if the stock actually went up in price and their clients' made loads of money; amazingly sometimes that happens. But that's so unusual. Brokers expect their recommendations to fail.

The real motivation is disguised from the client but it's always the same for the broker, to maximise their own commission first, which means the investor has to buy the worst companies with the highest profit margins.

It's a shocking incentive structure designed to promote the worst practices. The regulator worked hard to stop it by, introducing a series of measures forcing firms to change the way they pay their employees. However as with all scammers, it's a cat and mouse game and (some) principal firms have successfully circumvented the rules compliantly with the same end result.

One way to avoid attracting unnecessary heat is for the brokerage firm to occasionally place shares in higher calibre companies. The commission is much less but it's a necessary requirement because like all good scams, a few genuine investments have to be thrown into the mix for good measure, just to even things up a little.

The analyst can't just write about and recommend extremely high-risk companies, any more than principal brokerage firms can only raise capital for companies that go bust within twelve months.

There has to be a balance.

These better companies are far less risky, so their directors won't just give away the stock for peanuts to any brokerage firm. This means the profit margin is low, and the individual brokers will usually put up some resistance to selling their stock to their clients.

It's quite a difficult thing to get your head around. You would think that your broker, the guy who rings you up and becomes your best pal, would want you to get the best stock in your portfolio. But in fact, it's the opposite.

He wants you to fill your boots with the *worst* possible investments.

An upside-down business model

You might be wondering how principal brokerage firms can run a business in this way because presumably if clients keep losing money, at some point they just close their accounts down, right?

Well, yes, they do, but the business model works very differently to any other business.

Brokerage firms that make a million pounds of profit on a single secondary placing, don't care too much about client retention. When you make that kind of money, the collateral damage of clients leaving the firm is acceptable, even welcomed. That's because they know that if clients are losing money quickly, it must be because they are *making* money quickly. It's the zero- sum game again.

The money needs to come from somewhere. If clients are getting pissed off and closing down their accounts with some consistency, then money must also be moving with the same consistency to the brokerage firms.

The cost of settling the financial complaints, dealing with regulatory fines, and even the risk of being shut down, is all worth it when the money being generated is so great.

Remember that at the height of the principal dealing industry, hundreds of millions of pounds in revenue were being generated every year. That's plenty of money to spend on employing top salespeople to attract new clients and replace the lost ones. One in, one out.

Any other business sees client retention as one of their top priorities, but principal brokerages don't care about it in the slightest. When a new client comes on board, the ticking clock has started before they leave. In fact, a *low* client retention rate almost certainly means it's doing great business.

Of course, brokerage firms don't want their clients to leave. They just know that at some point they *will* leave.

Until then, their job is to take as much money out of their clients' pockets as possible.

Extending the lifetime of a client

Whilst client retention is always going to be poor, the brokerage firm still wants clients to stay for as long as possible. Therefore, a big part of the broker's job is to find justification, reasons and excuses why their last recommendation went down. They've prepared that apologetic speech long before they eventually have to make the call.

"Sorry, John this one didn't work out but that's the way it is with penny stocks. But don't worry because it's a numbers game. You really need to invest in at least five companies and one of them will do so well that they will more than pay for the others".

So that's what poor John does. Now he's invested in one failed company, he feels compelled to invest in another four in order to get back his original investment.

You'll be amazed how long this pitch can be stretched out. Sometimes clients stay for years and invest in not five companies but twenty-five companies, each one spectacularly failing.

It's easy to read this and think "I *wouldn't do that*" but once you're in the matrix, you'll be surprised how hard it is to get out. The lure of potentially getting your money back is enough to rope people back in. A gambler always has that last bet if he thinks he can make back his losses.

Most investors just never learn. It's not their fault, they just keep on buying, even after they lose. They are completely mis-sold to, they are surrounded by expert advisors, and they believe the analyst, the broker, the firm and, they still believe in the opportunity. Many of them are elderly, and don't really fully understand what's going on. They don't read their statements or valuations; they don't log into their account because they're not good with computers and have no idea about how their stocks are performing.

The penny share market also attracts gamblers who find it hard to stop trading. We've all heard of the penny stock that went from a penny to a pound, and it's that dream which   keep clients coming back for more. Nobody wins the lottery, but millions of people still spend money on it every week. It's the chance of winning.

They're searching for that one golden ticket, that one golden penny stock.

Sometimes that happens. Quite miraculously, even a dodgy penny stock in a failing business can sometimes go up! Despite the odds, something can happen in the business or the sector which sends the price up. This could be an unexpected contract win, a new technology, a favourable regulatory change or something else.

Every dog has a chance of making it big and just once in a blue moon, that happens in principal dealing.

When it does, there is a massive fanfare.

The clients are beyond elated, and the brokerage firms use that one example as a sales pitch to help sell the next ten placings. It's incredible how far the good news of one trade can be stretched to propel future trade recommendations. The company is shocked, the brokerage firm is shocked, and the individual brokers are shocked.

Nobody expected that to happen.

Ironically, if you are a client, it's also the *worst* thing that can happen to you.

That's because the broker won't allow the stock to go from a penny to a pound. As soon as it shows any sort of profit, even if it just from just 1p to 2p, the broker will be on the phone to his client telling him to sell. He knows there are another fifty brokers on the floor who all want to dump their stock so, he wants to get his clients out before the dumping begins.

Even if by some miracle you do stumble across that company which goes from a penny to a pound, you don't benefit from it anyway because you were told to sell it at 2p!

You end up with a measly £5,000 profit on a £10,000 investment which sounds amazing at a, 50% profit. But it's actually very bad news because it will be used as a weapon against you by your broker.

That one lucky winning trade is weaponised to give you belief again and before you know it, you've just invested another £10,000 on the next placing, and another one and another one. That £5,000 'profit' could end up costing you another £50,000 that you would otherwise not have invested.

You don't want profits like that. It's like the gambler who was about to walk out the casino before his roulette number came in. Now he decides to stay for a bit longer and loses even more.

A quick recap of the master mind team

So, let's just revisit the scene of the crime and its participants.

We have unsuspecting investors, most of them pensioners, who are being targeted by a team of highly skilled professionals whose sole task is to extract money. They have set up an effective scheme to promote, market, advertise and push highly speculative penny shares in near-bankrupt companies at artificially high prices using pressurised sales techniques. They are sucking money from the pensions of their clients and transferring it seamlessly into their own.

The owners of failing AIM companies have no genuine business and no money, so they want to raise capital by issuing shares to investors. They vary in degrees of dodginess and desperation, but the goal is simple – to transfer ownership of their failing business to people for a hundred times more than what it's really worth.

Then we have the directors of the brokerage firm, the pinnacle of this whole operation. They pull all of the strings, organise each of the team members in their respective roles, and source the stock from business owners. Their job is to find desperate business owners who were about to turn the lights out on their business and offer them an outlet using the principal dealing vehicle.

Working for the brokerage firm are the individual salespeople, aka the principal brokers and dealers, who have the relationships with their clients.

This used to be made up of hordes of uneducated twenty-somethings Essex school dropouts who struggled with joined up handwriting but have the 'gift of the gab'. Their ability to tell a good yarn to retired factory worker, Bob, on the telephone gives them the opportunity to drive brand new Porsches and wear gold Rolex watches.

Then there's the research analyst, who is usually the only intelligent person on the trading floor. He had big dreams after university to work for Goldman Sachs but didn't make it to the second interview stage. Now he's sold his soul to the devil because he's got bills to pay.

He's the spectacled, educated, oddball in the organisation. Socially awkward, uncomfortable around women, and the only person in the 'front office' who thinks coke is a fizzy beverage.

He conjures up different reports on demand, all designed to dress up a defunct and bankrupt company into appearing like an attractive investment proposition.

Across the floor sits the market maker. He's usually a little older, and more respectable looking. He thinks that he's above the brokers because he's a real 'trader'. He doesn't have to feel bad about himself because he's not having to tell porky pies to old grannies. He's the get-away driver pretending not to see anything. Even if he doesn't put the gun to the bank teller's head, he's still an accomplice.

At the end of it all, is the poor investor. He's just been gang-banged without any lubrication by some of the City's most professional, experienced financiers. He won't walk straight for the foreseeable future.

The £350 million Wild West scam

Principal dealing was massive business in the late 1990s and 2000s, and it still exists today, albeit to a lesser degree. It's still in operation now as is the DVP model but it's a very different animal.

Over the years, regulations have tightened up as they have with all areas of finance. But that doesn't mean there isn't a conflict of interest. Perhaps there are some principal dealers and DVP firms who genuinely care for their clients, who raise capital for good companies, and who are making money for their investors. I just don't know them.

It's like all of the scams that I'm alerting you to. There's always a genuine investment, a genuine firm, a genuine opportunity. But it's so well-hidden that you probably won't find it.

Besides, why would anybody jump into a sea of sharks just

to try and find one dolphin to swim with?

Over the years, the principal penny share dealing industry sold billions of pounds of worthless stock to unsuspecting investors until eventually the inevitable happened. Several high-profile, principal brokerages went bust, and those bankruptcies shook the market. It was the first time that things came to a head and there was wide-spread media coverage on it.

Pacific Continental (known as Pac Con) was one of the biggest collapses. It sold so much dodgy principal stock that the Financial Services Compensation Scheme (FSCS) paid out an astronomical £350 million to clients after the company went bust. A third of a billion pounds!

This wasn't a small, boiler room scam – this was an industrial scale problem.

Principal dealing firms were acting like cowboys and the financial market was the Wild West.

Knives are not responsible for knife crime

Despite the scandal, the concept of principal dealing isn't at fault. Just in the same way that knives are not responsible for knife crime, neither is principal dealing responsible for ripping off private investors.

The idea that a company can raise working capital and use a principal dealing firm to achieve that goal is entirely sensible. If a firm can raise money through issuing shares and allow investors to become part of their exciting business, why shouldn't it?

If the business is genuine, the research notes are accurate, and the risks are clear, then investors and issuing companies should be brought together. It's part of a free, market economy.

If the pricing is fair for all parties, then principal dealing can actually be a very good thing.

But when the pricing favours one party unfairly, and the interests are misaligned, that's when problems happen.

Without capital raisings, many of the businesses you see today wouldn't exist and that would be bad for everybody. It would be bad for the businesses, for brokerage firms, for investors, for the marketplace and for society itself. We need to support companies in their expansion plans and providing capital is the best way to do that.

As investors, we also want the opportunity to earn better returns than the measly sums the banks give us and so, we shouldn't be denied access to real investment opportunities.

Even raising capital at a discount which a broker can pass onto its clients, is an entirely sensible idea – on paper.

But as with so many things that look good on paper, human greed has a way of taking the beautiful and making it ugly. That's why I don't hold the FCA (or FSA as it was then) to blame.

I don't even hold all principal dealing firms to blame because I am sure there were some which would have acted correctly. They were certainly in the minority but that's not to say they didn't exist.

The point with this insider trading secret is the same as every other secret – first and foremost, you need to protect yourself. Don't listen to your advisor, don't listen to your broker, don't even listen to your family members, who may be giving you what they think is the best advice.

Do your own research and dig deep before you invest. Don't dabble in things that don't make sense. Don't play with matches and not expect to get burned.

If somebody tells you to buy a company that is issuing shares at 1p, think long and hard if that's the type of company you want to invest your pension into.

Yes, you might miss an investment of a lifetime, but you probably won't.

You're more likely to be dodging a baseball bat that was about to take your head clean off.

TIP 5 –
"LEARN TO TRADE" SCAM

You all know by now that I really don't like the idea of the professionals scamming retail investors – because it's an unfair match up; rich against poor, educated against uneducated, strong against weak, secure against vulnerable, young against old. In short, it's not a fair fight.

But there is something even worse than that.

You see, now that we are in the final stretch, things are about to become even more interesting. There is a growing number of people who are impersonating professionals and ripping people off. In my mind this is even worse than a professional ripping you off because it's like having your own family member turn their back on you.

As a society we have come to expect the worst from professionals, especially in the finance world. We already know that many of them will try and rip us off to make a profit. We've seen that happen for decades.

So, when a new financial scandal is uncovered on Wall Street or in the City of London, it doesn't make the headlines in the same way it once did. When you see yet another hedge fund fined a few million pounds for money laundering, collusion, price- fixing, mis-selling, market abuse or something else, it's water off a duck's back. We hardly even think about it anymore.

However, to have somebody who is just like you, another retail investor, try and rip you off, well in my book that's so much worse.

The retail scammers

I first had my suspicions a few years ago when I saw a sponsored Facebook advert pop up on my feed. I had no idea who the guy was, but he was talking about achieving 'financial freedom', how he had made millions in foreign exchange and was now teaching others how to do the same. Unfortunately, this chap is very prevalent on the social media scene even today, which is why I can't mention him by name.

So, I watched his introduction video, which involved him driving a flash car, as well as the usual nonsense, and realised that he was holding seminars at weekends for free. I became intrigued. I hadn't heard of this guy, so I did some basic due diligence and couldn't find anything to support his claim that he was a qualified trader. He hadn't worked for any firms, big or small, he had no trading accounts that he had disclosed, he hadn't worked in the industry and, he wasn't on the FCA register; there was nothing.

I checked him out at Companies House, he had various business interests but, again nothing related to trading. Nothing. My immediate thought was that this guy was a fake.

I continued to view his videos and content, it was all was hype. He was talking not just about foreign exchange, but also property, and later on he moved on to commerce and cryptocurrency. He was obviously an expert in just about everything.

So, I delved deeper into this rabbit hole and uncovered a growing movement of people, most of them quite young and troubled, who were paying hundreds, and in some cases, thousands of pounds, to enrol on foreign exchange courses, just like his.

Since then, I've seen more and more con artists like him openly scamming people online. It's a massive problem and it's getting bigger.

This is also a problem that nobody appears to be addressing. It's outside of the reach of the regulators, it's not picked up in the media because they don't understand it, and it's very difficult to uncover as a scam.

Social media and the internet are teaching our children that hard work is not the way anymore. Instead, we should all be posting videos, getting likes and subscribers to earn money. Sure, that's a business, and some people have done and will continue to do, really well.

But it seems to me it's encouraging our children think that taking short cuts is ok. It's telling them that the only valuable skill society needs is the ability to record yourself on a smart phone doing a stupid dance and posting it on TikTok.

It's all part of the wrong philosophy, that 'quick money' can be made. It can't.

But when you see the fast cars, beautiful men and women, and sprawling mansions, it's hard for an impressionable, young man or woman not to want those things.

It's promoting the idea that not only are these things attainable they're within everybody's grasp in just a few short, months. That's ridiculous. For every successful YouTuber, there must be a hundred thousand who failed.

It's not just the younger generation. There are many men and women who are in the 30s, 40s and 50s who are chasing the same 'get rich-quick' dream. Quite frankly it's destroying lives.

Instead of working hard, contributing to society and developing skills that will serve them and their communities well in life, they're going down a path that leads to nowhere but unhappiness and unfulfillment. It's the soul-destroying, make money quick strategy.

The fake FX gurus have picked up on this changing societal mood and taken full advantage of it, too.

Financial freedom

It all begins with individuals wanting to become rich quickly doing the least amount of work. The scam artists know that everybody is on the hunt to make money. They know that trading and finance is particularly alluring because of the vast amounts of money that is involved.

If you Google the words 'learn to trade foreign exchange' you'll see at least a hundred 'foreign exchange experts'. Each one has allegedly found the 'Holy Grail' of trading, a super system that is unbreakable, and how they hold the key to untold riches.

What a joke.

The foreign exchange market is actually one of the hardest asset classes to learn to trade. It's the biggest and most serious market of them all. It's also the must unforgiving cut-throat market. It takes no prisoners because it involves the very elite traders and banks, strictly the professionals. It's where Central banks, massive hedge funds, and investment houses are constantly moving money around the world in fractions of a second. It's where commercial deals to facilitate imports and exports worth billions of dollars are being settled. It's where UBS and Deutsche Bank are going head-to- head, trying to nick a few pips here and there in massive eye-watering deals using the most sophisticated trading systems.

It swings wildly from one direction to the other. Its price is almost impossible to predict as it depends on so many factors over which you have no control. Political events, interest rate decisions, inflation numbers, unemployment data, wars, military coops, economic sanctions, floods and other natural disasters, civil unrest, flu pandemics and much more besides.

It's also the most volatile, scary and risky market in the world. That's because it has unparalleled leverage and gearing which multiplies the slightest price movement by ten, fifty, even one hundred times or more.

Leverage (gearing)

Leverage is instrumental in this scam because the majority of people being targeted are financially weak. They don't have a lot of money so they need to trade in a product where they can start off with a small amount, maybe £500 or £1000 but gives exposure to a much larger sum of money, say £10,000 or

£20,000. The FX market is perfect for this and much better than equity trading which, with the exception of spread betting and CFDs, doesn't give you the same level of margin.

To be clear, there's nothing wrong with margin if you understand how to use it. In the same way, there's nothing wrong owning a Ferrari when you understand how powerful it is. But when you're barely 18 years old, and still only got a provisional driving licence, it's probably not a good idea to take out a fully loaded sports car as your first spin.

Leverage gives you the false illusion you're invincible when things go well. That's when you hear of somebody who invested £500 and made a £500 profit. They just made 100% in one day, which is impossible to do without margin.

But in the FX world it's entirely possible because you either win big, or you lose big.

Typically, half of the people get wiped out on their first few trades, while the other half make a few hundred per cent. Armed with that poor, get-rich-quick mindset, the winners assume they've found the system to unlimited riches, and it works for a while, until things go wrong; then it goes badly wrong.

The Alpari Disaster

The collapse of the FX house 'Alpari UK' is just one example of how dangerous this vehicle is. On one Friday evening in January 2015, the company had assets under management of £800 billion and was doing just fine. But on Monday morning, just three days later, the company was insolvent and was ready to file for bankruptcy. That's all because of margin.

It turns out that the Swiss National Bank would do something that nobody had expected. It shocked the market by announcing that its currency would no longer be pegged to the euro. That caused the Swiss franc to plummet by 30% and wipe out a big chunk of Alpari's trading positions. Alpari was banking heavily on the fact that the Swiss Bank would never unpeg against the euro so, it built all of its trades around this false assumption.

It seemed unlikely, almost unfathomable at the time, but it happened and that's the point.

If you put all of your eggs in one basket, even if the basket is supposed to be made out of impenetrable steel, one day you'll realise it was in fact made out of paper. It's time to say goodbye to your eggs.

That single decision was enough to blow up all of Alpari's live trading positions and decimate their collateral. Margin calls couldn't be met, and trades were forced to close.

The business blew up. All client portfolios blew up. People's life savings blew up.

That's how serious the FX market can be.

Easy to learn and pitch

The FX market is also one of the easiest to pitch because it has a very low barrier to knowledge.

In comparison it would be a huge challenge for a scammer to learn and teach about the equity market. It's not easy to pull the wool over somebody's eyes when discussing balance sheets, profit and loss accounts, dividend income, price-earnings ratios as well as all the fundamental analysis that is part of stock trading and portfolio management. The scammers know they can't pass themselves off as experts in this field which is why they target the FX market.

The foreign exchange market, despite its risk and volatility, is the simplest to teach. That's because it can be traded entirely on technical analysis, which involves reading charts. Reading charts at a basic level is actually pretty simple stuff but sounds really impressive.

You just need to learn a few basic charting principles and away you go. You can apply it to the FX market and pretend to be a guru.

Before you enter the technical analysis world it sounds complicated but once you're on the inside, it's so easy. There's no better way to learn than being a student yourself.

That's why ironically the majority of FX scammers have previously been scammed themselves. Once upon a time they were students too. They enrolled on a course, learned some chart patterns that didn't work, traded for six months, lost all their money, realised what they knew was worthless, and figured out they could make much more by teaching somebody else what they knew.

It was time to sell the pipedream to some other sucker. Of

course, this makes sense.

The genuine traders who are genuinely successful do everything possible *not* to disclose their secrets. They spend all their time trading making lots of money rather than teaching or trying to convince other people to trade. It's blindingly obvious really but as humans desperately searching for success, we want to believe any narrative that might help support our biggest wish that there's a way to make money that doesn't involve hard work.

That's why the FX market is a breeding ground for liars, deceivers, con-men and women. A couple of days studying, and you can set yourself up as an expert. A couple of basic pattern formations, like a 'reverse head and shoulders', or a 'diverging wedge' and gee, it all sounds so impressive.

Foreign Exchange is also appealing because it's unregulated and doesn't trade on a single exchange. That means less compliance, fewer rules, and the ability to trade anywhere in the world at any time, twenty-four hours a day, five days a week.

It fits perfectly with the digital world of today where everybody dreams of making money on a laptop, as they sit on a sandy beach while sipping a cool Sangria.

An explosion in online courses fuels this insatiable appetite which means people are now being scammed all over the world.

Trust is for sale

Building credibility and trust via social media can take many years if executed organically, but that's too long to wait. Instead, it's much better to 'buy' a reputation, and buy trust.

All you need is to spend a little money and you can get thousands, even tens of thousands likes, followers, and subscribers. You can pay people to write posts, create video content, write blogs, and design websites. It's so easy; you just need a little cash.

You can even become an overnight sensation on the internet, which can catapult you into a huge target market that is primed and ready to be scammed if you partner with the right influencer.

It's also easy to build social proof by partnering with existing social media 'celebrities'.

A simple endorsement from somebody who has a hundred thousand followers, can cost a scammer as little as a few hundred pounds and can quickly provide a ready-made target audience for an online course or presentation. These social media celebrities either receive a cash payment from the scammer or will earn a percentage of the course fees via a JV (Joint Venture) or an affiliation fee.

Even big celebrities can get greedy. I know of famous actors, singers and even ex-football players who are very willing to put their face to a brand, just to receive money on the back of it. Some of them have no idea they're promoting a scam while others are up to their necks in the scam.

To get the bigger A-list celebrities is more challenging because they've already made their money. But there's another way to get them on board which is by tricking them.

Scammers often attend black-tie events and charity balls, where they ask for an 'innocent' photo with the celebrity. I've seen this with the likes of Sylvester Stallone for example. He had no idea he was associating himself with a known scammer, but that one photo was used hundreds of times over social media.

I'm sure he still has no idea how that one innocent photo is being used to this day.

The glitzy presentation

As part of my journey to understand this game better I attended one FX scam presentation a few years ago in a very prestigious, five-star hotel in Central London.

It was fascinating. From their online company records, I could see this was operation was turning over several million pounds each year. This wasn't a small business and from the crowd of several hundred people crammed into the auditorium, I could see why.

The presentation from start to finish, from morning to late afternoon, was flawless. There were multiple speakers on stage with various courses for sale covering everything from Forex to property, and from crypto to e-commerce.

There were plenty of upsells too, including mastermind classes, investor summits, private mentorships, annual subscriptions, lifetime memberships, and referral programmes. It was all about maximising revenue.

The event was free to attend which would explain the big turnout, so their game was simple, *conversion*; to convert somebody from a 'no' to a 'maybe' and from a 'maybe' to a 'yes'.

All mobile phones had to be switched off before entering the presentation and strictly no filming allowed.

Funny that, isn't it?

These social media whores literally post everything in their life including photos of their egg and avocado toasted sandwich on Instagram. Yet, for this event they were shy of the camera. Why didn't they want anybody to record their presentation?

Probably because a lot of what they say isn't true. It's misleading at best, lies at worst, full of false guarantees, wrapped up in lots of pressurised selling, and mind manipulation techniques.

There was also an NDA (Non-Disclosure Agreement) that all attendees had to sign which means we couldn't disclose what was being presented. Ah well, never mind about that. If you want to sue me, get to the back of the queue behind St James's Place and Aston Martin.

There were various times throughout the day when the audience was encouraged to sign up to one of their courses. It was very well planned and orchestrated, and all of the offers were for 'today only'. Of course, that was never true.

I obviously didn't sign up to anything, and unsurprisingly, I was bombarded with telephone calls and emails for many weeks, with the same 'today-only' offer I was given at the presentation.

They also played a theatrical show where they drew members of the crowd onto the stage and performed various manipulation games to entice, cajole, and pressure people to sign up. I saw some people who were embarrassed, even ridiculed to signing up.

At the back of the room were rows of desks manned with members of their team who were armed with credit card machines. They're all paid a commission and were eager to push people to sign on the dotted line.

To my shock, there was even instant access to credit facilities. Quite literally, there were loan companies at the end of a telephone, ready to talk to anybody who couldn't afford to pay for the course in full. Yes, quite incredibly, 100% financing available and waiting.

It's really full-on because the scammers know the opportunity to close the sale *after* the face-to-face presentation, significantly diminishes. When people get home, the opportunity to be scammed falls very quickly.

But in that room, on that day, the energy is so high, it's contagious. You look around the room, and people are literally running to the back of the room to sign up to courses. It's easy to get washed up in the euphoria of it all. That's why they apply the pressure at the event and hope enough people will buckle.

This of course inevitably leads to buyer's remorse, where people get home and realise they've made a terrible mistake. But the scammers have prepared for that scenario too.

Kicking out kickers

The scammers use a genius way to eliminate 'kickers', people who agree to buy the course on the day, pay a deposit, but then go home and change their mind. They do this by simply providing something of *value*.

In other words, as soon as the deposit is paid, the student is immediately sent an email giving them full access to the course, including a downloadable 'secret investment guide' which is a thirty-page PDF that's supposedly worth a few hundredpounds.

This acts as a counter against the statutory fourteen-day 'cooling off period' because the investment guide and the online course can't be taken back. Once you see it, you can't un-see it.

From what I learned, if a consumer receives something that has a *financial value* they cannot pull out of the deal, the fourteen-day period becomes null and void, and they are now committed to the process.

Legally I have no idea if this would ever stand up in court, but I do know that it's being used as a deterrent and it's working very well.

The paying student signs the paperwork, receives the firm's terms of business, various high-valued documents, plus full access to the course, meaning the deposit is now the scammers, and the deal is done.

The scammers argument is that the student could have

downloaded the whole course already.

If the student still isn't budging, they'll use persuasion techniques, hide behind clauses, and, in some cases, they can be quite threatening or aggressive. They'll stop answering the phone, ignore your emails and pretty much do anything they can not to return payment.

Faced with your only other option, which is to sue the scammers, report them to the regulators or trading standards, most people won't bother. They assume that the Ts and Cs are water- tight, and they don't want to get into a legal battle with a multi-million-pound company.

So, either they accept and lose their deposit or if they've already paid for the whole course in full, they'll just do the course. They still have no idea that the course is a scam; they just decided they may as well do the course now, because they've paid for it.

But that's another big mistake.

When they attend that two-day workshop and learn the 'strategies', they take themselves further down a black road which ends in misery. Now they are committed even further. The course is never the end of their journey, it's always just the beginning.

Extra revenue streams

The most successful scams have multiple revenue streams.

An easy, add-on revenue stream takes place *after* the course. This is from the trading commissions of the students because the scammers recommend which FX brokerage firm their students should use.

The brokerage firm pays an upfront payment of a few hundred pounds for each client the scammers refer to them, then up to 50% of the recurring commission of the trading commission the students pay.

When a student has already invested thousands of pounds with a scammer, it's highly likely they will also take their advice on which broker to use. In fact, it's actually sold as part of the package "We'll even get you fully set up with a brokerage firm so you're ready to trade."

The brokerage firms the scammers team up with are never the cheapest. In fact, the scammers go out of their way to find the most uncompetitive FX brokerage firm they can work with because that increases their commission share.

If the student had little chance to make money before, those odds have just been slashed again. Of course, the FX teacher never discloses the back-handed arrangement, and the students are blissfully unaware as they continue to line the pockets of the scammers long after they finish their course.

Another way of converting all of those loyal students into cash cow machines is by offering them an opportunity to invest in the scammer's business through a planned IPO.

I've seen this happen with one particular scammer who conned thousands of his students and online followers to invest in his 'financial freedom' business on the pretence that it was about to float on the stock exchange. It was an easy pitch.

Why mess around with a £1,000 trading account when you can get exclusive access to invest in the business itself. What an opportunity!

I know exactly how this scam was pulled off because one of those investors found me as he was randomly searching for a stockbroker firm to help him get his money back.

He explained to me in detail how he had invested a staggering £120,000 in a pre-IPO and now the directors weren't even returning his phone calls. I had to break the news to him that his shares were worthless. Unless the company floated on the stock exchange, which was never going to happen, he had just given his money to the directors. I was shocked at the figure of £120,000 but that just shows how convincing these scammers are.

The pre-IPO scam is like the IPO scam but worse because you don't get anything for your money. The shares issued are literally worth zero because there is no secondary market.

A broken dream

The worst thing about this scam is the emotional impact it has. Scammers play with people's dreams by giving false hope. It's much worse than just a straight rip-off.

Every year there are literally thousands of people in the UK, and tens of thousands of people across the world, who attend FX courses in pursuit of a dream. While the courses are not cheap, the money they spend is actually the least important thing.

The biggest investment is their hope. They commit to something with more than just money, they commit with their heart. So, when it bears no fruit in the end, it's more painful than just losing money.

So many FX students are excitedly sat in their bedrooms at this very moment, wasting their precious time trying to trade in search of this false notion of 'financial freedom'.

Some will make a little money for a while, but eventually they all end up losing. It might take a few months, or even several years, but they will all reach the same realisation that what they are doing is not consistently profitable. They will have up days and down days like all traders, so it won't be obvious to begin with but over time, their account value will deplete and so, too, will their confidence.

At best somebody might get lucky and put together a string of winning trades but just like gambling, lady luck eventually turns her back on you.

When you don't have a proper risk management strategy in place, you don't understand the power and risk of leverage. When you haven't been taught the fundamentals by a real trader, then your demise is inevitable.

The problem is that with trading, as is the case with gambling, getting a win is the worst thing that can happen to you. We saw this in the last chapter with principal dealing and it's the same with FX trading. The danger is that you begin to believe in the system that you're using.

When you win, it reinforces a false belief that you really know what you are doing. You don't. You can't beat math or probability. It's impossible. You can't beat the FX market, or any other market, if you learned your strategy on a two-day course taught by somebody who has no previous trading credentials.

If you have ever paid for a Forex course from anybody other than a qualified FX trader, who either works for a hedge fund or investment bank, then I'm sorry to break the bad news, but you have been had. If you haven't bought an FX course yet, but were thinking about it, then count yourself very lucky. The small cost of this book has just saved you not just the price of the course, but a whole lot more.

At the risk of sounding totally over the top and melodramatic, allow me to explain how this chapter may have just saved your life.

It ruins lives

The reason that this scam is so bad that it literally ruins lives. When a professional trader rips off a retail investor, the retail investor eventually realises he's losing money and moves on. He stops buying whatever is being sold, he closes his account, gets his money back and moves on.

Some of the greedier retail investors might carry on for a bit longer and try to win their money back, but eventually they all stop in the end.

Either they blow up their entire trading account up or the

proverbial penny finally drops, and they realise there is only one winner; that's the broker earning his commission every time a trade is executed. Either way, it's game over and good night.

If a retail investor goes to a CFD brokerage firm and ends up losing £10,000, that's painful, but that's where it stops. When that same retail investor spends £5,000 on an FX course, and then loses another £5,000 on a trading account, the cost appears to be the same, £10,000 – but the hidden cost is actually much *more*.

That's because when you learn a new skill, you're investing more than just money. You're investing your emotions, your time, your heart – you're investing and attaching yourself to a dream. It's a whole new ball game.

You are committing to something that you truly believe will be life-changing, for you and your family. So, you make big, life-changing decisions.

People go on these courses to improve their lives. Many of them end up quitting their safe, full-time jobs, and put everything on the line. So, when it goes wrong (and yes it always does) they can lose everything.

They lose their job, they lose their confidence, they lose their patience, they lose their relationships, they lose their sanity. Investing months, sometimes years, of your most precious resource, time, into something that fails has terrible psychological implications.

It can often be the catalyst for even worse financial decisions where the victim won't give up the fight – he chases the dream even harder than before. He doesn't know when to stop, he doesn't know *how* to stop.

He's already in for £10,000, £20,000, £50,000 - he's already invested six months of his life, so why not invest another six months? He could make it all back, couldn't he?

He's already committed – he can't walk away now. He's lost his job anyway, so what else can he do? He wants that opportunity to make his money back, to get his time back. He wants to prove to himself and to everybody else that he has what it takes to be successful.

He finds himself with no choice – he has to invest more and more in a dream that was never attainable. He borrows money, sells his car, re-mortgages his home, cashes in his pension. It's just one poor decision after another. That's the cycle of addiction.

All of this in pursuit of something that isn't real; a mis-sold dream of financial freedom that doesn't exist in the real world.

The victims lose their self-esteem and self-belief. It changes them in ways that we simply couldn't understand, unless we've lived through it ourselves.

I have seen it affect marriages, cause divorces, kids being separated from their parents, messy court cases and the list goes on.

In the most serious of cases, it can literally be life and death. People who get caught up in serious gambling can end up homeless, alcoholics, on drugs, and in extreme cases can even commit suicide. It's the same with trading.

When you lose everything there's no reason not to jump.

Thankfully only a small number of scammed victims will fall all the way down to the bottom of this greasy pole., But most will slip far enough down for it to take years off their life.

It's even *worse* than gambling.

At least with gambling you know what it is and, you know that it's bad for you. As bad as gambling is, at least it's an informed decision. It might be addictive and difficult to control but you still know you have a problem, or at the very least, somebody else can you tell you that you have a problem and seek help for you.

But FX trading is very different, and here's why.

Help that could kill you

If you put yourself in danger, your loved ones will see that danger and jump in to save you. That could be anything from hiding that bottle of whisky, to sitting down with you and telling you to stop gambling. The problem with FX trading is that your loved ones don't know that it's a danger.

This means that even your loved ones can't protect you. They don't know what's going on. You went on the course, they didn't. So, they see your suffering, your distress, and they do what they think is best – they *support* you.

They tell you to believe in yourself, to keep going, keep trading. What they don't realise is that they're passing you a shovel to dig your own grave.

Trading happens twenty-four hours a day, in the morning, evening, or the early hours. It happens behind closed doors and, locked bedrooms. Your partner sees the screens with all of the charts and numbers and feels proud of you. They think you're onto something special. She wants you to succeed, she believes in it as much as you do.

This is the ticket for that more beautiful life for the family; it's the opportunity for a bigger house in that nicer area, a better school for the kids. This is your chance to prove you have what it takes. It's all on you.

But she doesn't know the truth, that you're losing money hand over fist. She doesn't know that you've just taken out a loan from the bank and have maxed out your credit cards.

You're doing it for her, for the kids; that's what keeps you going.

But what you don't realise is that you're walking down a road that leads to nowhere. In five or ten years, you will have lost everything. When you stare into the mirror, you'll see a grey- haired, exhausted, unfulfilled shell of your former self looking straight back at you.

I'm not suggesting that you shouldn't follow your dream; you absolutely *should* follow your dream and you *should* try and reach that lofty goal of being financially free. But the dream must be real and the path to get there must be genuine.

Most important of all you need a teacher who is honest and really can help you. We all need mentors and advisors in life to help us reach our goals. But when those people are con artists, illusionists, and scammers, they set us back years, decades even, and that's unforgivable.

Because that is time none of us can ever get back. They take away our most precious years.

Imagine spending just five years of your life when you're in your twenties or thirties trying to be an FX trader at the expense of working in a job, starting a new business, improving your education, learning new skills, or even travelling around the world.

Think of the missed opportunity.

Maybe you lost the chance to save up for a deposit on that house. Perhaps you missed the opportunity to experience that once in a lifetime back-packing adventure across the Amazonian rainforest. Could it be you were so busy trading, that you missed the love of your life who has since settled and married somebody else?

These scammers come into our lives for just a moment, but that moment can last a lifetime.

The 'never give up attitude' life

To make matters worse the scammers encourage a 'never give up' attitude. It's built into the scam, which makes it even more difficult to walk away. They will tell you, "It *will be hard at times, but you must keep pushing*".

They'll even warn you to ignore your loved ones if they try and persuade you to stop. They warn you; you mustn't listen to them. They warn you that your wife or husband mean well, but they don't understand what you're doing.

"Don't let them ruin your dream. Remember that you're doing it for them, too".

You'd think that the scammers wouldn't care if their victim traded for a week or a decade, after all, they made their money. But there's a good reason to keep you trading.

They know that the longer they keep their victim trading, the less likely it is that he or she will complain about the course. It's like money laundering, the layers create confusion. In this case, more trades executed over the longest possible period of time, maximise the clear space between the crime (the scammer selling the course) and the end-result (financial ruin).

They want their students to keep going for years. If they quit after a week, imagine what sort of negative reviews and online feedback the scammers will get?.

"I quit my job, traded for a month, lost all of my money and now I'm looking for work again. Don't go on this course – it's a scam!"

But if that same person trades for several years, he will put the blame on himself. Even if he did complain, the scammer has probably already moved on to his next scam. Besides nobody wants to listen to a disgruntled student who supposedly went on a course five years ago. Too much water has passed under that bridge for their opinions to be relevant today.

But the scammers' mind-control and games don't end there. Here's the worst bit.

You are told during the course, that if you don't make it, it's because *you* had the wrong mind-set, *you* didn't follow the program closely enough, or *you* allowed others to interfere with your judgement.

In other words, you are pre-programmed into believing that if after all of the work, if it doesn't work then it's YOUR fault. That's why most students never complain because they never realise it was a scam.

At the end, after the poor victim has lost everything, he still never really understands what happened. After defeat will come the time for reflection, to question oneself.

This is where the victim tries to work out why he wasn't successful. Thoughts run wildly through his or her head – *"What went wrong? I did everything I was told, I studied hard, I committed, I didn't listen to the nay-sayers, I quit my job- so why didn't it work out?"*

Now the voices are in his head.

"I must have done something wrong! I'm not smart enough. I'm a loser".

Then it's time to panic.

"Oh God, my wife told me this might happen – what do I say to her? How can I ask my boss for my job back? How could I be so stupid? I'm such an idiot! There's something wrong with me.

I should have known that I'm not cut out for this. I'm stupid...".

So, the personal abuse carries on, as does the internal frustration, bitterness and self-hate.

At no point does it occur to this person that he was scammed. Never is the course scammer even questioned. That's a tragedy.

At least when you know you've been scammed you can close that door and move on. It hurts for a while, but you can rationalise it in your head. But without that closure, the person ends up blaming themself for the rest of his life. They can even take that hurt and pain to their grave.

An FX course sounds so trivial, but when you see how it affects lives, it's anything but trivial.

When you get committed people, who want to change their lives, they will go to extreme measures. Not every case will end up with depression and mental health problems, but many will be left feeling dejected, deflated, with years taken off their life that can never be recovered. It's a huge price to pay for a scam.

The wrong rules to the wrong game

99% of so-called "FX gurus" are nothing more than failed students who realised they could make more money by teaching and not trading. It's the blind leading the blind, except everybody's following somebody who supposedly has perfect 20-20 vision. What a circus.

It happens every single day. It's happening in a city near you right now.

It makes a mockery of the people who really put in the time and effort to learn their craft.

It's the same for every industry and profession. When imposters come into an industry and impersonate the professionals, it damages the reputation of the entire industry. It means that the public is denied access to the truth, to the skills and knowledge that they could otherwise to acquire.

It diminishes the effort of the genuine people in that field who have invested their blood, sweat and tears into perfecting their craft.

The financial game is one of the most important games we all need to learn.

Our stock ISA, our pension, our tax allowances, our understanding of inflation and interest rates, our ability to understand and use debt effectively, our mortgage rates, our disposable income, our cashflow, our assets.

These are the financial foundations that we all need to learn and while it takes a bit of time to become proficient, these are critical life-skills. It's like eating healthily and taking regular exercise. It's part of your well-being.

If you want to learn about financial trading, I would strongly suggest you look at the stock market. It's the equivalent of learning to swim in a shallow swimming pool.

It's much easier than the FX market, and far less risky.

Why? Because the stock market always goes up over time. It's directional. Yes, it can go down with market crashes just like every market, but over time it only ever goes up. You must be patient, that's all. That's a massive advantage.

The FX market is the opposite. Because it operates in a pair and has two competing currencies, it's *two*-directional. What is up for one currency is down for another currency. So, it can never just go up in one direction in the same way that the stock market can.

Just look at the chart of any stock market index in the world over the past fifty years and you will see that the chart goes up. Now compare that to any currency index in the world in the past fifty years and you will see that the chart goes up and down. There's no clear direction.

Think about that for a moment.

Please, let this sink in and fight the urge to allow it wash over you. Read this last paragraph again and let it really impress itself into your knowledge.

What you've just read is one of the biggest secrets to becoming very wealthy. This book is not about making money, it's about not losing money. What I've just shared with you is so, so important, that it might just be the single most important paragraph in this entire book.

The property market works in the same way, it always goes up long term. That's why you can't lose. So, if you want to become wealthy, learn the stock market game and the property market game. The end.

If you want to make money, learning the game is the second part of the equation; the first part is to play the *right* game.

The FX game is the wrong game and even if it was the right game, you're being taught the wrong rules, the wrong strategy and by the wrong person. If two wrongs don't make a right, three wrongs definitely don't make a right.

If you really want to learn about investing and trading, then do one thing, forget about FX and learn about equities. In fact, I'm going to make it super-easy for you.

Email me at info@londonstonesecurities.co.uk and I'll send you a FREE copy of my book, *Dividend Income Plus* which retails on Amazon at £34.95. (You just need you to cover the postage of £4.95 but the book is yours for nada).

That's the starting place if you really want to know about 'financial freedom'.

The most vulnerable

Unfortunately, the people being affected by this scam are the most vulnerable in society. They are often working class and poorly educated, with low paid jobs, and just scraping by. It's the blue-collar worker, the labourer, the person on minimum wage.

He's the person who can least afford to be caught by this scam. But he's also the person who is most desperate to break-free from his poor lifestyle. Low income families, often on state benefits, are enticed disproportionately more than those in higher income families.

The 'middle class', and higher-income families typically have well-paid jobs where there is too much to risk. The accountants, the doctors, the lawyers, the architects and so on.

They're less likely to be enticed by the get rich quick schemes because they have too much to lose. They're already comfortable; they have their house, a nice BMW on the drive, two-point-four children and three holidays a year. Why risk all of that?

Even if they do make the move and go on one of these fake courses, they can typically afford to lose a few thousand pounds and get straight back to employment. They don't suffer lasting damage.

No harm done.

That's very different to the poor working-class guy, the electrician, the plumber, the bus-driver, the gardener, the guy who just wants a better life for his family and gives up everything in pursuit of a mirage that doesn't exist. The margin for error is too small for that guy to mess up. The risks are too high and the negative impact is too big.

Educational courses

I'd like to be clear. Attending educational courses and learning a new skill set or improving an existing one is probably the single best investment that you can ever make. If it's a genuine skill being taught by a genuine expert in any field, then you should be able to recover the cost of your investment within just a few months.

After the initial investment of your time and money, you should be able to use that skill repeatedly, for a lifetime and hopefully make money for yourself in doing so.

Therefore, I'm not suggesting you can't learn to trade in FX because you can. It's not easy, you won't learn in one day, and it's very difficult to find somebody genuine who will be willing to teach you. But it's not impossible – I just don't recommend it. However, there are other things you can learn with far less risk and more potential upside like I've shown you.

Education is the single most important thing that will change this world. That's the beauty of self-development, learning, and growing to be the very best version of yourself. I'm absolutely in support of education.

I also support the people who want to learn; the people who attend FX courses, or any other courses should be applauded for wanting to improve their lives and for wanting to take positive action. It isn't easy to make that decision, to venture along a path of uncertainty.

That's why the FX scam is particularly painful because. I know what it is to try and push yourself out of your comfort zone, when others around you think you are crazy for doing so. It's not easy to do something that you truly believe in, especially when it's not even for you, but for your family. That comes with added pressure.

I don't want you to feel discouraged from learning, from pushing yourself to grow as a person. I just want you to know that you must learn the truth and that means finding somebody who speaks it.

TIP 4 –
BOILER ROOM SCAMS

Professional investors ripping off retail investors is terrible; retail investors ripping off retail investors is even worse. However, and as bad as they both are, the victim still needs to be the one who makes first contact with the scammer. He or she must reach out and open that share dealing account, invest in that IPO, respond to that Facebook post, or attend that hotel presentation in London.

It all requires action from that person because nobody can drag them kicking and screaming out of bed.

So, in a way, and as harsh as it sounds, the victim puts themself in that position. That doesn't make the action of the scammer any less disgusting, but there is an element of blame, however small, to be put on the victim for falling into the trap in the first place.

But the next scam is even worse than all those that have gone before it.

No blame can be apportioned to the person who gets ripped off with this scam. In fact, the victim was just sitting in the comfort of his own living room minding his own business. He wasn't searching for anything on the internet, he wasn't replying to social media adverts, he wasn't looking for investment opportunities to become rich.

He was simply watching the snooker World Cup Final on television, and just when Ronnie O'Sullivan was about to sink the black ball to win the match, the telephone rang.

Welcome to insider trading secret four, welcome to the 'boiler room' scandal.

Professional operations

The words 'boiler room' probably send a chill up your spine, even if you haven't fallen prey to it yourself. The concept of the 'boiler room' originates from the idea that *high-pressured* selling in this type of business is akin to the high pressure within a boiler.

While we've all heard of the term, most people don't really understand how boiler rooms work.

You may think they're a thing of the past but unfortunately, they're still very much alive and kicking in the City of London. They haven't gone away; they've just morphed into something quite different, that is about to shock you.

Firstly, the best boiler room scams today look nothing like traditional boiler rooms. They're the complete opposite and are run like very successful businesses. They have a corporate structure, a detailed business model, excellent banking and credit facilities, watertight legal documentation, scores of employees, official training programmes, marketing budgets, advanced technology, IT systems, and all of the infrastructure a normal, successful business would have.

They have even won 'prestigious industry awards' (another

scam as I previously mentioned).

Of course, there are still one-man boiler rooms which run out of somebody's bedroom in Southend, but you don't need to be concerned about this lone, entrepreneurial scammer because he is unlikely to reach you.

The ones that you have to watch out for are the ones I'm about to describe in this chapter. These scams are the ones that have the ability to get straight into your living room and pull your wallet from your trousers pockets. You won't even know that it happened. That's how good they are.

These are very well-run, slick companies with highly intelligent and incredibly competent people behind them.

They operate like all successful businesses; they adapt very quickly to changing market conditions so they can stay ahead of the game. In particular they are always three steps ahead of the police and the regulatory bodies.

Boiler rooms have always come in different disguises. But in recent years, the biggest shift has been this movement away from the traditional, small boiler room scams that were hidden away and run out of derelict, buildings, to very large, internationals scams that are brave, bold and brash.

So, what happened, what changed, and why are boiler rooms now such a big threat to you and your savings?

Regulatory squeezes

Over the years, the regulator has done a pretty good job of

clamping down and making life difficult for those regulated individuals who played fast, loose, and wide. The FCA has faced its fair share of criticism, but I have some sympathy for them; it's a huge challenge for any organisation given the number and complexity of scams operating at any given time.

I'd even go as far as saying that we have one of the best regulatory systems in the world but somewhat paradoxically that comes at a cost.

When I first began my career in the City of London in the late 1990s, it really was like the Wild West. Telephone calls weren't even recorded and there were aggressive sales targets, which means it was all about the money, not about the client. It meant that brokers could say anything with impunity. They could make guarantees and empty promises just to close a sale, and that's what most of them did.

But it wasn't just corruption in the small firms.

I also saw corruption in the larger investment banks that I worked for, but it was a different type of corruption. It was more subtle, less in your face, and it was never talked about openly. I couldn't see the full picture because I was just a small fish in a big pond and didn't have access to the top managers. But I could see the culture was the same, it was all about maximising money.

It was about banker bonuses, hitting sales targets, and ultimately, conning the client without raising suspicion and avoiding complaints.

A good depiction of what went on back then was captured in

the film starring Leonard Di Caprio, 'The Wolf of Wall Street'. If you've not watched it, I highly recommend it.

Given that the film was about exposing the pre-IPO and principal dealing scams on Wall Street, it's ironic that the person who funded the film was found a few years later to be a massive scammer. His name was Jho Low, and his scam raked in not a few million, but *billions* of dollars.

With the Malaysian Prime Minister, he set up a fund called 1MDB that raised more than $5billion between 2009 and 2015. Think about that number for a moment. This was not $5 million, it wasn't $50 million, not even a staggering $500 million – it was a mind-boggling $5 BILLION.

It was raised for the country's economic development. However, the money wasn't spent on the people of Malaysia; instead, it was diverted to buying private jets, superyachts Picasso and Monet artwork. It was even used to buy entire hotels, massive real estate in Beverly Hills, and squandered on huge gambling sprees in the casinos of Las Vegas.

The US Department of Justice estimates that at least $4.5billion was laundered into offshore bank accounts and shell companies, many linked to Low.

It's no surprise that London and New York are the two cities where a big chunk of all of the funds raised in these global scams end up.

Remember Leonardo Di Caprio wasn't depicting a made up, fictitious person. This was based a true story based about the principal penny share dealer, Jordan Belfort. The UK at that time also had their own fair share of Jordan Belforts.

The City of London in the 1990s was all about high-tempo, pressurised cold-calling, selling high-margin, low-value products for maximum commission. It was about parties, alcohol, drugs, and testosterone filled young men with lots of money, all simultaneously going crazy.

What might surprise you is that none of this was a boiler room scam, in fact it was completely regulated. But the Wild West couldn't stay like that forever, the Sheriff eventually had to tidy things up because it was all out of control.

So, over time and with improved regulations, tightened rules, and larger financial penalties, the regulated firms had to change their approach, and this crazy commission-fueled, sales culture was eradicated.

The new intense level of compliance that the regulator introduced became too over-bearing for those brokers who were used to making a quick buck. Mandatory risk warnings before each trade were so long and tedious that clients would be put off. Business slowed to almost a stand-still overnight and sales ground to a halt. The game was over.

The easy get rich-quick lines being used by City hustlers to close clients in a single call suddenly disappeared, and in its place, came the 'balanced risk warnings' pitch. It was a big shift and clients sensed it. They could feel the caution and weigh up whether they should invest or not. Something didn't feel right, and clients stopped buying.

Instead of listing all the reasons why a particular investment was the best thing since sliced bread, brokers now had to list all the things that *weren't* so good about the investment. They had to disclose all the reasons *not* to invest. For the first time the risks were being properly explained.

The fast tempo, quick decisions that clients were previously forced to make were replaced with time delays, cooling off periods, and mandatory signed documents, which demonstrated that the client had understood the risks.

Clients who were previously pressured into making on the spot, fast decisions under duress, were now better informed than ever before and had time to consider their options. This wasn't because the brokerage firms suddenly became ethical. It was out of regulatory necessity. They had no choice. Either they complied or they lost their licence.

The unrecorded telephone calls that allowed brokers to make exaggerated financial promises of 'becoming rich' and offering 'guarantees' were replaced with recorded calls. Now brokers had to self-regulate what they said or face the consequences if their calls were ever listened to.

The entire industry of dodgy penny shares, principal dealing, IPOs, CFDs and other unsavoury regulated areas were decimated.

It was the final nail in the coffin for many of the East End barrow boys who had become 'stockbrokers' and were making a financial killing in the regulated world. The cockney 'apples and pears' banter that previously rang through the City of London was gone. Now it was all very subdued and quiet.

A few stayed from the 'old school' they reskilled and retooled, but the majority formed an orderly line as part of a mass exodus out of the City.

As brokerage firms collapsed from the increasing number of complaints, compensation pay-outs, bad publicity and new suffocating regulations, several hundred young, hungry salespeople, were forced to find an alternative source of income. They were not educated or qualified to make the leap into the investment banking world, and neither could they make the switch into wealth management sales, where they were less able to connect to this new middle-class demographic; just their Cockney accent was enough for them to lose the trust with these new types of clients.

Their cheeky chappie sales pitch was okay to sell penny shares to retired pensioners, but it wouldn't work in the more serious world of portfolio management or investment banking.

So, a new home had to be found.

Mass migration

As a wave of unemployed financial advisors, penny share brokers and CFD traders hit the London scene, all in search of a quick way to make easy money, there was an inevitable and mass migration out of one area into another. They were being squeezed out of the regulated market into the unregulated market, resulting in an explosion of boiler rooms.

Boiler rooms have been in operation since the early 1980s, and there's been a fairly clear line between the regulated and unregulated world. Boiler rooms stayed well away from the regulated world, far from the City of London, and away from the long arm of the law. They preferred to operate out of European overseas jurisdictions with Spain and Germany being amongst the most popular.

So, while there were regulated firms selling dodgy penny shares, financial advisors selling dodgy endowment mortgages, and banks selling dodgy loans, the traditional boiler rooms were living it large in Barcelona and Berlin.

That's because the scammers were close enough to home if they missed mum's cooking but far enough away from the UK law. The scammers knew that as long as they didn't rip off local residents, the police in those jurisdictions quite frankly didn't care about their crimes. The police already had enough on their plate dealing with their own local crime than to spend resources chasing boiler rooms that were scamming British citizens a thousand miles away.

You can imagine how crazy the lifestyle might have been back then for a young man in his early twenties. It would have been a dream come true for any alpha male to make £5,000 or £10,000. Monday to Friday and then blow it all on booze, drugs, and women over a single weekend.

These kids were literally doing penny share deals, taking cocaine, and sleeping with prostitutes all in the same twenty-four hours; they were having the best time of their lives. They'd work for a couple of hours in the morning and spend the rest of the day sat on a beach in the sun, surrounded by scantily clad ladies and, getting blindly drunk.

Compared to the alternative of working in wet and windy Basingstoke as a plumber's apprentice, it was an appealing proposition.

However, by the time the mass migration took place from the regulated to unregulated world, the overseas cities had lost their appeal. The regulators had done another good job in their big publicity drive warning the UK consumer not to take phone calls from overseas numbers. As a result, boiler rooms began relocating back into the UK in their droves.

At the same time the regulated brokers and advisors were also looking for work. They found themselves going into the dark shadows of the unregulated world.

With boiler rooms there are no checks or balances, no recorded telephone calls, and a free rein to do whatever the hell you want. It was what the regulated brokers were used to before the new sweeping regulations came in.

It was a perfect storm, a perfect alignment of the stars. Overseas boiler rooms were finding their way back to the UK at the same time that out of work ex-regulated brokers were also looking for work.

It resulted in a mass migration to London's unregulated world; a tsunami of hundreds, even thousands of hungry cold callers were ready and able to apply their aggressive sales skills. They had the market knowledge, the sales training, and they knew the game inside and out – they just needed new, innovative products to sell with high-margins, and boy, they were not disappointed.

That's when the explosion happened. Brilliant scammers came together, formed groups and alliances, then took over London and the whole of the UK.

That's when the boiler room products hit the market like never before, in the late 2000s.

Carbon credits, solar panels, MLMs, car park spaces, cemetery plots, forestry, storage, graphene, pink diamonds, and fine wine, to name just a few. The list has just kept growing every year. Some of these scams were around in the 1990s but they've changed now. They've been repackaged, restructured and they are unrecognisable to what they were before.

Most recently we have seen new scams due to the new technological advances. There are massive crypto currency and NFT (Non-Fungible Token) scams which are already running into billions of dollars annually. By the time you're read this, no doubt there will be many more new scams doing the rounds.

The boiler rooms made a lot of money, and the scammers were back to their winning ways. However, there was one big problem. UK investors were constantly being warned of unregulated investments and this was beginning to really affect how much business scammers could do.

So, the scammers had to find a solution and they did. It was genius and it's called cloning.

Cloning

Boiler rooms know that it's difficult to convince investors to part with large sums of cash without holding the 'badge of honour' which comes from being regulated and approved by the Financial Conduct Authority. They can still scam a few thousand pounds here and there, but they can't easily get the big, mega deals they want.

The FCA was also spending a lot of money on television and radio adverts warning investors to be wary of scams and boiler rooms. So, it was becoming difficult for scammers to operate.

Cloning was their answer. This is where an unregulated firm simply lies and tells their potential clients they're a regulated firm. They literally steal the name and goodwill of a regulated firm and pass it off as their own.

It sounds almost too simple to work but it does. And the reason I know this is because it happened to me and my business just a few years ago.

One day and without any warning, two police officers came into my office to explain that a boiler room had cloned my business. The scammers had built a fake website that looked identical to mine, they had the exact same headed paper, the same glossy brochures, business cards, the whole nine yards. They even had an internet domain name identical to mine except with a hyphen. My business and the scam business were barely indistinguishable from each other. It was frightening to see their material. It was a carbon copy of my firm's documents and literature, the same terms of business, fee schedule, privacy policy; the list goes on. It was all identical.

Unbelievably, the scammers were even operating out of the *same* serviced office building as me, just on a different floor!

You can imagine my shock.

This doesn't just happen to small, independent businesses like mine, but also to massive investment banks, too.

A few years ago, one of my clients was on the cusp of transferring a staggering £150,000 of his personal money to a firm that purported to be Morgan Stanley for an investment. Luckily, he told me just hours before making the transfer and after a few checks I realised it was a scam. I saved him from what would have been the biggest financial mistake of his life.

I'm very happy to say that over the years I've been able to help so many people from being scammed. The amount of money that I have saved people from losing certainly runs into many millions of pounds. I'm hoping this book will save people from losing many more millions.

However, there are times where unfortunately I'm too late to the party and I only get to speak to investors *after* they've already parted with their cash. That's always a difficult conversation because when I tell the person what's happened, they usually become defensive and angry. Nobody wants to believe that they've been scammed. I've had people slam the phone down on me in disgust only to call me back several months later, profusely apologising, saying that I was right, and asking if I could help them try to recover their money.

Of course, I always try and help. There's always a chance of recovering some money and on occasion that has happened. Usually however, the scammers have long gone, and the money is never seen again.

Thankfully, there is a simple process you can follow to protect yourself if you're unsure if a firm is pretending to be regulated. Just go to the FCA website - www.fca.org.uk - and enter the name of the company that called you, into the 'financial register' section. You will see the firm's details including address, email, the name of the director's names, who is on the FCA register, any fines, disciplinary actions against the firm, when the firm received its licence, what permissions it has, and a host of other useful information.

There is, however, one piece of information which is more important than anything else, and that is the telephone number.

Simply call the telephone number on the FCA website and ask to speak to the person who has been pitching you. If that person comes to the phone, then you know you are dealing with an FCA regulated company. If the firm has never heard of that person, you have your answer.

Imitation is the highest form of flattery

Cloning isn't an easy thing to pull-off and it's fraught with problems including having a very short life span; usually a few weeks, especially if you're operating out of the same building! It also takes just one person to report the boiler room to the firm that's being cloned, and it will be game over.

That's why many boiler rooms decided to *imitate* regulated firms rather than clone them. It meant their operation could run for many months, even years.

The boiler rooms knew that if they wanted to thrive and not just survive, they had to make themselves look as if they were regulated. That means no more hiding away, no more overseas jurisdictions, no more fake websites and no more cloning.

They had to come out fighting and that's exactly what they did.

Instead of hiding away, boiler rooms became more brash than ever before.

Right now, they are leasing some of the most luxurious office spaces and properties in the City of London that money can buy, including the world famous 'Gherkin'. They also hire the best accountants, lawyers, and auditors. They're paying the best salaries, so they have the best IT contractors, marketing teams, PR companies, and HR. They recruit the best by paying the best.

That's happening today, right now, as you read this.

Of course, each boiler room is unique and follows its own business strategy. Like a normal business, there is a scale of sophistication, from basic boiler room to the highest level of sophistication.

For example, some businesses don't operate out of the City at all but pay for exclusive postal addresses in Mayfair or the West End to give the illusion of being a reputable business, without the overheads. Some scammers prefer having no physical location at all but operate from a PO box address because it means they are never raided.

It means that if things really do get a little heated, it's relatively easy to relocate. For example, if the authorities come knocking on their door, there's nobody there to arrest.

It's also helpful to protect against disgruntled investors. If an unhappy client armed with a baseball bat, takes a three-hour train journey from Newcastle to London to meet the advisor who has taken all of his money, but has stopped taking his phone calls, he's got nobody to swing at.

I know of many investors (usually without the bat) who have taken long journeys from different parts of the country to surprise their advisor, only to find a vacant building, a window shopfront, or just a letterbox.

Whether a firm operates out of a plush office in Liverpool Street, a dodgy building in Stratford, or a PO box address in Knightsbridge, it all serves a purpose. The game is always to imitate a regulated firm, in its stature and appearance.

That's why you should never be fooled by presentations, face to face meetings or seminars.

Serviced, swanky offices are easy to rent in expensive locations all over London. They're quite literally next door to the genuine firms, the big investment banks, stock brokerage houses, and hedge funds.

The smaller boiler rooms may have a presence in cheaper locations on the fringes of the City, such as Aldgate East, but even for them, it's not difficult to hire an office for a day. They can organise some actor stooges to sit and look busy in front of a few screens, while they give a presentation for a few hours.

Offices all come pre-kitted with furniture, including desks, chairs, telephones and, storage cupboards. They even have plants, wall clocks, wastepaper baskets and all of the little things you would expect to find in an office. It's easy for even a one-man boiler room outfit to create an impression that he has a full, bustling team of busy employees.

But the big money spinners, the big scammers, don't have the time or patience to rent offices for a day. They just rent out huge office spaces for the whole year, even two or three years. They have full teams of salespeople out on the front line, 'smiling while dialing'. They're not hidden away; they're in your face.

The most sophisticated boiler rooms refuse to cower anymore. You can meet them at their offices, see their operations, meet the team, read their prospectus and, attend their events. They've got nothing to hide, they'll give you their real and answer all of your questions, they are who they are.

You would think that acting in this way puts the boiler rooms at risk. By openly parading would seem financially suicidal, but actually it's not. That's because there is good reason for this new-found bravery.

It's because the scammers found another brilliant loophole, and this one's going to shock you even more.

Price v value

Boiler room operations are based on one of two business models.

The first and most basic boiler room scam is one that literally rips you off. The scammers might try to steal your personal details, transfer money out of your bank account, or they'll convince you to buy something that doesn't exist then run off with your cash. This is obviously just plain theft. The victim has not received any product or service and the boiler room has made off with your money, with a 100% profit margin.

When somebody takes your money and gives you nothing in return, this is criminal activity, it's theft. No questions asked.

However, what happens if a boiler room buys something for 5p and sells it to you for 100p?

Is that still theft? Well, it might feel like theft, but actually, it isn't.

If you think about it, that's how all businesses work; they try to maximise their gross margin.

For example, it is exactly how most telecoms and internet companies operate. The cost to supply an internet connection to a house might literally cost just a few pence but you to get that line, you might be charged £30 per month. That doesn't make British Telecom a boiler room operation. It makes it a business looking to make the biggest possible profit.

How about if somebody buys a car for £500 on E-Bay, and

then sells it to somebody else for £5,000 on Autotrader – is that fraud or theft? No, of course it isn't. That's good business again.

It's this high-margin business model that sophisticated boiler rooms are now adopting and applying the same logic to; and it's creating a big problem as you're about to find out.

Diamonds and metals

One boiler room operation that has operated for many years and is still thriving today is the 'pink diamond' scam.

A genuine, pink diamond can be sourced from any number of places around the world, including many African countries, for literally just a few hundred pounds, depending on quality.

That same diamond can be repackaged and sold through a boiler room for £5,000, £10,000, even £20,000. In fact, it can be sold for any price that somebody is willing to pay for it.

Boiler room scammers are therefore moving away from illegitimate theft and fraud to the lesser charge of an *unethical* business model. The difference is legality. Before, they would convince you to buy a pink diamond but then give you nothing in return and simply steal your money.

Now, they actually give you a diamond, it's just not worth very much.

Even if this new strategy in a court of law is not deemed to be completely legal, at the very least, it creates a grey area that sits between the black and white of illegal or legal. Boiler rooms can still be shut down and brought to justice but it's not as easy. The consequences and penalties are also not as severe.

The same logic applies to the graphene scam, a product used in Nano technology. A scammer buys it for a few pounds and sells it to an investor for a few thousand.

Then there is the 'rare earth metals' (REM) boiler room scam which follows the same pattern. The scammers buy a kilogram of REM for, say, £500 and then sells it on for £5,000, or even £25,000! These metals are bought from mining exploration companies in China or Africa, then shipped and stored in secure facilities in the UK. That's where the extra pricing is hidden. The scammers blame packaging, shipping and, insurance costs to justify their ludicrous prices.

Even physical gold bullion is being used by boiler room scammers. They slap on a margin so high that the price you end up paying is much more than the actual spot price. However, it's still 'within reason' and bears some resemblance to the underlying asset price, even if it's exaggerated. For example, it could be 10% - 30% or more above, the spot price.

The scammers are pushing back the envelope and going as far as they can, which keeps them on the right side of the law whilst still maximising their rip-off potential.

That's why they are more heavily involved in things like graphene and pink diamonds where the price is more elastic; there is no fixed price or starting point. The scam is always better when investors are unable to compare the price that they are paying to the real price.

Consider this question.

How much do you think it a factory polished, ten-carat, high quality grade four, pink diamond that weighs 100 grams costs? Just take a guess and write it down on a piece of paper. Even if you have no clue, write a number.

Now, how much more is that same diamond worth if its authenticity has been independently verified by the world's recognised and leading authority on commodities, none other than South Africa's PMSE, Precious Metals and Stones Exchange (PMSE)?. What's it worth now?

Finally, what's that same diamond worth if it also comes with a certified thirty-year guarantee against weather damage and atmospheric salt erosion?

Now, write down your new number on the same piece of paper. You should have three numbers in ascending order.

Have you got your answers?

Well, I'm sorry to say but whatever numbers you wrote down, they're all wrong. There is no correct answer because I just made up the questions.

In fact, I just made it all up. There's no such thing as 'grade four' diamonds, and there is no such thing as a 'Precious Metals and Stones Exchange'. The thing about salt erosion was made up too.

Sure, there might be a few people who try and Google those words and won't find anything, but there will be many more who won't.

In any case, it would be silly for a scammer just to make names up like I did. There are genuine organisations out there who really do verify the quality of diamonds so the scammers would clearly just use those names instead.

Therefore, when you do Google those names, you'll find that they are genuine, they really do exist. They know anything about the scammer or his product, but the mere association creates more uncertainty and greyness within which to operate. Even if a product was genuinely verified does it add a further £500 or £5,000? Does it add anything at all?

The point I'm making is that nobody has any idea about what the fair value of a product is if they've never seen that product before, let alone bought or sold it before.

That's why the scammer can charge what he wants. Because they're unregulated products, there are no rules or guidelines as to what can or can't be charged, or what can or can't be said.

If it's not complete fraud or theft, where they just steal your money, the scammers have found an (almost) risk-free way of printing money. Of course, in between theft on one end and immoral business on the other, there is a lot of space for scammers to manoeuvre.

The victim can't even get an independent assessment of what he has bought because usually it's a plot of land sitting about 8,000 miles away, or it's locked up in a secure, storage facility like a bonded warehouse on some random industrial estate in Milton Keynes.

The only thing he physically receives is an official looking certificate, which, in itself is worthless.

Even if he wants to 'see his investment', that's easily taken care of. A sales rep meets the victim at the bonded warehouse and opens a box with a lump of grey metal in it. That's it; job done.

Some of this may sound almost hard to believe but it happens. I have spoken to many people who have physically travelled to bonded warehouses in Milton Keynes and many other locations across the UK, and have literally been shown a box with grey metal in it. That's it.

That's their £20,000 investment just sitting there. It's crazy.

I've even known investors who took delivery of their graphene only to find out years later that it was nothing more than a worthless piece of junk metal. Sure, there was a little graphene in there, but it was so heavily diluted and mixed with other metals that it had less than 20% purity.

I shudder to think how many proud owners there are right now in the UK holding a worthless box of scrap metal which is going to sit under their bed for the next ten years until they decide to sell it.

A shift in business model

The calculated shift from theft to the lesser charge of being immoral, is what allows business owners to show their faces and give their real details. Instead of setting up fake businesses with fake names and fake bank accounts, more and more boiler rooms are now establishing themselves as 'genuine' businesses.

They have transitioned from *stealing* to *selling*.

The police are also finding it hard to intervene if the scammers have genuinely sold something that has some value, however small that value might be. It doesn't matter what the profit margin is, the question comes down to — did they sell you something, or did they steal from you?

Boiler rooms have morphed from fraudsters and crooks to brilliant businessmen.

Of course, there are trading and business standards, and many other rules, regulations and laws in place to protect consumers from getting ripped off. So, it's not quite as clear-cut as either being lawful or unlawful. But it does make the whole game decidedly opaque, which is good news for the scammers and bad news for you.

Remember, the lack of liquidity, transparency and visibility of an investment is directly correlated to the size of the opportunity for the boiler room.

When you spend £10,000 on a piece of agricultural farmland in Nigeria which is actually worth £250, you may find that the boiler room has done nothing technically illegal.

If they can package a deal so that the price you are paying includes their marketing, research, travel costs, administration, salaries, legal charges, and consultancy fees, they can pretty much justify whatever price they want. The price will include for example travel visas, flights, hotels, entertainment and a hundred other things that costs money.

You could end up paying £10,000 for a piece of land that has a resale value of just £250 and it could still be completely 'justified'.

Even if the scammers are brought to justice by the police, it's a difficult charge to uphold in court. Besides, what does a judge know about the intricacies of forestry, land, sunflower oil, corn crops, car park space, micro-chips, gold coins, cemetery plots, time-shares, apartments, carbon credits, diamonds, precious commodities, graphene, fine wine, whisky, collectible stamps, vintage cars, crypto currencies or rare earth metals?

Answer: not a lot.

To summarise, there are three simple lessons to remember. Don't buy anything 1) highly specialist 2) unregulated or 3) difficult to price.

But that's not where it ends, the scammers are not quite finished just yet.

Fake investor certificates

The thing about boiler room scams is that they are unbelievably versatile and fluid. There are so many different forms that it's the insider trading secret covering the widest number of products.

But out of all of those products, there is one in particular which is the hardest to spot.

After all, it's easy to be doubtful if a complete stranger calls you out of the blue and tries to sell you a plot of woodland in the Amazonian rainforest. That's not everybody's cup of tea when it comes to investing. Without wishing to be cruel, there are a few things that need to happen before that deal can be closed; 1) the scammer must be good at selling, 2) the operation needs to be reasonably sophisticated, and 3) the victim must be at least a little bit gullible or desperate.

The fact that the product isn't regulated, can't be accurately valued, and sits thousands of miles away is usually enough to put off most sane people. Yes, we can all have a bad day and make a poor investment decision in the heat of the moment, but it's still easier to walk away from somebody trying to sell you Sao Paolo's finest submarines, or whatever the deal of the day happens to be.

On the other hand, it's a lot harder to walk away from investing in something we are familiar with, and where we do know the price. It's even harder to say no to that product when we're being offered an opportunity to buy it at a big, juicy discount.

So, get this.

Scammers now offer investors the opportunity to buy into companies like Amazon, Microsoft, BP, Sainsburys, HSBC, and many other similar blue-chip companies.

You'll recognise that the above names are not just your regular, listed companies; they are some of the largest and most established businesses in the world, quoted on some of the biggest stock exchanges in the world.

The question is, how do the scammers get away with this and where's the scam?

It works like this.

The boiler room identifies a big, well-known company that has been in the press recently. It could be that the company is raising money through a share issue, executing a share buy-back, involved in a take-over, the directors have recently been buying shares or perhaps the company has just announced a big contract win. There just needs to be some 'story' which can be used for the scammers to hang their pitch to.

The scammers then cold-call people and offer them the opportunity to either buy or sell shares in this company, depending on what the corporate news announcement is. The actual pitch will vary and be tailored according to the news story surrounding the company.

For example, if it's a share buy-back, they might convince their victims that they're able to secure the investment at a discount to the market price because they are one of several appointed brokers who work closely with the firm's nominated advisors. The scammers might say they have been tasked to contact shareholders directly and raise £10million. The person might be dubious at first, but that doubt will slowly fade and be replaced with trust, as the scammers prove the news announcements that show the buyback news.

So, their pitch goes...

"...The company is making two offers; one is through the public stock exchange but that is restricted to a fixed number of shares per investor. The second approach is privately by approaching shareholders directly. This is through a network of approved

brokerage firms where investors can buy direct if they wish.

The private buy-back price is also set at a price 3% higher than the one being offered to the public. In other words, a higher price can be secured for a shareholder's shares if they go with the nominated advisor rather than through the stock exchange..."

None of this makes any sense, but to an eighty-year-old pensioner sitting at home, it's perfectly plausible, especially from a slick, fast-talking, seasoned salesperson.

Once the prospect is hooked into the story, the logistics are explained which again depends on the scam but usually involves a 'share certificate'.

If the scammers are promising to *buy* the stock from the victim, then the victim must post their certificate to the scammer. If the scammers are promising to *sell* stock to the victim, then the scammers will post a share certificate to them.

The scammers prefer to sell stock to the victim because then they receive cash from the client rather than receive a certificate which is more difficult to liquidate. It's not impossible but holding a share certificate and trying to dematerialise it into your own name is not straight forward. Besides, the victim being scammed can cancel the certificate at any time by contacting the Share Registrar.

On the other hand, making a bank payment to the scammers is irretrievable. Once it's gone, it's gone.

If a victim agrees to buy shares, the scammers will post a fake certificate *before* the victim makes payment for the investment.

That gives the victim peace of mind. However, the agreement will be that the payment needs to be made within three working days of the certificate being received.

This is intentional because the victim has no way to verify the validity of the certificate that he's just received until he posts it to his stockbroker firm or deposits it with his local bank. This process of moving from paper to electronic format, known as 'dematerialisation', can take several weeks, during which time the victim has no idea if the certificate is a fake or genuine.

During this time, the scammers will be pushing very hard to get paid.

The pressure becomes real when the scammer refers to the terms of business, which the victim has signed and agreed to. If the scammer is not paid within three working days, the victim is warned that interest is payable. A strongly worded letter talking about late payment penalties, solicitor fees and, and debt collection charges is usually enough for people to panic and make the payment.

But it gets worse.

Most victims never even try to dematerialise their certificate. They don't take it to the bank, and they don't give it to their broker, so, they have no idea they are sitting on a worthless piece of paper. They just feel the thickness of the high-quality paper, see some reassuring watermarks and official looking stamps, and their name stamped across the top of it. It all looks impressive and authentic.

But there's one final twist to this plot, which is that the scammer knew all along his victim would never even verify the certificate. But how could he possibly know this?

The scammer already knows their victim will never even try to dematerialise their certificate. In fact, he knows that his victim doesn't have a share dealing account, he doesn't have a stockbroker, and he doesn't hold any investments online.

He already knows his victim will just store that certificate away in a drawer the moment that he receives it in the post.

But how?

Laser guided targeting

The victim was never randomly chosen. He was intentionally picked out of the millions of investors in the UK. He fulfilled certain criteria and, he was hand-picked to be scammed.

The people who are being cold called are not randomly chosen out of a telephone directory. They are being targeted with laser-guided precision because of the investments they *already* hold.

Once the scammers have chosen a company that is in the news and has some form of corporate action or market news they can use in their sales pitch, they contact the Share Registrar of that specific company. For a small fee they can attain the names and addresses of the thousands of people who are shareholders in that company!

In fact, for less than £50, and in less than ten minutes, you could buy a list of all the shareholders of any UK listed company.

You would have the name, address and in some cases even the telephone number for each of those people. Even with no telephone number it's a short step to retrieve their telephone numbers as most people are not ex-directory.

These 'shareholder lists' reveal the details of all those people who hold *share certificates* at home. It excludes shareholders who hold their investments in an ISA, SIPP, or any form of electronic account. Bingo.

The scammers immediately know that when their victims receive their dodgy share certificate, they won't be rushing out any time soon to put it on their share dealing account because they don't have one. They're old-school and prefer to hold paper. They don't trust things online and that means they keep their investments off-line.

If they hold paper, there's no way for them to know the certificate about to be sent to them, is a fake. The victim will just file his new certificate away with his other certificates. That's why the scam works so well.

Only 2% of UK investors hold certificates whilst the remaining 98% hold shares electronically which protects their identity from scammers. The problem is that the 2% who hold certificates, who are visible and open prey to the scammers are typically the elderly, and most vulnerable.

Pensioners are overwhelmingly the biggest group of people in society who prefer to hold their investments in certificated paper form at home in a cardboard box. That's because it makes them feel safe. Little do they know it exposes them to more risk.

So, the scammers are specifically targeting the very group in society that requires the greatest protection, those who are not computer literate, who can least protect themselves.

The only time the investor has any chance of knowing he's been scammed is when his dividend cheque doesn't turn up in the post. That's usually several months by which time the scammers have long disappeared.

If the company isn't a dividend payer, then the victim might not find out he's been scammed for years, if at all.

Over the years I have personally heard of many horrific stories and seen many fake certificates. Victims who have fallen for this scam have sent me their certificates and straight away, I can see they're fake. Unfortunately, there are even cases where the victim never even gets to find it.

He keeps his treasured certificate in his drawer for the rest of his life and after he passes away, his children must deal with the grief of learning that their father was ripped off by a conman.

I have had countless conversations and heard the heart break of pensioners over the telephone when I have had to tell him their investment is worth nothing. In some cases, they have lost their life savings over this wicked scam.

Sales training

All scams are based upon carefully constructed sales pitches and like every pitch some deals will be closed, and others won't. Sometimes the cash register rings and other times it stays silent.

It's the same when you go fishing; when you hang a worm on your fishing line, you expect some fish to bite and others to swim away. In sales, the number of fish that bite is known as the 'closure rate' which depends on three things: a) how good the salesperson is, b) how good the product is and c) how credible the company is.

If you have a great salesperson, you can sell some really shitty things.

It's always a numbers game. More marketing, means more leads, means more telephone dials, means more brochures, means more presentations, means more offers, means more closed deals, means more victims, means money for the scammers. That's the full circle of a scam product sale.

There are of course a hundred different pitches and ideas that the scammers have running through their heads at any given time. Just like legitimate businesses that spend millions of pounds on product development, testing, as well as research and marketing, the scammers do the same. They try different sales approaches, techniques, offers, deals, pitches and scripts.

The sales guy's roleplay in the office between themselves to overcome each other's objections. They perfect their scam craft just like any legitimate business perfects theirs. Therefore, stories change, sales pitches adapt, the telephone call is continually tweaked and altered to improve the closing ratio.

Whilst responsible for executing the close, the salesperson on the phone is at the lowest end of the food chain. The managers at the top and the directors above them are the ones that control the narrative, the sales pitch, the hooks, the offers, the guarantees. They know what works and what doesn't work as they were once the lowly salesperson themselves.

The managers will listen to a live a phone conversation and 'call-barge' which means they can speak to their salesperson during the pitch, but the prospect (soon to be victim) won't be able to hear him. The salesperson can be guided word for word about what to say to his prospect. He's given perfect timing and direction on how to overcome the prospect's objections.

That's why an unsuspecting pensioner sat at home is no match for a professional salesperson who is drilling and practising all day, every day, to perfect his scamming skills. Even an average salesperson has the support of the managers and expert scammers in real-time whenever he needs it.

The sales pitch

Going through the shareholder list and calling the names is not difficult. It's just a numbers game; most won't fall for the scam, but a few will, that's all that the scammers need, a few willing victims.

But as time goes on, and with a better pitch, better sales training, and better objection handling, the end result is quite scary. Even switched on, educated, sceptical people can get caught out in this scam.

Imagine you were called with this pitch:

"Hi, this is John from Mayfair City Capital, you might have heard

of us. We are the nominated advisors for one of your shareholdings Vodafone. Our records show that you are a registered shareholder in Vodafone, which last week announced a share buy-back at 145p. We're contacting shareholders to advise them on the different options they have available before the cut-off deadline of 3rd August.

Before I go through the options, can I just make sure that I'm speaking to the right person?, The shareholder I have here is for a Mr Mark Reynolds and the postcode is XXX XXX? I can only speak to him for GDPR and confidentiality reasons, can you let me know if he's available?"

Pretty good, isn't it?

What if the scammers wrote to you first?

What if you received a letter in the post explaining there was a corporate action on Vodafone, which is one of your shares and that you need to act in the next seven days, or you would lose that deal. If you failed to act, it would mean that you would relinquish your right to those free shares, or that cash payment, or whatever the offer was.

The letter goes on to say that a nominated advisor to the firm will call you in a few days and you should make a note of your unique reference number which is detailed in the letter; this will prove you are the shareholder. (The reference is of course, just a made-up combination of letters and numbers).

When you receive a call two days later, what's the chance that you pick up the phone and at least a conversation with that 'advisor'? Pretty high, I would say.

Think about it. The advisor knows your name, postcode, and the fact that you hold shares in a particular your company.

He also has detailed accurately the corporate action that is pending on that company, (which of course, you checked independently and verified to be true).

That's usually enough to convince most people that it's not a cold call. If somebody calls you with information that ther people don't know, you automatically assume you need to take the call. You'll wonder what else they might know about you. You'll believe that you need to speak to them, so you give them those precious few minutes to deliver their pitch. Even if you're sceptical you will give them the benefit of the doubt.

That's all they need, one chance. Now they're through the door, and you're in deep sh*t.

They've cracked the hardest part of the whole scam which is getting through the first 30 seconds of the first cold call. That's when the phone gets slammed down. The goal of every scammer is to not be stonewalled on his first call.

Now they're through the first tricky part, they have a chance. It's still a small chance but it's gone from maybe 0% to 30%. It's not ideal but it's a big shift in their favour, and you're one step closer to getting rolled over.

Now the scammers need to deliver their story, give that extra bit of spin, build some rapport, and eventually over a few more calls, lay down the final trap and hope that you, the victim, walk into it.

The scam won't be completed on the first call. That's a 'one-call-close' and doesn't happen often. More likely, is that there will be a second, third and fourth call, perhaps a face-to-face meeting, some paperwork sent in the post etc. It all depends on the victim and where they are in the sales buying process. Are they warm and ready to buy or are they cold and need more convincing?

If they've bought the story in the first five minutes, an experienced salesperson will go for the jugular, right there and then. They will smell blood and take their chance to close the deal.

But the big deals take time to nurture and develop. It's easy to convince somebody to part with £100 over the phone but a big- ticket item of £100,000, well, that requires more patience and strategy from the scammers.

That's where a fixed time deadline has a massive advantage that the scammers can use. All corporate actions have defined dates by which action has to be taken and this is publicly announced. Therefore, the share buyback or share issue or takeover or whatever the announcement is, will typically have a date before which shareholders must act. This is great news for the scammers because it forces the victim to decide.

Scammers want to get their money quickly, and so will often pressurise the victim. But this can backfire because the victim senses desperation and this increases the chances of the scammer's cover being blown.

However, with a looming deadline that the victim can verify on

Google or the London Stock Exchange, the 'pressure' becomes real. But now the pressure isn't coming from the scammer. The scammer no longer looks desperate. He's simply stating the facts that if the victim doesn't decide before next week, the company's offer will be revoked. He gets the same result from a pressurised sale but without any of the drawbacks, without his cover being blown.

Scam size and sophistication

Amateur scammers will take any kind of business no matter who the client may be, because they are desperate for the short-term cash fix. A professional scammer however will be more selective in their approach and will qualify their potential client before they sell a dodgy investment.

Pitching to the wrong investor at the wrong time potentially has terrible consequences for the scammers; that investor could bring the whole party to a premature close if he smells a rat and goes to the authorities.

That's why scammers prefer to deal with people who are less inquisitive, not very vocal, not well-connected, unlikely to question things, and not financially savvy – these are their prime targets.

Sadly, this qualification process also means that those targeted are often the ones who can least afford to lose their money; the ones living alone, elderly, with limited income, poor knowledge, as well as a lack of family and network support.

However, there is a potential conflict of interest here for the scammer to contend with.

While they can more easily target and scam pensioners, their reward per victim will be less.

They might get away with low-ticket sales of a few thousand pounds but not the big bucks, which means they would have to scam hundreds of pensioners. They might get lucky with a big deal every so often but in the main they're always fighting for the scraps.

On the other hand, if they can rip off just one wealthy investor, even though he might be more switched on and likely to pose greater resistance to the scammer, the pay-off is much bigger. For example, a single high-net worth investor could invest up to £250,000 or even £500,000 into a scam. That's worth a lot of pensioners.

It's like a thief choosing to either hold up a petrol station or a bank. The petrol station is easier to steal from, but the reward is also much less. A bank is harder to break into but if you make it into the vault, you could retire on what you find in there.

Like all business owners, the return and risk pay-off is considered by the scammer.

The ideal customer, of course, would be somebody with lots of money but low financial intelligence, somebody who has millions in the bank but doesn't really know the game, has no network of advisors, and is trusting of everybody. They do exist but it's a dying breed.

Firstly, because there aren't many of them to begin with, and secondly, if they are rich and gullible, they won't stay rich for very long.

The problem for society is that the bar is being constantly raised by the scammers. Their sophistication is increasing, their skill set is improving, and their ability to scam is becoming a little bit better every single day.

This means that in order to compete, in order to protect ourselves, we also have to improve our level of financial intelligence, and our understanding of these scams. The scammers are constantly acquiring new levels of competence while the rest of society is being left behind.

99.9% of people aren't going to be learning about anti-scam techniques, why would they? Are you going to commit the same time and resources to combat being scammed as the scammers will commit to scamming you? Nope.

Are you sitting at home role-playing with your wife to prepare yourself for that next boiler room call in the same way the scammers are role-playing every day to scam you? Nope. Of course, it would be unreasonable for you to do that. You have a life; and maybe you have a job.

This is the life and full-time job of the scammers. It's not your full-time job to become scam aware. Most people only spend the time necessary to learn about scams *after* they've been scammed.

The scammers can only get better which means that relatively speaking the rest of society can only become more susceptible to those scams.

Rich pickings

I have spoken to quite a few smart, intelligent people who were very rich once upon a time, and in the space of a few months, they lost everything, in some cases quite literally millions of pounds. That's because the scammers up their game for individuals like this – it's not just about calling them over the telephone and sending a glossy brochure.

For the big players, the scammers go to their house, they befriend them, they play golf together, they go for weekends away, they even go on holidays together. That's the commitment of the most serious scammers.

It's not a quick sale over the phone. It's a slow, deliberate sale over several months or even years. It's one massive pay-out in the future rather than a quick, small pay-out today.

It doesn't matter where you are, even if you are abroad. If you've got enough cash to interest them, they will even fly to your house and give you a presentation. The money is too great for them not to. That's how they get you. A legitimate business which works on sensible margins will not fly to Dubai first class for a meeting with you. But an illegitimate scam business which will make 95% profit on whatever you give them can afford to take that trip out.

The next time somebody is being overtly nice to you, spending time, money and resources that appear to be disproportionate to the value of what you think they should receive in return for your business, then think about their margins. It all comes down to profit margins and remember, *you're* always paying for them.

Scammers love the long term

There are other ways in which boiler rooms can extend the life of the deal. This is more important for the more sophisticated, lavish scams because they require large amounts of upfront capital investment, which can only be recouped over a number of years. Therefore, the scam has to run and collect income for at least three, four or five years for it to work.

In the first year the scammers might invest say a million pounds or more to get the business going so that's a very different business model to the low-cost entry boiler room game of 'get in quick, make money quick, and get out quick'.

There's one key element that scammers must control in   order to ensure longevity, that's to keep the lid on complaints and bad press.

The scam usually only gets found out if enough investors complain. So the trick for the boiler room is to ensure their clients never complain. One clever way to stop complaints is to only sell 'long-term' investments. From this starting point of their desired outcome, they have cleverly managed to reverse engineer the range of products they can sell.

Whisky and fine wine are two examples of long-term investments where investors don't cash in for at least a few years. Therefore, the illegitimate copy-cat versions of these two products are perfect for scammers to promote.

A boiler room scammer might offer an investor the opportunity to buy into a 'fine wine collection' which is expected to increase in price by say 5% to 15% per annum, but the investment can't be sold for five years. This means the boiler room has five years to make as much money as it can before buyers of their product can even begin to ask for their money back.

Genius yet again; another master stroke by the scammers. Remember, the authorities, and in particular the Serious Fraud Office (SFO), are already swamped and overloaded with work, so they won't be looking into any company unless its's flagged. This means that either the company has to go bust or there has to be a sufficient number of complaints from the public.

Offering just a five-year investment is great but alone it's not enough.

During those five years it's important the scammers can identify any unhappy investors quickly and quash their complaint before it's even raised. The job of the boiler room is to keep their clients happy and not to raise suspicion at any cost.

This means that as a client you're going to be given everything you need to keep you happy. That includes regular email updates, annual statements, valuations, market updates and positive trading announcements. This is all part of the illusion.

The boiler room will also routinely call their clients just to make sure they are happy with everything. This is important because the scammers need to be sure there are no disgruntled investors who might be tempted to set off the alarm bell. If a client is unhappy and is demanding his money back, it's better for a scammer to just pay him off to keep him quiet than to risk one loudmouth bringing down the whole operation.

Upsells and false valuations

Regular telephone calls not only help to identify and eliminate unhappy clients, they also play a critical role in the 'upsell'. That's when an existing investor buys more, and more and more of the same investment. This is only possible because of the long-term timeframe.

But there's another important element to this which is the valuation. Because the product is unlisted, unregulated and doesn't have a quoted price, the scammers can make up *any* price.

In the same way that an unlisted, privately held share can be given any price, so too can a limited version, twelve-bottle case of the rarest, fine wine. So, if an investor spends, say, £400 on that product and the scammers write a letter to him six months after the purchase, telling him that the price is now £780, but it's expected to reach £1,290 by next year, what do you think he might do?

Yep, he's going to buy more. So, these false valuations are regularly pumped out either by post or over the telephone, and that entices investors to buy more. Of course, the scammers encourage their clients to buy more than just one or two crates this time. They also encourage them to go big by offering sizeable discounts. Why invest £5,000 when you can invest £20,000 and get a 25% discount on the price?.

The scammers will also tell the victims that as existing investors, they can acquire more stock at a lower price than is available to the rest of the marketplace. Another hook to whet their appetite.

How about you get a letter telling you that the stock is in short supply and that the price is going up quickly so there are some new investors who want to buy your wine from you?. Would you sell? If the price is going up, of course not.

This is a 'reverse' or 'take-away' close in sales. It makes the person want the product even more. If the person decides to sell, the scammer says okay and then an hour later calls you back to tell you that the order has been filled by another client. So, you never get to sell even if you want to.

If you do want to buy, they will create false scarcity to make you want more. They'll tell you that unfortunately you just missed out on that deal. You're going to think "Wow, this can't be a scam because they're actually refusing my money!"

It's a case of casting the fishing net but intentionally not catching any fish. The scammers will tell you that you're now on a 'priority list' and next in line the next time new stock becomes available. They also tell you to have your funds ready because the stock won't be held just for you. If you can't satisfy the payment within 48 hours, it will have to be given to the next person on the list.

That's the scarcity game; it's to make you want something.

Eventually a few weeks later, by some miracle, the scammer says that he's had a distressed seller who needs to liquidate his portfolio because he's going through a divorce. The price is still going up and the scammer needs a quick decision if you want to take that new stock. Of course, you say yes. You've been waiting on that priority list for a reason!

There was no distressed seller and there is no divorce. The scammer has unlimited amounts of stock ready to be sold at any time.

There are lots of tricks and nuances to this game, too many to be covered here, but it always favours the scammers. They make the rules of the game so that only they can win.

For example, sometimes scammers even pay back a small amount of money to the victim at a massive supposed profit. If a victim invests say £1,000 into a scam, they might say that it's now worth £2,500 and encourage them to sell 20% of their holding, i.e., £500. They still hold £2,000 in stock. So, the scammers simply pay back £500 out of the original £1,000 and keeps £500.

That makes the victim go stir-crazy with greed – "Wow, I made so much money, this is crazy," he's thinking to himself while waiting for the next opportunity.

A few days later the scammer calls the victim and asks if he wants another opportunity for a new product, but this time there is a minimum buy in of £20,000. It's even better than last time and due to the short supply, he thinks this investment will be worth at least £100,000 in the next two years.

The investor wrongly assumes he made 5x on his last investment (even though he made nothing), so, now he jumps at the chance.

So, the scammer has turned his own £500 investment into a £19,500 profit. Of course, sometimes the victim may not do the £20,000 deal and that's a risk for the scammer but it's a great trade. The scammer only needs to be right once in forty times to make his money back.

He increases his odds by financially qualifying the victim first and making sure that a) he has more money to invest and b) he is open to investing. That's all part of the information gathering exercise before the sales pitch is even made.

This long-term approach also works really well because it fits in perfectly with most people's investment objectives. Most investors don't want the headache of short-term trading but would rather invest for the medium to long term. It plays beautifully into the hands of the boiler room.

Be careful of new trends

One final thing to remember is this, boiler rooms always favour new trends.

For example, in recent years a big thing has been made of the relaxation in cannabis rules. So, many boiler rooms are now offering investments in cannabis farms. Investors get excited when they see something new. They think they'll be the first ones in and will make the big bucks.

But what they don't realise is that they pay a massive price to be the first in. They're entering a market where regulations don't exist, and where true price discovery hasn't yet taken place.

You need a market that is at least half-mature before you invest, otherwise you open yourself up to huge amounts of risk.

The only time to invest early is when you have excellent information and contacts in that industry. If you are relying on somebody to pass on that information to you, to put you ahead of the pack, that's a mistake. Nobody gives that information for free, and you should be suspicious of anybody who is suggesting they will.

Investors, on the whole are too worried about missing the big opportunity; they're worried about the market becoming saturated, of being too late. But you're never too late because genuine markets don't come and go, they stay forever. It's never too late to become rich in property or the stock market. Besides, it's better to be too late than too early.

The scammers play on this human disposition that we all have, the fear of missing out. It's why IPOs are so popular because investors want to be in first.

Remember, it's better to be second, third, tenth or a hundredth. Don't be at the front. Those people might make a lot of money, but they are also the ones that sometimes fall off the edge of a cliff.

Let them go first, and then let a few more go past you, then a few more. Once you know what the market looks like, what the fair value is, what the risks are, then you make your investment, if you still want to. Once you see that a hundred people haven't fallen off that cliff and they aren't sitting in a pool of their own blood by the side of the mountain, that's your signal to get in.

Eventually, one short-lived craze will die down, the market will become saturated, and a new craze will unfold. But the real investment products stay around forever.

As new products continue to hit the marketplace each year, avoid the temptation of trying to be the pioneer. This isn't space travel and there are no prizes for being the guinea pig.

The scammers will entice by telling you that the new opportunity is where the 'juice' is, it's where the big money can be made. Sure, you will miss a few good deals, but you'll also miss a lot of bullets.

Whether it's a sea-fronted apartment for sale in Madeira or cutting-edge security systems in Swansea, there's always a deal to be had. The new products just entering the marketplace will always get the maximum attention.

Electric cars, solar panels and green energy products have already been targeted by scammers but expect even more innovation and cunning investment ideas in the future.

The next technological wave of Artificial Intelligence (AI) and investments in the fintech space is the same; another hotspot for the scammers. The information in all of these new areas is limited and constantly changing so, that's where the huge price-value discrepancy thrives.

What I have touched upon in this chapter is just the tip of the problem. It spreads far and wide, and doesn't discriminate against background, gender, race, or religion. If you have money, you are a target. It affects us all, which is why you need to educate those around you, especially if you know people who live alone.

Maybe they are being targeted right now through telephone calls, post, emails, even visits to the door. The scammer could be masquerading as an entirely different person before they go for the kill. He could be building trust as a 'charity' worker or as a handyman, or as somebody who works in the local hospice.

The scammers can go to extraordinary lengths to build trust – then comes the sales pitch and the rest, as they say, is history.

To finish this chapter off, I'd like to share a story from somebody that I came into contact with quite recently. His name is Vince and he's a lovely guy who was unfortunately scammed for a lot of money using some of the techniques I have outlined here. When he found out that I was writing a book, he was keen that I should share his story so others could learn from his painful lessons.

My new pal Vince

Vincent, known as Vince to his friends, at the time of writing, is 76 years of age and a truly, wonderful, kind person. He contacted my stockbroking firm through an online internet enquiry, but due to my busy work schedule, I didn't get back to him until two weeks after the enquiry. I regret that decision very much because if I had called him when I was supposed to, I would have saved him from what happened. As it turned out, the scammers managed to get to him before I did, and it changed his life for the worse forever. For that I'm truly sorry.

When we spoke for the first time, Vince had absolutely no clue he had been scammed.

We chatted for a while, and he told me how he had made several online enquiries to invest his life savings, I was one of the firms he had reached out to. It was £150,000; the sum of his entire life's work, and he wanted to find a safe home for it because he had no other sources of income other than a small state pension. He was getting older, and his health was not great, which meant he needed to plan for medical care in the years ahead.

I dreaded what he was about to say next, but I already knew where this road was leading. I had heard the same story a thousand times. I let him continue talking without interruption and heard his horrific story unfold.

He told me that he had spoken to a company and had invested £90,000 with them. He was planning to give them other £60,000 next week. My heart dropped. I asked tentatively what he had invested in. It was in the fund 'AXA Framlington,' a well-known global fund.

It was of course the name of a legitimate fund, but I knew differently. People don't cold call to sell legitimate funds.

A few minutes later he gave me some more details, including the name of the company he had invested in. I asked him if the firm was FCA regulated. He said that it was.

Vince is a smart guy. He realised that boiler room scams exist so he had made all of the sensible checks. He had gone to the FCA website, checked Companies House, checked the directors, and the address of the office.

As we talked, I typed the company name into Google and my heart dropped.

I immediately saw that it was a scam – there was even a great big warning sign on the FCA website saying that the company had been 'cloned'. Vince was still talking excitedly about the investment, so I knew I had to break the bad news to him slowly. As I told him about my concerns, I could hear him almost go into shock.

Silence. I was worried that something was going to happen. I called out his name a couple of times, but he didn't respond. I could hear his heavy breathing.

Eventually he tried to speak, and stuttered "*But – I didn't... – No– I don't think that – '*. It was the typical response. Denial. Shock. I knew the emotions of anger and resentment would follow shortly.

He'd be angry at me first. Then he'd be angry at the scammers, and finally, he'd be angry at himself. It was the usual script being played out, which I had seen so many times before.

I was worried that Vince might even suffer a heart attack with such news, so I realised that I had to calm things down and regain control. I told him that everything would be okay, that he should come and meet me and I would help him. In that one moment I could hear him break. There was no sound, but the silence was deafening.

This poor man was completely lost, and now he was talking to a stranger who was breaking the devastating news to him that he had just lost more than half of his entire life savings.

It was a horrifying experience for us both.

We spoke shortly after that initial call, and I invited Vince to come and see me. We agreed a date, and he was set to catch a train from East Yorkshire to come and see me in my office in Central London. But he had to cancel at the last minute because of a hospital appointment.

Unfortunately, we never did get to meet but he told me that he was eternally grateful for the information and advice I gave to him during those difficult times.

Vince had already planned to invest the remaining £60,000 with that same boiler room firm and had it not been for our phone call, he would have lost the rest of his savings, he would have been completely wiped out. I gave Vince the various numbers of organisations that could potentially help him. I also called the company that had scammed him, but they denied responsibility.

Several months later, I called Vince and spoke to his wife. She remembered me and told me some amazing news. Vince had managed to get most of his money back. It wasn't the full amount but a good chunk of it. I was so happy for them both. I don't think Vince realises how lucky he was; I've seen so many times scammers vanish in thin air, so, for him to recover most of his money was nothing short of a miracle.

There are countless stories of pensioners losing their life

savings. It happens all the time. In the work that I do, I have heard more than my fair share of stories. But for every story I hear, there must be a hundred stories that I don't hear. There will be many more stories that are never reported.

The problem is much bigger than anybody can imagine.

Vince wanted me to pass this message on to you personally, and simply said this,

"Please just check what you're getting into. Much better you keep any cash under your mattress than try and be too clever. Don't take the risk like I did, just don't it."

TIP 3 –
THE EQUITY INVESTOR
SCANDAL (EIS)

The classic boiler room has for several decades been one of the scams responsible for destroying the greatest number of lives. Therefore, the question is, what can possibly be worse than this?

Well, this next one beats it and I'll explain why in just a moment. Welcome to the murky waters of the **Enterprise Investment Scheme (EIS)**, or perhaps it should be more accurately described as the **Equity Investor Scandal (EIS).**

Another government c*ck up

The Enterprise Investment Scheme (EIS) was a government initiative set up in 1994 to encourage investors to support small, start-up companies. These companies often find it difficult to borrow money from banks but because they're the backbone of our economic society, providing growth and jobs, the government naturally wants to support them.

The government therefore actively *encourages* investors to buy into EIS approved schemes by offering income and capital gains tax incentives. In other words, if you have a tax bill to pay, you could write off a big chunk of it simply by investing in an EIS investment.

After the financial crash of 2008 when bank lending dried up, the popularity of EIS products sky-rocketed and this became the new fertile land for scammers to make millions of pounds.

To date, nearly 30,000 companies have received EIS funding of almost £20 billion from UK investors. Those numbers are staggering - 30,000 companies and £20 billion!

Clearly the scheme is well-intentioned and on paper it makes a lot of sense.

However, the EIS market has been heavily infiltrated by scammers to the point that today, I believe there are more EIS scam companies in the market than there are genuine EIS companies. Nobody knows the exact numbers, but I would estimate that out of every genuine EIS, there are at least two fake ones.

So, if you're an EIS investor or thinking about buying an EIS, the odds of you getting caught out on this scam is incredibly high.

Big ticket size

To see why this is product is favoured by so many scammers, we need to compare it to the alternatives.

For example, trying to convince somebody who lives in a quaint, little cottage in the Cotswolds, to buy a crate of Senegalese palm oil is not exactly the easiest pitch in the world. Now compare that very difficult sell to offering the same person the opportunity to reduce their income tax bill by 40% by investing in a government approved scheme.

You can see why the scammers love it.

The sales pitch is much easier which means more sales with fewer calls. In fact, the product sells itself. If you want to reduce your tax bill (who doesn't?), the demand is already there. You don't need to create the demand, you don't need to excite the prospect, you don't need to entice them with those big juicy profits.

No, all you need to do is to find somebody who wants to pay less tax - which is pretty much everybody.

This means the conversion rate from prospect to client, is so high that pretty much every fish in the pond is tempted to have a nibble.

But what's even better than this, is not the volume of fish but the *size* of those fish, i.e., the *deal* or *ticket* size.

The average EIS deal is much bigger than a typical investment in any of the other scams we've discussed so far. That's because it's based on the tax rebate as a percentage; if you have a large tax bill to pay, you *have* to invest more in an EIS to offset it.

So, if an investor wants to write off a large income tax or Capital Gains Tax bill, he has no other option but to invest heavily into the EIS. He's *encouraged* to invest more.

It's brilliant for the scammers.

The scammers are usually worried about asking the victim for more money because that could jeopardise the deal; it might appear desperate and salesy. Now, the scammer simply has to run through the maths – "*Mr Client, if you want a tax saving of X, it means you need to make an EIS investment of Y*".

It's brilliant.

Just like the boiler room fake certificate scam uses the corporate action deadline to persuade the victim to make a quick decision, the EIS scammer uses the tax benefit to persuade the victim to invest more than they otherwise would. In both cases the scammer detaches himself from the sales process but can still apply plenty of pressure indirectly without looking like the sleazy salesperson.

The numbers aren't just big; after the purchase of a house, it's usually one of the biggest investments that somebody might make in their whole life. It's a jackpot scam.

Indeed, many EIS investments are linked to property deals. That's because the biggest Capital Gains Tax (CGT) bill that most people face is when they sell a buy to let investment property. For some people, that tax bill could literally run into hundreds of thousands of pounds.

That means a £50,000 or £100,000 EIS investment is not uncommon.

One large deal of £100,000 is worth a hundred clients who each invest £1,000. That means the scammer gets all that money without any of the headache. Instead of having a hundred clients to deal with, which require a hundred identification documents, a hundred account opening forms, 1a hundred risk disclaimers, a hundred payments, a hundred certificates or products to manage, and of course a hundred potential complaints, that's all gone. Instead, you have just one person to keep happy.

It could be much more.

Let's say an investor has a £200,000 CGT bill and wants to write it off. Depending on his tax-bracket, he might have to invest say £500,000 into an EIS! The scammer typically makes a margin of around 70% after costs; that means a profit of £350,000!

That's a single deal. Imagine that.

Inheritance Tax

EIS investments are also 100% exempt from Inheritance Tax! That's terrible for investors but great for the scammers because it pushes up the deal sizes even more.

An investor who has an estate worth, say, £5 million might think nothing of dropping a £1 million across a handful of different EIS schemes. Some of my own clients have invested over a £1 million in EIS schemes. I tell them to be careful of scams but many of them don't even seem to care. They'd almost rather risk being scammed than give it to the taxman.

That's because they write off 40% from their Inheritance tax straight away. Put yourself in their shoes for a minute.

You're on your last legs and, your health isn't what it used to be. You want to prepare your paperwork and finances to make things easier for your loved ones before you depart this Earth. Most importantly you've worked bloody hard for sixty long years, and you'll be damned if you're going to let the government get their grubby hands on your savings.

That's the main thing keeping you awake at night; it's the thought of your kids not receiving your assets. You can't make sense over why your children should only receive 60% of your assets after you're gone; that you are giving away 40% to the government. How unfair is that?

That was YOUR hard work!. That was decades of sweat and graft. You find yourself becoming more and more angry, and your blood pressure is rising.

"Over my dead body", you mutter to yourself with clenched teeth.

You'll do anything to make sure your money goes to your kids, not the taxman.

To add insult to injury, you remind yourself that you've *already* paid income tax on this money in the first place! Now the government wants to tax you again?? The cheek of it.

You're faced with this insurmountable problem that keeps you awake at night.

So, one day you decide to find a way out; you Google *"How to mitigate Inheritance Tax"* and you see a company offering a free PDF report called "5 Ways not to pay IHT".

Hmmm…. that looks interesting. You download the report in exchange for your telephone number and learn about the five ways; one of them is an EIS. You've never heard of an EIS before, but it's got you thinking. Finally, and for the first time, you feel a bit of hope.

But you don't think too much of it. It's something you might explore later, and go back to watching the telly.

What you don't realise is that in that small moment of madness, in that one simple internet search, in those innocent keyboard clicks as you typed your telephone number, you've just made the worst mistake imaginable. A mistake so incomprehensibly damaging that you wouldn't believe it if somebody wrote a book about it.

You literally just lost your entire life's work and blown your kid's entire inheritance. Technically speaking you've just royally fuc*ed yourself in the most spectacular fashion. You just don't know it yet.

This is where the theatre show starts.

An hour later you get a call from an EIS scammer and so the play begins. You're sceptical at first but hopeful. You want to believe it; you want there to be a solution. You want to sleep at night.

You listen intently to the polished sales pitch and the more you learn about EIS schemes, they more intrigued you become. Wow, it's real, government backed schemes, they're true, they actually exist.

Within a few weeks of back and forth with the scammer, due diligence checks, background reading as well as maybe a call or two to HMRC and your accountant, you realised that it's all completely legitimate. Incredible. Why didn't you hear of this before? Finally, God has answered your prayers.

The day has come when you can finally put two fingers up to the government.

For the scammer you've gone from a cold lead to a burning hot prospect.

Little do you know but your name is now hand written in BLOCK CAPITALS in a big red circle, sitting proudly at the top of the scammer's white board, in some derelict back-street office in East London.

You have no idea but if you care to look down, you'll see that your belt is undone, and your trousers are edging their way slowly towards your ankles in preparation for the party of a lifetime. It's your leaving party.

Suddenly the EIS scammer becomes your best friend. Just what you were looking for.

This is your final piece of work, your final responsibility as a parent. It's your job to ensure your children succeed in life, for them to be happy. That means you need to provide for them financially. They shouldn't struggle like you did; you want your grandchildren to have the best education, the best start in life.

Now this is your last and final act. It's on your shoulders and you are so relieved; finally you found it, you cracked it. Daddy did it.

The scammer offers you an incredible solution. He tells you to invest in a series of highly profitable, small, start-up companies. Not only will it reduce your income and Capital Gains Tax bill, not only does it give you a great opportunity to double or triple your investment in the next few years, not only does it beat inflation and protects your cash from erosion, but on top of all of that – yes on top of all of that - and most importantly of all, a big chunk of the investment you're about to make is automatically *removed from your estate.*

It's not taxed at all. As if by magic, you waved a wand and now your money can magically go straight to your kids, not to the government.

So, instead of throwing 40% away, now you can invest that money, and your kids can receive that investment tax-free. Brilliant.

All you have to do is hold the EIS investment for three years and you've just dodged the 40% tax. That's it. What could be simpler?; Your children get to inherit a brilliant investment, which, in five years' time might be worth 10x what's it worth today, and they pay NO tax.

It's almost impossible to lose – in fact the investment has to fall by more than 40% before your kids lose a penny. What's the chance of that happening? Not much, you convince yourself.

You my friend, can now go to heaven in peace.

It's an incredible sales pitch. It's an incredible story and it's one of the easiest things to sell because it solves a problem people genuinely have.

Buying graphene doesn't solve any problem for anybody.

In fact, eliminating IHT doesn't just solve any old problem, it solves the single, biggest problem for a big, rising group of people. This isn't just for the rich.

Inheritance Tax used to be for the rich but with house prices and inflation going up, more and more people are getting caught in the IHT tax band. The government isn't exactly complaining about that.

This 'death tax' is one that everybody hates. Nobody thinks it's fair, even those who don't pay it. This means there is a huge desire to find a solution. The demand for the magic pill that solves this problem is unprecedented. Everybody wants that pill.

For the scammers, finally, after all these years of searching for that miracle product that sells itself, you just found it.

The EIS racket was born.

The get-rich formula

As with all scams, the start-up cost, which includes the financial costs as well as, the time and effort needed to execute the scam, need to be weighed against the potential upside.

The upside, or profit, depends how easy the product is to sell, what the profit margin is, and for how long it can be sold. Scammers also need to price in the level of risk involved, and the likelihood of getting caught.

For example, if a scam is very expensive and time-consuming to set up, requires a lot of effort, is hard to sell, and is very risky, it would need to have a massive pay-day on the other side of the equation for it to make any business sense. If a scam is easy to sell, not very risky and relatively cheap to set up, the deal can work even if the profit margin is low.

So, let's run the EIS scam through this get rich formula to see how it scores.

On the cost side, it's a very easy sell because it's a government backed scheme with huge tax benefits. EIS shares must be held for a minimum of three years for the investor to receive his tax break which gives it a long time-period, another big advantage. There is however a fair bit of work to do in order to set it up. On the complaints front, very few investors make a noise so, the risk is low.

On the profit side, the average ticket size is much larger than your traditional scam. Profit margins are also very high, typically around 70% after costs. There are some built-in added benefits such as time deadlines. For example, investors have to buy an EIS before the end of the financial tax year in order to offset their tax for that year.

It ticks so many boxes. If you're supposed to 'make hay while the sun shines', you can regard the EIS scam as one never-ending summer. The stars align almost too perfectly for this scam.

When you punch the numbers into the get rich equation you can see why the scammer's love it. It's also why the scammers don't mind putting in the extra time and money on setting it all up. A big dollop of effort now is worth a big pay-day tomorrow.

Patience today for a bigger pay day tomorrow

The professional scammers are in no rush.

They might take one or two years to set up an EIS scheme properly because they recognise the importance of building up a track record. Like all scam companies they must resemble a legitimate business.

A solid board of directors, audited accounts, reputable accountants, online content, social media presence, high-quality brochures, information memorandums, an engaging website, positive customer reviews, prestigious office location, professional marketing, and so on. It's the same game that all scammers have to play if they want people to invest in their company.

It can't just be window-dressing. It has to be real.

There must be some turnover in the business, it must produce or sell something, at least for a while.

You can't just set up a business today and raise money tomorrow. That's too obvious. Even if HMRC give you EIS authorisation, you won't be able to raise much capital.

Taking a short cut during the set-up stage means you're now back at the bottom of the barrel again with the other boiler room outfits. An EIS is a classier outfit, a different breed of animal; those scammers are cut from a different cloth, and they know it.

They're not looking for the quick, easy goal; their goal is not to rip off a few gullible punters. Their game is to annihilate the whole market for years and still never get caught.

That's why they build up their credit score, their brand, their reputation. It takes time and patience. You might think they do all of this for HMRC so they can acquire EIS status but actually the HMRC checks are pretty flimsy. It's not difficult to run a fake business for a couple of years and be approved for an EIS. The threshold to join the HMRC club is surprisingly low.

The window-dressing is not for the government, it's for the investor. All that extra work and shenanigans is to increase their chance of raising more money. The charade, the theatre, the illusion, it is all for you. It's to give investors like you many reasons to part with your cash and as few reasons not to.

Quick short cut

Of course, not all scammers want to put in all of that hard work in setting up a business. They want a short cut to avoid all that time, effort and money. So, there's a solution for that, too.

Instead, the scammer just buys an *existing* limited company off the shelf. It's easy to do and not expensive.

In fact, there are hundreds of businesses in the UK that go into administration every year. They're not difficult to spot. The scammers   simply reach out to these firms and buy their business off them. The business owners are thankful for getting any sort of money because they're on the brink of administration and the scammers get what they want more than anything else – a long trading history.

The scammers don't care about the profitability, the assets, where they're based or, what their balance sheet looks like. All they want is a business that's been around for a few years that they can now make into their own.

Not all businesses qualify for EIS status so, having the right product or service is a bonus. But even that's not essential because the scammers can apply for a change in business if necessary.

With a few small changes to the business model, they can quickly accelerate the EIS scam into operation. Dig deep into the Companies House records and you'll see the sale, the change of ownership and the full history.

But from a sales perspective, they just say, "This business has been running for eight years".

Here's the other helpful thing.

The whole idea behind the EIS scheme is that it's designed to help businesses that need money. By definition, that means businesses that are struggling, short of cash, are not profitable and have poor cash flow. That's perfect for the scammers because it means they can buy a failing company for peanuts.

Big margins give options

EIS schemes can raise up to a staggering £5 million in one year and up to £12 million in its lifetime.

Now put yourself in the shoes of a scammer on say a 75% gross profit margin. A £12 million EIS raise would bring home a clear £9 million of bacon. That's a lot of money.

This gives the scammers great options, and almost unlimited choices. Unlike a legitimate business on say a 15% gross profit margin, a scammer already knows he can spend literally millions of pounds to make the scam work, because he's got up to £9 million to spend.

Therefore, his goal is always to *shorten* the sales cycle. Rather than make £9 million over a seven-year window (four years to set the EIS up and another three years selling it to investors), he wants to know how he can trade 'money for time'.

Instead of doing what most people do which is to sell their time for money, he does the opposite; he sells his money for time. One example of this is to recruit talented team members into the scheme.

By recruiting a big-name non-executive onto the board, a scammer might instantly buy himself twelve months of credibility. That's what this name brings to the reputation of the firm. In return the scammer pays the non-exec , say £100,000 year to 'work' just one day a month (although, of course, he doesn't actually do any work). His sole purpose is to shorten the time it takes the scammer to get EIS approval and how quickly it can be sold to investors.

Another way to shorten the sales cycle is where the directors invest themselves. This helps massively with the pitch because the sales advisors can say, *"The directors have invested their own money into this EIS, that's how confident they are that it will be a success".*

However, the 'personal money' being invested isn't personal at all. The money is coming straight out of the future £9 million profit, it was never the director's own money!

But to an investor it appears that the board is fully committed. It gives the perception that the business must be worth investing into, because the directors are investing. The directors must know something nobody else knows. It builds confidence and credibility.

These little shortcuts help to reduce time, but for some greedy scammers, it's still not quick enough. They want to build credibility even faster.

FCA legitimacy and Section 21

The best way to earn instant credibility in the UK financial world is to mention those three important letters, F, C, and A. The problem for the scammers is that they can't use them.

We already know that scammers love to align themselves to the regulated world, because that's how they make bigger sales. EIS is no different.

The trick used is something called 'Section 21 FCA *approval*'.

The Financial Services Market Act 2000 (FSMA) is a piece of legislation which requires certain investments to obtain a Section 21 approval. In these cases, the firm has no choice but to comply. However, it's not required for most businesses.

The reason an EIS scam firm will *voluntarily choose* to become Section 21 approved is because it raises the legitimacy of the proposition in the eyes of the investor.

It means an FCA regulated company, typically for a fee of around £20,000, will independently perform a number of checks on the firm.

Note - the EIS investment is NOT regulated, it's simply being checked by a regulated firm.

This is where the problem lies.

Most people won't have even heard of a 'Section 21 approval', let alone know what it means but it sounds very official, doesn't it?

The scammers take something which costs very little and spin it into something that helps to align them with a regulated business. It helps them to artificially push up the perceived value of what they are selling and thereby reduces their sale cycle.

The sales pitch can now become, "*This EIS is Section 21 approved which means it's been approved by an FCA regulated firm...*".

Hmm...did I just hear that that the EIS is regulated. I mean I'm sure I heard the words 'EIS' and '*regulated*' in the same sentence. Did I catch that correctly?

Somebody who hears that sentence when told by a professional salesperson will assume that the EIS is regulated, or at the very least has some form of regulatory protection.

Even if they didn't fall for the firm being regulated, the fact that angulated firm has done checks on the EIS, is itself a very big selling point.

In fact, the actual checks carried out for Section 21 approval are minimal and quite basic, usually surrounding the auditing of the accounts. Nonetheless, the perceived value is huge and that's because of the expert skills of the salespeople who present the story.

But it doesn't end there.

There's also another huge benefit to the scammer having its dodgy EIS attain Section 21 approval. It allows the EIS to be financially promoted, i.e., advertised, to a much wider group of investors.

Once the marketing material including the prospectus has been approved by an FCA firm to be 'fair, balanced and not misleading", it gets the seal of approval to be mass-marketed to a much larger audience.

Suddenly the fake business has just received a massive green light to be openly marketed to retail clients.

It can be sold to pensioners, single mothers, and people on low incomes. Of course, it can also be sold to everybody else, the rich and wealthy, and professional investors. The Section 21 whilst appearing to protect the investor, paradoxically paves the way for the scammer to run riot.

Without the Section 21, the scammers are restricted in targeting a much narrower market, which consists only of high net worth and sophisticated investors. With section 21 approval, they can target anybody and everybody.

Buying shares from directors

Once all the credibility techniques have been exhausted, there's one final way to fast-track money to the scammers and it's the oldest, dirtiest trick in the book.

A credible EIS with a good reputation will help to lubricate the pipes through which money can flow from the investor to the directors, from the scammed to the scammers. But it's not the only pipe.

With the EIS scam, there's an extra flow of money that is easy to capitalise on and it works like this.

Imagine an EIS company is valued by its scam directors at, say, £5 million (this could be justified by some flimsy IP rights, a medical patent, or some form of technology expected to be released next year etc.). Now, let's say, they issue EIS shares worth 10p and totalling £2 million; so, the directors are giving 40% of their business away. This means that twenty million EIS shares are issued and available for purchase.

Therefore, it also means the directors retain thirty million shares at 10p = £3 million.

Remember the money is in the valuation. If the directors can convince HMRC the business is worth £5 million and issue shares accordingly, it has created a fixed, reference point from which all future deals can be measured. It means that 20p for shares in that company are expensive and 5p are ridiculously cheap.

The directors have basically turned themselves into paper millionaires. However, the thirty million shares they have awarded themselves are actually worth nothing because the company is worthless. It has a 10p price tag only because that's the price the directors have given it.

So, now the goal is to offload the thirty million shares to investors in addition to the twenty million shares.

This opens up not one but two potential markets. The first one is for investors who are looking to save money by mitigating their CGT, Income Tax or Inheritance Tax liability. The other market is for investors who are looking to speculate and make money.

By manipulating the price, it attracts the speculators. Even if you don't think you are a speculator, you soon become one when you're offered an amazing deal. Everybody loves a bargain.

Imagine what would happen if the scammers offered investors the opportunity to buy EIS shares worth 10p, directly from their *own personal shareholding* at just 5p!

Yes, they wouldn't get the EIS tax benefit to offset their tax, but they'd more than make that up by buying shares with a 50% discount!

Can you see the attraction?

Investors are duped into thinking they can buy shares at

half-price because there is an official EIS document, stamped and approved by HMRC which says that shares in this company are worth 10p. You could even ring HMRC and they'll tell you that it's genuine.

Now you're being told by an IB (Introducing Broker) who has a relationship with the firm that he can arrange an Over the Counter (OTC) deal directly with one of the directors.

He might say something like, "Hey John, you have a couple of opportunities here. You can either buy the EIS shares, which obviously have great tax breaks and will help you wipe out next year's Capital Gains tax bill or, if you don't care too much about your tax and just want to make some money, I have access to a small number of restricted shares which you can buy directly from the directors.

Because it's from the directors, you can pick them up for just 5p. That was the previous trade price they sold their shares for and under Best Execution rules, the directors have now snookered themselves; basically, they have no choice but to sell their remaining shares at 5p, at least until this first round of the EIS is complete. After that they will put up the price to probably a minimum of 15p, but right now, their existing shares have to be sold at less than the EIS price for compliance reasons.

Obviously, we have much more demand from our clients at 5p than we have shares available, so, I don't know at this stage how many shares I can get for you at this level, if any at all. However, I can put an order request on the trading book, so your name is on the list. It's an aggregated order so, everybody gets the same price, and it's guaranteed to be at the 5p level.

Now, just one thing to bear in mind – there's a very good chance that everybody will be scaled so, whatever number of shares you apply for, you won't get your full allocation; at 5p, which is literally half price, there's just too much interest. If you think about it, you're paying half the price as somebody else for exactly the same company, the same risk, the same opportunity.

Also, remember that you have the added benefit of not having to hold them for three years. As soon as the company floats which we expect will be towards the middle of next year, you can sell your shares straight away.

If you want to sell them sooner, I'm sure that I'll have buyers myself willing to pay at least 8p once this batch of shares is filled, because that's still 2p below the current price.

By the way, the directors don't want to sell now. They would rather wait for the EIS to be complete but as part of the EIS terms they're obliged to reduce their stake because they're majority shareholders and they need to drop their allocation down to 49%; at the moment it's 60%. That's the only reason you're getting such a golden deal."

Do you see how easy it is?

It doesn't matter if any of the above is true or not. It sounds true and that's all that matters.

If you think you can buy something today that's worth 10p and pay only 5p who doesn't want the deal?

Technical information and 'market lingo' put together in a seamless pitch by an experienced salesperson always sounds so sexy and appealing, it's hard not to become seduced. That's what your broker is doing to you, he's serenading you back to his apartment for some kinky sex games.

Unfortunately, it ends up with you being handcuffed to the bed posts while your wallet is emptied. It's not emptied once, but twice. First your cash will disappear and then your credit cards.

First, you lose money through the EIS and then a short while later, you get an opportunity to buy shares straight from the directors. Without warning there are now two massive money pipes sucking cash straight from your bank account to the scammers.

The scale back

Creating demand is all that matters. That can be done by manipulating the price upwards or by artificially restricting supply. The supply side is where the broker creates the illusion of scarcity by saying that investors will be 'scaled back' on their orders.

This happens with genuine companies on the stock market all the time which makes the story feasible.

It's a ploy to encourage investors to put in exaggerated buy orders. Somebody who might typically invest, say £10,000 could be tempted to put in an order for £20,000 or even £30,000 because he believes he is going to be scaled back.

But here's the thing. He is never scaled back. That's just another lie.

Because he has to put up a deposit, usually 10%, of the full allocation of shares that he's applied for, he's already committed to £2,000 or £3,000. This means he has to follow through or he loses his deposit. The salesperson turns this into a positive by saying how lucky he is for securing his full allocation, and that it's never happened before.

But the investor is now left scrambling to find the money for a £30,000 investment when he only intended to invest £10,000.

The scammers can only pull this trick once but that's enough. It's the equivalent of three normal sized deals and it also gives them valuable information because it tells them who the 'big whales' are within their client base. Who's really got the dough?

Of course, some investors will often try to back-pedal at this point, but because they're already committed to the deal the broker will put pressure on them to pay the full amount.

Losing a hefty deposit is usually enough to seal the deal.

Extracting more money

Scammers are never short of ideas when it comes to extracting more money from their victims and strategies quickly move from the creative to the outlandish.

Using made up prices is, of course, at the heart of it all.

That's where professional scammers *create* their own fake market using an official looking website with 'live prices'. This could either be on their own website or better still what appears to be a type of exchange. To buy a domain URL costs peanuts and it's easy to update prices on a site.

The prices don't need to be live or change second by second like equity prices do. After all investors know that these are illiquid investments. So, even a price that changes once or twice a week, is sufficient. How hard is it to change a couple of numbers every few days? Not very.

But that fake website, which looks official, with links to market news, and regulatory announcements, and advertising billboards, with maybe live prices of gold, bitcoin, the Dow Jones, etc. creates the perfect illusion.

Somewhere on that page you will see the price of that box of fine wine, or graphene, or pre-IPO, or, in this case, the EIS share that you just bought.

The price is of course made up and the investment can't be sold but having even a 'quoted' price on a screen is enough to get investors very excited. If you see a website showing a price of an investment that you hold, you're probably not going to think it's fake.

As a result of this new-found confidence, existing investors are often duped into investing even more money.

The scammers convince investors that their original investment has already doubled or tripled in value. Not only does the IB tell his client over the phone that the shares that he bought at 10p are now worth, say, 30p, but he directs the client to the website so that he can verify it himself. The price actually says 30p on the website. Amazing!

You know what the next step is, yes – more money please.

The IB now offers the client the opportunity to buy another tranche of shares, at say, 18p which is still 12p less than the new current price of 30p. There are different ways to present this data to maximum conversion and sales but at the heart of it all is a massive price-value discrepancy, which acts as the bait. The opportunity is too good to miss. We all want a great deal.

Investors will even borrow money from family and friends or take out loans from a bank or even re-mortgage their homes. They'll do anything to get that 'sure-fire' profit.

Then there's the extraction trick where an announcement is made about a new issue of shares being launched after the initial batch of shares is bought. If the first tranche of shares is issued at say, 10p, an EIS could announce to the marketplace that it will issue another batch of shares at some fixed date in the future at 40p. They might suggest a corporate restructure, or a big contract win, or some positive news which justifies the share price jump.

It could even be that the first tranche was priced artificially low to attract investors and it was intentionally under-valuing the company; the second tranche was actually in line with the company's true valuation.

Faced with the opportunity to buy something today at 10p or to wait three months and buy the exact same company at four times the price, you'd be forgiven if you wanted to buy today.

Whether the company ever does issue more shares at 40p is

irrelevant. You're already invested.

On paper the company share price has quadrupled in price, but that's all it is; on *paper.*

If an investor puts in £10,000 and now it's worth £40,000, in their mind they've just made a clean, and very easy £30,000 profit. Wow.

When they look around and see that their bank account is giving them 1% interest, they realise they have something very powerful. They feel special, as if they have somehow stumbled across something lifechanging.

The broker will feed that appetite. He'll use the 'profit' as good news to then sell even more EIS scams.

Once you're in the spider's web, you're f*cked.

"Steve, I told you to trust me, didn't I? I didn't let you down, did I?

Well, look here's the thing. Yes, you've made some good money on this EIS, but honestly, it's nothing compared to the next EIS that I've got coming up. We've almost fulfilled our whole allocation and it's not even be released yet.

In fact, we're being forced to take pre-orders on this one because the company has won a contract with British Aerospace to supply their electronic systems. That's the rumour we're hearing from a very credible source. If that's true, the company will fly out the door as soon as the EIS is open to investors. That's why we can't wait for when they go live.

You need to get in now, if you don't want to miss out.

My management team are ahead of the curve on this one thankfully and they have pulled in their contacts. We're one of just three companies that have secured an allocation already.

Here's the best bit, we can get the shares at just 4p, but the actual trading price is 11p and when the EIS is actually released it could come again at 18p or more."

Again, it's so convincing, isn't it? Just a few paragraphs on a piece of paper sounds plausible and I just made this up in my head. The real pitches would be ten times better than what you've just read from me.

Reading it is very different to somebody telling you the story over the phone, it has a ten times greater impact. Now imagine it's not just a call but somebody is actually presenting the EIS to you in person, with charts and graphs, or over the phone or on a Zoom call. Imagine being given prospectus documents, and other information to get you 'over the line'. What if a tax expert actually started going through your estate value, your Capital Gains tax calculations on a spreadsheet and punched in some numbers to see what your tax rebate would be?

It's no wonder why so many people just drop a hundred thousand pounds into these products, without a second thought. The pitch is too strong.

It's this fictitious pricing that makes the EIS scam even worse than principal dealing.

With principal deals, the share price is on an exchange so,

when the price drops, the broker finds it hard to sell the next deal to his client. The client sees his investment disappear and becomes wary of buying another one.

But with EIS investments, the opposite is true. It's as if every single deal makes money. Every EIS can't stop making money. That's because prices are all made up. You can tell your client anything.

This ultimately leads to the client raiding his and his wife's piggy banks to find more and more money to invest in more EIS scams. Before he knows it, he's re-mortgaged his house and is the proud owner of ten EIS investments totalling £250,000. On paper they're worth £2 million. In reality they're worth nothing. But the scammers have one final trick up their sleeve and this one catches just about everybody, even the most sceptical investors.

The false share buy-back

Some investors may not believe the price, even though it's on a 'live' website. So there is a brilliant way to make the price 'real'. The trick is for the broker to pretend he wants to buy shares back *from* the investor.

Let's say the investor buys an EIS at 10p and the price is now supposedly worth 20p.

The problem is that the investor realises that 20p is not a tradeable price so, he can't sell the shares. Therefore, he's not convinced in buying more shares or adding more to his allocation.

This is the time where a false price has to become a real price.

The broker tells the investor that because the firm is doing so well and the directors regret issuing as many shares in the business as they did, they want to now *buy back* some of those shares. Because the price is up to 20p they're willing to pay 15p for the shares.

Suddenly it becomes interesting! So, the shares that you paid 10p for just three months ago can now be sold for 15p, you make a 50% profit.

Even the hardened, sceptical, switched on investor falls for this one.

Did you fall for it? Where's the catch? If you make 50%, how can you possibly be scammed, right?

Here's the thing; the IB tells the investor the good news and makes the offer but warns him against taking the deal.

"Listen John, the directors are willing to pay 15p for their shares but think about this.

If they're offering 15p what does that tell you? It means their business must be worth much more than that. I reckon you should just wait a few months, they'll be offering at least double or triple that. They obviously know something that we don't.

Of course, it's up to you. If you want to cash in now, I can do that for you. Just give me your order and the directors will be more than happy to take those shares off your hands. But as your broker, I have to look after your best interests and my view is, it would be crazy to sell."

50% is a lot of money in share dealing and in the stock market but John, this is the EIS market. This is where you can make 5000%. It's where a 10p stock could float at 50p or 500p on an exchange, so to sell at just 15p is crazy."

What do you think the investor will do? Answer - he's not going to sell.

In fact, he's going to hold those shares closer to his chest than he did with his first new-born baby. In his mind, he's thinking this one investment is about to change his life.

More importantly, it's shifted the sceptical investor to the trusted investor. That's the first step required in order for the investor to buy more.

It's known as a 'reverse close' in sales or 'the take-away'. You offer something that doesn't really exist hoping that your cover isn't blown. It's like going all in with a shitty poker hand and bluffing out of your anus, hoping not to get called.

If you're good at sales, you won't be called. In fact, your clients are now more desperate than ever to buy more stock.

It's called the false share buy-back and it works night times out of ten.

But what happens on that one occasion where the investor says "Yes, I'd like to sell".

Well, that's easy. The scammers put the 'sell order in the market' but a few days later, they are informed that unfortunately all the stock buy-back has already been satisfied.

Oh dear, what a shame. So, that's right, nobody ever gets to sell.

Or better still for the scammer, is when the client actually receives money into his bank account. You'll remember this false buy back strategy in the boiler room scam. It's actually applied in all scam products because it's one of the most powerful tricks in sales. I've seen this happen where a scammer has made not one, but sometimes two or three payments to an investor.

You can imagine, as the investor, what that might feel like. Imagine you made 50% profit in three months! You got your money back into your bank account – you'd never think it could be a scam because the money is sitting right there. You can spend it.

You'd barely be able to control your excitement; you wouldn't believe your eyes. Well, that ecstatic feeling is what the scammer is paying for. That emotion of winning, the sheer elation is worth much more money than what the scammer has paid to you. It just has to be harvested correctly.

It means that your next move may well be the big one. After convincing yourself that you really have made so much money, the danger is you might loosen the purse strings and make that one big deal, that one life-changing investment.

That's what the scammer is waiting for.

The end game

After months, even years of skullduggery, illusions, misdirection, and just good old-fashioned lies, and only after the investor has been milked like an abused cow for every last drop, will the telephone calls from the broker finally subside.

It's the Pareto rule. Now that 80% of the juice from the lemon has been squeezed, there is too much hard work and effort to worry about the remaining 20%.

The investor also gets tired of hearing the same story, *"the company is going to float, it's about to come to market, be patient, just next month, just next week, just, just, just..."*.

At some point, and after all the money has been extracted from the victim, the scammer will eventually say that the EIS IPO is now on hold because market conditions are not quite right. That will be it.

He won't tell you it's a scam. Your investment on paper still appears to be doing great, and your hopes are just left hanging in the air.

That's the way it stays. Forever.

Until one day, many years in the future, you hear that the company is going into administration.

That's the story of every EIS scam that ever existed. None of them come to market, none of them float on an exchange, and none of them can ever be sold.

We all have patience that eventually runs out. Investors will at some point, give up the chase. They'll stop calling the broker, stop emailing, stop writing, and stop believing. The merry go round circus drags on for a few years but life moves on and enough water passes under the bridge until it's eventually forgotten about.

Investors finally give up. They just forget about their investment entirely. They've already written it off in their minds and besides they've got their tax break. Time to move on.

Investing in unlisted shares is a very dangerous game, it's one of the most dangerous games any private investor can do with their money.

Private equity firms know how to value businesses so, buying unlisted shares in private companies may be easy enough for them, but for everybody else, my advice is to stay at home and watch the telly.

The unlisted market is a swamp of crocodiles. Don't go swimming there.

Investors WANT their EIS to fail!

There's one final piece which is so hard to get your head around, that it's probably going to stun you for a while. It certainly did to me when I found this out.

We know the only way a scam can come under any real pressure is when investors complain. That can only happen when their investments fail, and they lose money.

But get this. With the EIS scam, investors not only expect their investments to fail but they *want* their investments to fail. Yes, you read that correctly.

Let me explain.

Statistically the majority of EIS companies fail and so investors are already expecting them to do badly. That's why they typically invest in several EIS investments rather than just one.

In other words, investors buy them hoping for the best but are already preparing for the worst. It's seen as an outside bet, a gamble, a punt. That's because the primary reason to invest in an EIS for most people is not to make money, it's to *save* money by paying less tax.

It's different to any other investment because of its unique tax rebate which shifts all of the power from the investor to the scammer.

Of course, if the EIS makes money, then great, that's a bonus, but it's never the main goal.

This is a real problem because it means that when the EIS fails, there's no investor uproar, no complaints and no investigation. Investors don't even blink an eye.

So, if investors don't care, who's going to alert the authorities and ring that bell?

Remember, investors already believe that EIS investments are *supposed* to fail.

Depending on the tax bracket, an investor might only put 50%, 40% or even just 30% of his own money into the deal! When somebody acquires an asset worth £100,000 but only puts in £30,000 of his own money, quite frankly he doesn't really care.

Even if the thing went bust, the investor never feels that he's losing his own money because he was going to spend it on tax anyway. It feels like fluttering a few quid away on the horses.

But it's actually worse than. You see, not only do investors not care if they make any money but in fact, they actually *want* their EIS investments to fail!

Sounds crazy but again, it's because of the tax-breaks.

If a scam EIS investment never floats on the stock exchange (which of course they never do), the investor is left with a worthless piece of paper in his hands. The investor holds the EIS for three years, qualifies for his tax-breaks, and that's all great, but what next?

Well, if the company never floats, it means the shares remain unlisted and can never be sold. So, it doesn't matter what the price of the EIS is. If, it can't be sol, it's technically worth nothing anyway. In that case, it's actually better for the EIS company to go bust because that way the investor can at least use the loss as a capital write-off to offset against his future profits.

So, yes, as crazy as it sounds, when an EIS actually goes bust, it's celebrated.

Just think about that for a moment. EIS investors WANT their investments to fail!

The scammers must be thinking it's Christmas. No complaints by the investors when the scam product goes bust, just celebratory cheers with glasses of champagne.

Mind-blowing.

We're all paying for this

You might be thinking what all the fuss is about. After all this scam is for the rich, so who cares?

I can understand why you might not shed a tear when a multi-millionaire property developer gets scammed with an EIS. After all he was trying to avoid paying a million pounds in

Capital Gains tax on a sale of flats in Kensington.

But we shouldn't think of it like that. Nobody deserves to be scammed, rich or poor.

Besides, EIS investments are not just for the rich. We all pay tax so there are plenty of people on low incomes who also get conned by EIS scams. They see an opportunity to save money and understandably they don't want to pay any more tax than they need to. So, the scam impacts everybody, rich and poor.

However, there's another even bigger point.

Even if you don't buy an EIS, you're still being scammed. In fact, we're *all* being scammed through the back door.

That's right – all of us - you, me, and the rest of society.

We're paying with our taxes. The person investing in the EIS is being scammed and loses, say, 50% of his money but the other investor in the deal which is of course the government, aka the taxpayer, is you and me. That means we're investing the other 50%!

So, if you're reading this thinking that you'd never buy an EIS and it doesn't affect you, guess what? It does.

Indirectly we're investing tens of millions of pounds worth of dodgy EIS investments every single year with our taxes. We're the other partners in that deal putting up the money, plus it's *without* our knowledge or consent.

The government diverts our hard-earned tax-money away from building schools, roads and hospitals straight into the bulging pockets of the scammers.

That's right – it's you and me, pal, getting stuffed together which is what makes this scam so unique.

Yep, we're all getting screwed on this one, big time.

The carrot becomes even bigger

We know that the EIS scam is powerful because of the tax breaks but this scam just seems to get worse and worse.

There's something called SEIS which stands for Seed Enterprise Investment Scheme that offers even *more* generous tax breaks than EIS schemes!

SEIS is the very <u>first</u> round of capital raising for the company which means the EIS will follow. Because of the higher tax rebates, the amount an investor can buy is restricted to £100,000 in the first year and £150,000 across the whole lifetime of the business.

Now think how easy that sales pitch becomes for a scammer to a high-net-worth investor.

"The company is raising £5 million in an EIS but the first £150,000 will be via the SEIS. The investment is the same, the risk is the same, the company is the same, in fact the only difference is that you'll get a much bigger tax rebate.

If you're interested in reducing your tax bill, and you'd like to use the EIS route to do that, then you should really take advantage of the SEIS. But as you can imagine, the demand is much greater for this. Would you like me to reserve you any shares?"

Powerful, isn't it?

The wrong incentives by the government inadvertently produce the perfect selling conditions for a scam.

The generous tax breaks mean less direct investment from the investor, which means less risk of there being an unhappy customer, meaning less risk of a complaint, meaning less chance of an investigation, meaning less chance of the EIS being shut down by the authorities.

It's just another juicy carrot for the scammer to wave in the faces of their soon-to-be victims.

Introducer fees

None of this is possible without a strong sales team which is typically outsourced to an 'Introducer Broker' (IB). That's an external professional sales team of unregulated 'advisors' and 'brokers' whose sole purpose is to push the scammer's EIS stock to their own book of clients.

Scammers don't have the time or experience to do the selling, so, it makes sense to partner with a company that can do all the sales and pay them a commission for doing so.

But IBs are not cheap.

The directors of IB firms will typically secure a commission rate of between 30% and 50% of the money raised. It's a lot of profit to give away but the scammers are prepared to do that because of what the IBs bring to the table, which is *volume*.

Partnering up with a decent-sized IB is ideal for the scammers because it gives them instant access to hundreds, even thousands of willing, pre-qualified investors who have money and are ready to buy. This means they can raise millions of pounds in just a few short months. To raise that kind of money on their own would otherwise take years so the 40% or so they pay away is a sensible investment. It buys them the valuable commodity of time.

The IB firms pay their sales guys between 10% and 20%, keeping the other 20% to 30% for their profit less their overheads of office rent, marketing and advertising, telephone and IT, compliance etc.

Scammers also won't work with just one IB but usually at least four or five different ones.

These brokers are unregulated and dotted around the City of London. They don't have to conform to the same rules as regulated firms which means they can say what they want over the telephone but they're usually not as 'wide' (reckless) as traditional boiler rooms.

So, they sit somewhere in the middle and when you hear their sales-patter they almost sound regulated. They know that the traditional method of 'guaranteeing' profits and high-pressurised sales not only puts investors off, it also attracts unnecessary heat.

Their job as always is to align and disguise themselves as genuine brokers by acting in the way a regulated broker might act.

A sound model

The IB model has been used for decades so, there's nothing wrong with the concept. In fact, it's entirely sensible for a business to pay an expert sales team a commission to market and promote its product. That's a marketing expense and happens in genuine businesses all over the world in every industry.

If one firm has access to a product and another has access to capital, it makes a lot of sense for the two to partner. You could argue that all forms of internet marketing are loose types of IB arrangements.

Google is paid by millions of companies around the world to advertise on their platform and gain access to their database of 'clients', i.e., basically the whole world with an internet connection. Amazon is exactly the same.

Whether it's affiliate marketing, referrals, or introducing brokers, the concept is the same.

The IB has access to investors with money who are specifically looking for EIS opportunities, and EIS companies should rightly pay a fee for that access. As the name suggests that's what introducers do – they *introduce*.

So, the model is sound, in theory at least.

The problem comes when the introducer either knows or at least, suspects the EIS is a scam but continues to actively promote it.

Most IBs have to be aware of the scam because of how much they get paid.

Think about the numbers again.

When a scammer pays an IB, say, 50% of any money that it raises, unless the company is going to make at least a 50% profit after all costs, then the investment has to fail.

As soon as an EIS starts to pay anything more than say 10%, the IB should know that it's likely to be a scam and stay well away.

IB choice – 10% genuine or 50% scam

Given the choice between a 10% fee for a genuine EIS or a 50% fee for a scam EIS, you will find that some IBs turn a blind eye and will take the 50%.

IBs aren't stupid; they can pretend to play dumb if they wish, but any IB knows that companies offering 50% or more are charlatans. They just pretend not to see or hear anything.

However, some dodgy IBs go much further than this. They don't just turn a blind eye; they are involved and complicit in the scam. They work closely with the scammers and that's when things become ugly.

That's when the scam firm and the IB come together and coerce on the marketing, sales, and presentations. There are no secrets anymore. They all know the game, and what their role is.

Of course, the IB doesn't disclose to the client the close relationship that it has with the EIS firm. This is for three reasons.

Firstly, if the EIS fails, the IB wants to distance itself as far as possible from the toxicity that comes with that failure. They'd rather plead ignorance to the whole thing, pretending that they were selling something which they believed was genuine. Whilst this protects the IB it also protects the scam firm because it means there are fewer people who know what's going on. Fewer mouths to talk and spill the beans.

Secondly, clients buy more when they think that their IBs are impartial. If an IB is not linked to a particular EIS, then his sales pitch is more believable. It also allows the IB to pitch multiple EIS schemes, not just one.

Thirdly, it reduces risk for the scammer. If a client does his due diligence and picks up on something to give him doubt, rather than go to the authorities directly, he's more likely to tell his IB. After all, the client trusts his IB because they're supposed to be on the same team.

The IB thanks the client for the information and says he will look into it, but then simply reports back to the scammer who then fixes 'the problem'. The problem is anything that affects the scammer's ability to raise more funds, such as a negative online review, something dubious about the history of one of the directors, a suspicious entry on the audited accounts, or a malfunctioning form on a website.

Whatever it is, big or small, if it raises suspicion for one potential investor, it will raise suspicion for others so, it's allvaluable feedback for the scammers to correct.

The very savvy investors who conduct high-level due diligence will always find some holes that put doubt in their mind. Therefore, this feedback is invaluable, and the scammers use it to plug those holes, making it more difficult for the next client to spot.

This constant feedback loop of information and problem solving, helps the scammers to fine tune and improve their product for their next victim.

The IB needs to be the first port of a call for the client, and this happens only through trust, which is why the IB must appear completely independent of the EIS issuing firm.

Not every person will invest, and the best IBs are trained to probe and question to find out why.

Like every business, including the scam EIS business, understanding why people *don't* buy, is at least as important as understanding why people do buy.

The dark underbelly of unlisted shares

Apart from the tax benefits, EIS companies, like all unlisted shares, are sold on the dream that one day they will float on a stock exchange.

Over the years, I have spoken to hundreds of EIS investors who all told me excitedly how their EIS was about to float on the stock exchange. Out of those hundreds of giddy investors, shrieking with unadulterated joy as they told me of how they were going to become rich, not one of their EIS investments ever floated.

Not a single one.

I don't blame the investors, but I do wonder at what point their common sense was replaced with a crazy, unrealistic pipedream. It just shows how good the scammers must be. The tax benefits alone are enough to sell the scam, but the possibility of quadrupling your money, well, is that really likely?

Maybe I've just been in the industry for too long and seen this story repeat itself a thousand times, that for me it's becoming glaringly obvious. But then a small part of me can't help but think *"Really...Did you really think that you were going to make 400% profit in eight months because somebody at the end of a telephone that you had never met, told you so?"*

I once spoke to an investor who had bought EIS shares in a cannabis company at 3.5p, and he excitedly told me how it was now trading at 37p. He went on to say that he was now buying more at a *discounted* price of just 25p, and that the company had already had clearance to float on the Nasdaq stock exchange in three months' time at 84p.

"It's all agreed, signed, and delivered", he boasted, feeling very chuffed with himself.

I could just imagine the sales pitch from his broker, *"This is the last chance to get in. There are only a restricted number of shares, so you need to put your order in now...blah blah blah"*

Honestly? Has it really to come to this? I didn't know what to say.

How do you even begin to have a conversation with somebody who thinks he has made a 24x return on his investment, from 3p to 84p? Those investments don't exist in the real world.

If they do, then rest assured that neither of us will be lucky enough to find them.

This chap had convinced himself that his £10,000 was now worth £240,000 and was soon to be worth even more. It was going to make him well over a million pounds he told me.

Worst of all, in his mind he had already spent the money.

That's the hard part for me in my job; trying to convince somebody that their dream is just an illusion. It's tough.

You end up being the bad guy because you have to break the devastating news them. They wake up happy one day and you don't just ruin their day, you ruin their whole year. You really hope that you don't ruin their whole life, but unfortunately sometimes that happens too.

Of course, they never accept the truth from you. It's always denial, anger, reflection, worry, misplaced hope, more worry, denial, more anger, we're back to the usual cycle of emotions.

They only realise the truth when their new best friend, their EIS broker, who just made them a gazillion pounds suddenly stops returning their telephone calls. Six months on, a year on, three years on, unsurprisingly the EIS never did float on the Nasdaq.

Eventually when the penny finally drops, I usually receive an email apology from the investor saying that they should have listened to me.

No apology needed. I'm just sorry I couldn't have helped you sooner.

What's the solution?

None of these EIS scams could happen if it wasn't for the approval from an institution as established and trusted as HMRC. This is what makes the whole scam legitimate in the eyes of many investors.

So, I think the solution for this scam is actually quite easy. HMRC has to really turn the screw on the scammers and make it much more difficult for any Tom, Dick or Harry to receive an EIS approval. This might also make things a little tougher in the short-term for the genuine EIS firms to gain approval but, overall, it would help them hugely.

That's because the genuine EIS companies are being starved out of any investment, they can't compete with the scammers. A genuine EIS business doesn't have the ability to pay an IB 40% or 50% of the money it raises so, it must raise capital the hard way, organically. That means it's denied access to investors. At the same time, the investors are denied genuine investment opportunities.

The IB in the middle acts like a dam, preventing real investors and real investments to ever meet.

They simply can't afford to pay an IB firms to promote the EIS companies because the EIS scammers pay too well. Genuine EIS firms are being priced out of the market.

However, if the dodgy firms were eliminated by a tighter selection process imposed by HMRC, IBs would have no choice but to work with the EIS firms available to them, i.e., the genuine firms who pay more sensible fee rates of say, 5% to 10%.

The scam IBs would disappear leaving just genuine EIS firms and genuine IBs.

The market would also benefit from a massively improved reputation. With fewer scam EIS investments available, a much higher percentage of EIS investments would actually perform well. They'd float on the stock market, and more investors would make more money. There would be fewer scams, and fewer investors would be ripped off.

The word would spread, and that would encourage more investors into the EIS market. This all feeds into a positive, self-perpetuating cycle.

By HMRC tightening up the selection process at the very top, this would also mean fewer casualties and fewer bankruptcies further down the funnel.

Our tax-payer money is not supposed to be used to support failing businesses. We should be supporting genuine small and medium sized businesses that have great vision, a solid track record, have a committed team behind them, have real assets on their balance sheet and most importantly can be trusted   to use the money we give them to legitimately expand and grow their business, not to expand the pockets of their directors.

We, the taxpayers, are not there to gamble on every start up, crazy idea that pops up.

Not every business will make it, that's part of free market economics and capitalism. But because HMRC literally supports almost every entrepreneurial idea that ever existed, including the notorious chocolate teapot industry, there is a massive failure rate.

With more hoops to jump through, you will find that only really committed businesses will apply for EIS funding. The scammers will realise that they'll fail the selection process and won't even bother applying.

Even genuine businesses are doomed for failure are taking the EIS route because it's an easy way to raise money. While they're not scams, they still have a very high chance of failure. If we eliminate these excessively high-risk businesses, there will be more successful investor outcomes, which, in turn would mean that HMRC wouldn't need to offer such lucrative tax-breaks.

The only reason HMRC has to offer investors up to 70% tax write-offs is because most EIS businesses fail. If more EIS investments were successful, investors wouldn't need the big dangling carrot and would be happy with smaller tax breaks of just 10% or 20%. That means more money for schools and hospitals and less money to scammers.

If one out of every two EIS investments tripled in value, who wouldn't want to take those odds? The only reason HMRC is desperately giving away 70% tax breaks is because the market is awash with scams and terrible businesses, which means that nine out of ten EIS investments fail.

Make it *more* difficult to join the EIS club, not less difficult, and that would be good for everybody, including genuine businesses, HMRC and the taxpayer.

TIP 2 –
BONDS

You may be wondering how any scam could possibly top the EIS scam.

After all, it's deception of the highest kind, it's rubber-stamped by the HMRC, it's almost undetectable, and it affects every taxpayer in the country. You might even describe it as the 'perfect scam'.

Well, all of that is true, but yet, the next insider trading secret is even worse. Because I have left the best, I should say the, worst, to last.

It's worse than the EIS scam because it affects the weakest and most vulnerable.

EIS investments are primarily for the rich and wealthy who don't want to pay tax. As we've seen, they can affect low-income earners too but as a whole it's mainly designed for high income earners, property landlords, business owners and wealthy estate owners who have a lot of money and want to shield it from the tax man.

There's nothing wrong with that and they certainly don't deserve to be scammed, but they are usually astute individuals and at the very least, have money they can afford to lose. They also go into EIS investments with their eyes wide open knowing and even expecting they might lose everything.

But this next scam is the exact opposite.

It hurts the people who have the *least* amount of money, those who are *most* vulnerable, and those who *don't* want to speculate. The victims of this scam are not looking to reduce their taxes. In fact, most of them don't even earn enough money to pay tax.

They don't even want to grow their wealth and they certainly don't want to speculate.

They're the exact opposite, they just want to keep their money safe. This is the group of people who want no risk at all.

Biggest and most vulnerable market

Think of the word 'bond' and you'll probably think of a *low-risk* investment; something where your capital is safe and protected, and where you receive a steady, fixed stream of income once or twice a year.

Now think of the words, 'shares' or 'stock market' and you're likely to think of something which is riskier, more volatile and where your capital is at risk.

In simple terms, bonds are low-risk and shares are high-risk, right? Wrong.

That's why the bond scam is so painful because the people who buy them do so with the intention of actively searching for *low-risk* investments. They don't want shares because they can't afford to lose their money, so, they look for bonds.

They've also most likely bought bonds before and so they're

comfortable with the concept, which means their guard is down and they're not suspicious. They assume that all bonds are low risk and reliable. As a result, it's where investors typically make much larger investments because they deem the risk to be negligible. That's great for the scammers.

With EIS investments, the deal size was inflated because of the tax-break. With bonds, it's inflated because of the perceived low risk.

The market for bond investors is huge. In fact it captures quite literally *everybody*. It's even bigger than the EIS market, which is those who pay tax. Bonds cover the entire population.

The market for cryptos, pre-IPOs, IPOs, pink diamonds, penny shares, CFDs and FX trading courses is quite small. EIS is more but still limited.

However, bonds are on the other end of the scale, it's for every person and their dog.

Every pension fund, every balanced stock portfolio, every diversified investment strategy, and every sensible risk strategy you can think of will somewhere along the line, include bonds.

That's because bonds are the lowest risk asset class. It's the number one tool used to diversify away risk and to bring stability to a portfolio.

In fact, the only thing lower in risk than bonds is cash, and as revered US fund manager Ray Dalio once said, "cash is trash".

The market for bond investors is probably suitable for 99% of the world. The other 1% don't invest anyway.

Not a bad sized market for the scammers to tap into.

A very big chunk of that 99%, maybe as much as 90% I would estimate, are retired individuals. So, this scam disproportionately targets the retired. Simply put, people who buy bonds are typically the most vulnerable in society.

Retirees who have no way of replacing their income and have a fixed amount of money sitting in their bank account are the prime targets for this scam. They typically earn 1% or 2% on their savings in their bank or building society so, in real terms they are depleting their savings through inflation. That's why so many decide to invest in bonds for a fixed return of, say, 3% or 4%. It makes perfect sense.

They feel obliged to take their cash out of the bank because they know that inflation is eroding their life savings, it's depleting their purchasing power. But, at the same time, they don't want to take on any risk, so they simply move their money to the next lowest risk asset, which is fixed income bonds.

Here's the tragic irony – whilst the people who can least afford to be scammed are being scammed the most, the speculators and gamblers who are openly searching for high-risk products are *put off* by the fixed rate of return, so don't invest!

As always, the problem is that the scammers have skilfully woven and integrated their scam bonds in and amongst the genuine bonds within the marketplace.

Genuine bonds really do offer safe havens for pensioners. It's where they put their money for a rainy day, somewhere safe and secure, and where they can park their funds comfortable in the knowledge they can draw on them at some point in the future.

Dodgy bonds look and feel the same but are nothing more than very elaborate schemes which steal your money and throw you out into the street.

Up until recently pensioners were shielded from the scammers antics because their product range was so out of touch with what the pensioners wanted. God only knows how hard the scammers have tried in the past twenty years to convince retirees to invest in carbon credits or pink diamonds.

That's a really hard gig and for every one hundred cold-calls, even a talented salesperson might be lucky to get one or two bites, where somebody shows even a fleeting bit of interest and can be closed on a sale. But on the other ninety-nine occasions, it usually results in the phone being slammed down in the scammer's face.

Bonds however, now that's a different story.

Now you're selling something that people not only want but are *actively searching* for. That makes all the difference. It's like the EIS in that regard, it's a problem that people are trying to solve.

There are literally tens of millions of pensioners all around the world, who all want the same thing, a fixed income return. They all want bonds. Think about how big this market is. Literally billions if not trillions of pounds, dollars, euros and yen are out there just waiting to be mopped up.

That's why the scammers had to go back to the drawing board. If they wanted to play in the big-league, they weren't going to do it with graphene or car park spaces. They could only do it with bonds.

They had to find a way to create a bond scam so brilliant that they could pass it off as a genuine bond, in such a clever way that it could con the world, it could con all investors.

They had to find a way to create something so amazing that it would have all the hallmarks of a bond that it couldn't be spotted even when under close inspection. If they could do that, then they had a mass-market appeal so big, that it would make any scam that went before it like kids' play.

Many years of hard work by the scammers have resulted in a plan so genius that it will shock you to the core.

Not only did they con the pensioners, but their final product was so brilliant; they managed to con everybody. They conned the advisors, the brokers, the custodians and even global stock exchanges all over the world.

I've been in this game for nearly thirty years, and I can tell you, that this was the biggest financial con of them all. Worst still, it's bigger today than ever before.

Pensions

Pensions give a seal of confidence that other products just don't have. If you have a stock ISA or a share dealing account or maybe even a corporate account, that's all fine, but a pension is something else. It's viewed differently.

There is a natural, default position which as investors we all assume when we deal with our pensions. There is an assumption that it's safe.

Therefore, if an investment, for example a bond can be invested into a pension, then we naturally think the investment must be legitimate. After all, pension funds and pension trustees are FCA approved, and they're swimming all day, every day in compliance, legal documents, regulations and paperwork. It's what they do.

With so many checks and balances, you would never think that your pension could be infiltrated by the scammers, right?

It's like breaking into the Tower of London to steal the Crown Jewels. It would be the heist of the century; it just wouldn't happen.

Add to the fact that you're investing in the lowest risk asset, a bond, just makes the whole thing even more secure.

It's this same level of confidence that investors give to their pensions. They believe that because there are so many rules governing their pensions, because they are so strictly regulated, it would be the last place a scammer could break into. But how wrong they are.

The bond scammers know this is the impenetrable product, the impossible safe for them to breach. If they cracked the code, it would mean their dodgy bond would become

'SIPP investable'. That's it, game over for potentially millions of investors in the UK.

But that's exactly what happened.

These dodgy scam bonds became SIPP investable. Suddenly the floodgates were finally open and the biggest financial scam in living history was about to take place and I was about to witness the whole thing go down.

The disastrous Pension Freedoms legislation

The government has never got to grips with how the City of London works. It's full of civil servants, think tanks, and academics who mean well but just haven't got a clue about how the financial markets work.

You only need to look at Kwasi Kwarteng's disastrous mini budget in late 2022. As the UK's Chancellor at the time, he announced £45 billion of tax cuts but didn't say how he was going to pay for it. The markets collapsed and Liz Truss, now enjoys the unenviable record of being the shortest serving Prime Minister in the country's history, at just 45 days.

However, go back a little further and you'll see an even bigger howler by the government.

In April 2015, it introduced the '**Pension Freedoms**' legislation which led to a catastrophic outcome for many tens of thousands of pensioners. This ill-thought-out law allowed individuals to convert their safe, stable work-placed pensions into SIPPs.

This gave pensioners the choice to invest in whatever they

wanted, equities, bonds, investments... anything. This would seem reasonable if an investor is financially astute and surrounded by good people. But most pensioners aren't.

Many are alone, have little meaningful financial experience, and are completely vulnerable.

The fact that the government then followed this up by making it mandatory for pensioners to seek financial advice before making any investment decisions, added fuel to the raging fire. Now these vulnerable pensioners were being thrown into the lion's den. If they wanted access to their SIPP, they had to engage with, build rapport and forge relationships with none other than our friends, the financial advisors.

If they got unlucky and found one of the hundreds of dodgy IFAs that now operate in the UK, they were on the cusp of losing their entire life savings. What happened next was an atrocity.

Pensioners were tricked and mis-sold the benefits of moving their safe, stable Defined Benefits (DB) or Defined Contribution (DC) pensions into SIPPs. They had no idea what they were getting themselves into.

A large number of pensioners were simply cold called out of the blue and convinced by financial advisors that it was absolutely the right thing to do. So even if it appeared that the client was initiating the pension transfer request, it was actually being orchestrated in the background by the financial advisor.

The dodgy IFA knows he can't make any money from a DB or DC pension, but from a SIPP, he can make a fortune. The wall of the dam that had stood for so many decades, which was designed to protect pensioners was finally broken.

Overnight literally *billions of pounds* became accessible to scammers. Some of that money found its way into carbon credits, dodgy pre-IPOs and other unregulated investments. However, most of it was channelled into dodgy bonds, with huge commissions for the advisors who had recommended it.

Moving money from a DB or DC pension to a SIPP was mistake number one for the pensioner.

His pension was previously protected because he couldn't touch the money but now his entire life savings were out in the open. It's like taking a lion cub away from its mother and throwing it in the middle of a pack of hungry hyenas.

Mistake number two was just a formality, as sure as night follows day. Now that the SIPP was out, with the cash and funds were accessible, it was a small step to convince the pensioner where to invest their money, i.e., which specific bonds to buy.

It made perfect sense.

If a pensioner had already taken his financial advisor's recommendation to move his safe, protected company pension into an unprotected SIPP, it follows that he'd also take advice about *how* to invest that SIPP.

Within the space of a few weeks, from living a financially secure, worry-free life with a guaranteed regular monthly pay-out, thousands of pensioners had moved their lifetime savings into a load of worthless dodgy bonds. It would just be a matter of time before they all went bust.

Within a few years, the investments would blow-up, and the pensioners, as well as their families, would be left with nothing. That's exactly what we're seeing today.

As those bonds mature, they are going pop, pop, pop, one after the other, just like a sprawling display of fireworks, except it's not New Year's Eve, and there's nothing to celebrate.

Above any other policy that I can think of in the past thirty years, this has to be one of the biggest own goals the government has made in the financial world. It should never have interfered, and whichever think tank or group of overpaid financial consultants were responsible for this catastrophe should be stripped of their jobs.

I'm not even sure if the paper-pushing, civil servants in Whitehall have realised the full extent of their mistake. The government is certainly back-tracking and trying to fix things.

It's not just DB pensions into SIPPs that are causing problems.

Even transfers between existing SIPPs are being questioned.

For example, at the time of writing, one of my clients was prevented from moving his SIPP, which he held with another firm, to my firm because his current SIPP provider insisted he must have a meeting with the government funded body 'Money Help'. This was apparently to ensure the SIPP wasn't about to be transferred into a scam.

The problem with this approach is that it creates a barrier to exit for the client, which could be abused by the original SIPP firm. If that firm doesn't want to lose clients, it can make things very slow, costly and painful for them to leave. It simply refers each client to Money Help on the pretense of protecting their best interest.

My client not only had to complete extra forms and answer numerous questions, he also had to wait eight weeks for his meeting! You can imagine how a lot of people, faced with the same inertia, might just give up and stay with the original SIPP firm.

Certainly, the government and regulator have done their best to undo the harm caused by this crazy legislation, but my fear is that it's too late now, the damage is done, and the genie is well and truly out of the bottle.

Worst of all, it's still happening today, and it could be happening to you right now.

Rotten financial advisors, with a little charm and persuasion, still regularly convince pensioners that a SIPP is the best product. Even though the rules to move into a SIPP are much tougher now, transfers into SIPPs are still taking place, so, the root of the problem is yet to be fixed.

Dare I say it, another pensioner will have been scammed of his life savings by the time you turn the next page.

Mandatory legal financial advice

Forcing pensioners to take mandatory legal advice is just giving another loaded weapon to their financial advisor.

I'm not suggesting that individuals shouldn't seek advice about something as important as their pension. But there should be better safeguards in place to protect them from all of the corrupt advisors out there who are circling above them like a flock of vultures.

When the government makes it a legal requirement that a person *must* seek financial advice, they are forcing at least some pensioners, who have the misfortune of running into a dodgy IFA, into a very precarious position.

It shifts the balance of power entirely to the IFA.

The average pensioner is already lost in the financial world and feels obliged to pass the reins to a 'professional' i.e., a financial advisor. The government has now made this mandatory and has put all IFAs, including the dodgy ones, onto a pedestal which is open to exploitation.

Dodgy IFAs follow carefully designed scripts that brainwash unsuspecting pensioners. It's become all too easy to convince pensioners to move away from their fixed, company pension schemes to personal pension schemes.

This is all detailed in their 'financial planning' call.

It goes something like this.

"You know Bill, I've reviewed all of your finances and noticed that your Defined Benefit pension really isn't doing much for you. A lot of my clients have moved into SIPPs and they're getting a

much better return. I think that with the change in government rules you should really think about doing the same.

In fact, I'm surprised that you haven't already. On average the stock market goes up every year by about 8% and you're missing out. Also, I don't trust these company pensions because they could default. If you manage your own portfolio at least you're in control and there is no risk of the pension company going bust.

Also, you can take out a 25% lump-sum cash payment tax-free. You can enjoy yourself. Just imagine, you could take Margaret on that holiday she's been asking for, she'd love that or maybe buy that new car you were looking at but couldn't afford. At your time in life, you deserve to enjoy yourself, and you can't do that with your current pension which is tied up.

Don't worry about the investments. I can manage the whole thing for you. In fact, I know some really good, low risk bonds that are paying 6% annual income. Maybe we should make the switch?"

Not a bad story. It's a shame that it has such a shitty ending.

It's completely unintentional but a big unnecessary push by the government to force pensioners to rely on financial advisors creates a very undesirable outcome. It compounds the problem.

It dangerously shifts the mindset of the investor.

The average pensioner automatically assumes he shouldn't even to try and manage his own SIPP. He assumes that if the government has made it a legal requirement, then he must listen. He assumes he is incapable of making investment decisions for himself. It's the start of the slippery slope of relinquishing control.

The government has unwittingly put at huge risk the one group in society that needed the most protection.

Do the maths

Now, we understand how a pensioner's money is accessible, let's look at the actual scam itself and how it works.

All bonds give a fixed amount of interest (known as a 'coupon') twice a year. Therefore, your money is tied up for a period of time, known as the 'term'. At the end of the term, your bond 'matures' or 'redeems', and you get back your original deposit.

Let's say you have £10,000 sitting in the bank earning you 1%, but you have an opportunity to buy a bond which pays 5% per annum for five years.

This means you can invest the £10,000 today and receive £500 every year for five years, which equates to £2,500. This will be made up of two semi-annual coupon payments a year of £250 each.

At the end of the five-year period when the bond matures (also known as redemption), you will get back your initial £10,000 investment. This means you will have received £12,500 after five years. Compare that to your bank account, which gives you £100 interest per year i.e., just £500 after five years.

You can see the attraction and why so many people fall for

it. Cash gives a £500 return and bonds give a £2,500 return!

Sounds great; where do I sign up?

Once again, willingly putting your capital away for a few years without wanting it back, plays right into the hands of the investors. Scammers know they have at least five years before they may be rumbled, which gives them plenty of time to make lots of money.

In the same way that an EIS scam can be rinsed for at least three years, a bond scam can be rinsed for even longer. Some bonds can operate for ten years!

The perfectly sensible investment strategy of investing in bonds for income and long-term capital preservation, has been hijacked into one of the most devastating scams of all time.

Pyramid scheme

We've all heard of the pyramid scheme scams which became so popular in the late 1990s and early 2000s. That's where you invest, say, £1,000 into a 'business', then you try and convince your friends and family to do the same. Your friends in turn ask their friends to invest and so on. The pyramid widens as money trickles down.

The only reason it can be sustained is because the fees generated from new members is used to pay the existing members. But it's just one big scam because nothing is being produced.

Eventually like a pack of cards, when new people stop joining the scheme at the bottom of the cash-funnel, the people at the top of the funnel can't be paid, and the whole thing collapses.

In the past decade, there's been an explosion in the reincarnation and repackaging of pyramid schemes via Multi-Level Marketing operations (MLMs). It's the same scam except with a product thrown in to make it look legitimate. Now instead of just asking people to join for a fee, members actually *sell* a product, usually a fitness drink, health gadget, make-up product or something similar.

There might be a few genuine MLMs out there but in the most part, if it looks like a duck, walks like a duck, and quacks like a duck, then it probably isn't a cat.

The Bernie Madoff Ponzi scandal was one of the most highly publicised Ponzi schemes worth a staggering $60billion! This wasn't some back-street operator hiding in the bushes. He was very-well known, in fact, at one point, he was the chairman of the Nasdaq Stock Exchange, one of the biggest exchanges in the world. That's before he was caught in 2008, sentenced to 150 years in prison, before eventually dying in his cell in 2021 aged 82.

We shouldn't forget that he very nearly got away with it. It was only because of the financial crash of 2007-8, when spooked investors demanded their money back, that the whole thing folded. Otherwise, it would still be operational today.

Well, the modern-day bond scam is the latest reincarnation in a long list of reincarnations of the pyramid scheme. It's also one of the most sophisticated and untraceable.

It works like this.

Coupon payments & Escrow account

An Escrow account is simply a separate bank account is set up to hold funds specifically to pay for the bond's coupons. For example, if pensioner, John invests £100,000 into a five-year bond which pays a coupon of 8%, he will receive £8,000 every year for five years, which is £40,000.

Because the scammers know that paying John his coupons is critical to their scam working, they immediately transfer £40,000 from the original £100,000 that John paid them into a designated Escrow bank account. This means that the coupon payments are now secure for John regardless of what happens to the business.

This allows the scammers to ensure that John will get paid on time, twice a year with no risk. In other words, the firm returns 40% of John's investment and keeps 60%. That's not a bad profit margin for the scammer. However that's not the real money-making game here.

The bigger play is that the scammer can generate millions of pounds, even tens of millions of pounds from *new* investors because of the Escrow account. It's the segregation and therefore guaranteed coupon payments which ensures that John and all the other investors are happy really happy.

They're getting paid.

So, while John is over the moon that he's getting paid what he doesn't realise is that **he's actually paying himself!**

Because the coupon payments are being funded in this way, there is zero chance of it failing – it's completely self-sufficient.

This is where the Bond scam is an improvement over the original Pyramid Scheme scam. The reason that Pyramid schemes collapsed as often as they did was because investors were allowed to get their money back at any time. If enough investors became worried and asked for their cash back, the scam would quickly collapse.

The way that bonds work is that the initial capital can only be redeemed at maturity, so there is no risk of investors wanting to get their money back sooner — they can't. That's part of the agreement.

It also means that if you invest in a bond during the early stages, you're going to be sitting further towards the top of the pyramid. That's 'good' news for you because you're going to receive more coupon payments.

Using the example of an £100,000 investment in an 8%, five-year bond where you invest right at the beginning you *might* get back, if you're lucky, 40% of your investment. That is assuming the company doesn't default on any of its coupon payments.

But if you bought in year five, you will only get back one year's coupon i.e., just 8% of your investment. So, you lose a staggering 92% or £92,000!

In all cases, the Escrow account is what protects the scammer from himself. It stops him from taking the money and running. By providing income on a regular basis to existing investors, it means that he and his pals can keep milking the cash cow using new investors.

Free marketing

Another benefit of investors receiving regular coupon payments is the free marketing that it gives. The biggest advertisement is not on billboards, in newspapers, on the internet, or television. The biggest (and cheapest) form of advertising is word of mouth from the thousands of investors who have already bought the bond and are getting paid their regular coupons.

Can you imagine the conversations they'll have with their spouses, with their siblings, their friends, and their work colleagues?

You could even forgive them for bragging. It's hard not to become excited when you're getting 10% a year on a bond when everybody around you is being stuffed by the banks and receiving just 1%.

Investors who really believe they've found a way to beat the system are more than happy to share their knowledge and good fortune with others. They think it's their duty to let the secret out. Why wouldn't they want their loved ones to also make money, just like them.

It doesn't take long for others to get involved in the action. Suddenly you have large influxes of new investors all scrambling to get onto the money train before it leaves the platform.

The second issue…and the third…and the fourth…

Once a bond has raised as much money as stated in its initial prospectus, you might think that's the end of the scam. Far from it. Just like EIS scams, the bond scammers rarely disclose their true intentions during the first round of capital raising because disclosing their true ambition of how much they want to raise would put investors off.

In other words, if a company said that it planned to raise say £50 million from the outset, that would attract too much attention and might raise a few eyebrows. It would be better if the company started off by saying that it wants to raise, say £5 million. This is especially true if the company doesn't have a big balance sheet, or isn't very well-established.

A larger initial bond raise wouldn't create any urgency for investors to rush out and buy because there's such a huge supply. Investors could delay their purchase and not worry about 'missing out'.

On the other hand, a smaller bond issue of £5 million is likely to get investors far more excited which means more deals can be closed over a shorter period of time.

Investors will quickly buy into the false narrative that there is only a relatively small supply and they need to buy now, not tomorrow. In other words, people are encouraged to take immediate action.

The goal of the scammers is to raise as much money as possible. That's easier to do in several smaller tranches rather than trying to go for that big home run and potentially scare off investors from day one.

The sales story is also a lot easier to tell for those unregulated trading floors and IBs across the City, that are being paid to sell the bonds. Limited stock availability helps to pile on the pressure to what is already a very high-pressured sales pitch.

After the first bond issue sells out, the bond issuer simply creates a second issue. Easy peasy.

It's the equivalent of a shopkeeper telling his customers that he's got a closing down sale and everything must go. Customers rush in so they don't miss the huge discounts, but the next month when they walk past the same shop window, it's full again, with more of the same stock proudly displaying the same 'closing down' sign.

Once the initial issue is fulfilled, there comes the second issue, and then a third, and sometimes a fourth and a fifth.

It's these later issues where most of the money is made.

In the first raise, there is speed because investors don't want to miss out on the deal; there is also uncertainty because the bond is an unknown and untested quantity.

On the second raise, there is less speed but more certainty. This is because investors on the first issue have already received coupon payments so, confidence levels are high. Word has got out and usually the first batch of investors will dig deeper into their pockets and buy more.

The first investment is a taster. When you go swimming in

the sea, you're always going to dip your toe in first to check that it's not too cold. But once you see hundreds of people swimming in the sea, all happily smiling it makes you want to jump in.

It's the same with investing; when we buy something that's new, untested and without a track record, we might only commit a small amount of money, say, £5,000. Once we're sure that it works, that's when we raid our bank accounts for another £50,000, £100,000 or more.

The goodwill and marketing that is generated by the timely coupon payments that are being churned out for existing bond holders can't be over-estimated. That's why the Escrow account is so critical.

The regular cheques being received by investors reduces the perceived risk of the bond significantly, to the point of being negligible. That's why the second and third issues is where the biggest deals take place.

The market suddenly opens up and floods of new investors jump in.

The final piece of the jigsaw – default

Like any good film, the bond scam has a twist right at the end.

Throughout the bond raise, things always go well. The bond always pays its coupons on time, the investors are happy, there are plenty of smiley faces, as well as lots of back-patting and high-fives.

The scammers make regular contact with the investors, producing eye-watering reports and positive market updates, and everybody is feeling good, good, good. They're all now best pals with each other. The positive company reports continually reinforce how well the business is going, which translates to the IB saying, "See, *we told you what a great investment this was*".

The backslapping and high-fives are also important because investors need to be constantly reassured. They're important forms of communication specifically set up to keep the existing investors happy, while also being used as a marketing tool to attract more investors.

The goal is to keep raising money for as long as possible, right up until the eleventh hour, which is that's usually a year or so before redemption; that's when the plot suddenly thickens.

That's when something 'bad' happens. It could be a big contract loss, a loan payment that's gone wrong, poor market conditions or something else. But it has to be big enough to impact the company's ability to pay back its investors.

If it can be linked to some macro event, like a recession, a pandemic, or a war, then so much, the better. Any negative news, that might impact the business is warmly received by the scammers so the news can at least shoulder some responsibility and blame for the collapse of the investment.

Because it's big news, it can't be released on the week or the month before the bond matures. That would be too suspicious.

Ideally, it should also be a series of negative news announcements rather than a single one. The scammers will begin to seep in this bad news over a period of time, usually six, twelve or eighteen months before the bond matures. The exact dates depend on the maturity date of the bond and the strategy of the scammer.

A short-dated bond of, say two years might experience their Black Swan moment just three months before maturity. A ten-year bond might experience their Black Swan point maybe two or three years before maturity.

Following the 'bad news' announcements, the next step is the company fails on its next coupon payment. That's the first major crack appearing.

The coupon may be cancelled completely, or it may just be delayed and paid out in full later. In both cases, the scammers are setting the scene. They're letting investors know that conditions are changing and they're preparing investors for the big default further down the road.

Remember, by this time the scammers already know exactly what's going to happen and the exact sequence of events about to take place. What you see as an investor was already discussed and agreed two or three years ago. It just looks like 'breaking news' to you.

The negative news could be anything. It might be that the company they loaned all their money to goes into liquidation, or it may be that the first charge the company once held on particular properties, buildings or land has been removed. Perhaps it's that their expensive machinery was stolen, and their insurance company is refusing to pay out, or maybe a mysterious fire burned down all of their expensive artefacts and precious items.

Perhaps there was an IT security breach or a physical theft or maybe their unregulated, offshore business bank account collapses and it's forced into in administration.

Or could it be that the company was forced to carry out a fire sale of an asset, resulting in a big financial loss. It could even be that the directors made some terrible investment decisions, were ripped off and scammed themselves, how ironic.

It could be anything.

The important thing is that the basis upon which the entire company once stood, is taken away. The assets, the cash, the legal charges, the securitisation of buildings, in fact all of the things that were boasted about in the prospectus, they're all systematically removed one at a time.

All the reasons why the company was a good investment in the first place is no longer there. Each of those positive points have been taken away from the business. In their place are now unsecured loans, IOUs, failed debtors, a list of empty promises and poor management decisions.

It's not long before a profitable business that had such great dreams is now nothing more than an empty shell of a company.

When there's nothing left in the business, there's no money to pay for the coupons.

Even the beloved Escrow account is emptied out in the last year because there's no reason to keep up the façade.

The scammers have been busy scurrying away their money for years in advance. They were already preparing cases with their lawyers, accountants, and financiers. They've spoken to their pals with those loan companies and worked out how to circle back the money to themselves through a complicated structure of offshore company structures.

They had already conducted the heist, now it's time to execute the getaway.

The Great Train Robbery

A Bond scam is like the Great Train Robbery of the 21st Century. As soon as the coupon payments are compromised, the scene is set for a dramatic showdown. It's the final and most disturbing scene of the play.

Investors become very worried because for the first time the good news isn't there anymore. They come to the realisation that they've over-committed to something which looked great but now looks like a train-wreck. They still hold hope because that's all they have left, but the risk facing them is slowly becoming more and more real.

It's only one missed coupon payment, of course so investors want to stay positive. They have no choice but to hope for the best.

But the scammers, over a series of carefully constructed announcements, make it clear that things are not improving.

The company continues to issue statements and updates, each one becomes progressively more depressing than the last.

Eventually they issue the inevitable statement to the market, "It is with regret that the bond cannot meet its payment obligations."

Accompanied with this distressing statement is an equally worrying explanation of how things have gone wrong. Investors start to freak out, but they can't sell the bonds because they are illiquid.

Even if there was an OTC (Over-The-Counter) market to trade them on before, (and usually there isn't), after the coupon is missed, all liquidity quickly dries up and investors are stuck.

It's only a matter of time before the final judgement day comes. That is when the bond is supposed to redeem and repay the principal to bondholders. But, of course, it doesn't pay. It can't pay. It's bankrupt.

Now the company is officially insolvent.

The directors won't completely run the bank accounts dry because that would stink too much and bear all the hallmarks of a smash and grab bank job. If the company loses, say, 80% or 90% of its assets but still has a little cash left over, which can then be distributed to the bondholders, that makes the story far more plausible.

There might be a couple of million pounds left over from a bond issue that raised £100 million. That will barely cover the fees for the administrators to wind up the company, and any outstanding creditors. But it gives the bankruptcy more credibility, rather than posting a zero bank account on the last day of trading.

Whatever's left over, is subject to a massive 'haircut' as the paltry sum is divided among the thousands of investors. As an investor you'd be lucky to even recover 5% of your original investment.

The company goes into administration, and the bondholders lose everything.

The Great Train Robbery is complete and the bomb, I mean bond, finally detonates.

The authorities

Before the bond self-implodes, investors will naturally start asking questions.

They'll email the company, call the corporate advisors, and may even make a visit to the Introducer Broker who sold it to them.

There will be emails, telephone calls and, letters. There will be confusion and uncertainty, slowly this will escalate into heightening levels of concern and worry. But it never turns into full-blown panic because the information is released bit by bit by the scammers. That's their strategic plan.

They don't want a thousand disgruntled investors stood outside their offices waving placards and, shouting, "*We want our money back!*", while they're still filling up their getaway car with petrol. They want to elongate the whole process.

The scammers know that different investors will react differently to the news being released.

Some won't react at all; they won't even read the email and are oblivious to the whole thing. Others will take immediate action and be straight on the phone to the regulator, the police, or the local newspaper.

Some investors will see the announcement but either won't pay attention or will choose to ignore what they're seeing and hearing, hoping that it will sort itself out. Some will pray and look for guidance.

In all cases and unless the investment can be uncovered as a scam, it's very difficult for the authorities to do anything. The regulator may already suspect something, they may be aware of what's going on, but are usually powerless to act.

Their hands are tied because they can't open an investigation until there is some wrongdoing and they won't know there's any wrongdoing without an investigation. Tricky.

Therefore, any investigative work must be undercover.

They also don't want to alert the scammers if they are investigating.

What if the business is in fact not a scam but completely genuine? There are firms which really do fall into troubled times and miss coupon payments. It happens, even with the big blue-chip companies when they miss a dividend payment.

A missed coupon doesn't mean it's a scam.

The business might have looked dodgy, but what happens if it turns out that it wasn't. That creates much bigger problems, and lawsuits undoubtedly will follow if there is reputational damage, which there will be.

Any public announcement of an investigation could lead to mass hysteria as investors panic and run for cover. Investors will try and sell their bonds which would be devastating for the business. If the bonds can be sold, at best it will collapse the price and potentially force the company into insolvency. Investors will be scrambling to try and get their money out.

Even if the company doesn't default and pays back all the investors, it will never be able to raise any money again. Investors don't want to be a part of any company that is being investigated, not now and not in the future.

That's the quickest way to kill off any company.

Reputation is everything and once it's gone, it's gone. If somebody is tried for a crime they didn't commit, they'll always be remembered for that crime, even when the jury delivers a 'not guilty' verdict.

In short, publicly accusing or even questioning a firm for a scam that it didn't commit has serious, far-reaching and irreversible consequences.

That's a problem for you as an investor because it means that you'll only find out if a bond is a scam *after* it's already defaulted.

Money in, money out

I've already mentioned in this book some of the ways in which scammers can extract money out of their business, but bonds are different.

Remember, these bonds are not cheap boiler room frauds; they are high level, sophisticated operations. This means the money raised is substantial and often runs into tens of millions, even hundreds of millions of pounds.

It's not easy to move that kind of money.

That's why the money can't just be cleaned by layering through different paths and channels. The movement of capital from one company to another, or to multiple suppliers for goods and services, is useful but it won't be enough. The more people, companies and parties involved, the more overseas jurisdictions, the more exchanges, the more bank accounts, the more complexity... again. It's all helpful but again, it's just not enough.

Even with a lot of time, patience, and planning, there is only so much money that can evaporate into thin air for salaries, marketing, advertising, office costs, insurance, IT and legal fees.

To make a hundred million pounds disappear requires something different, something a little special.

That's where bond scammers have come up with the 'big money' disappearing acts that would even impress Houdini.

Asset purchases

The asset purchase scam is, once again, a genius piece of brilliance on the part of the scammers. It's where scammers buy very expensive plant and equipment at vastly over-inflated prices. The company they buy it from is indirectly connected to, and 'friendly' with the scammer.

The purchase results in a single large cash payment leaving the scammer's business and being replaced with an asset on its balance sheet. A few months later, 'market conditions change' and the asset is subsequently sold at a massively reduced price, either to the original company or to a different company, that's connected indirectly to the scammer.

Buying machinery, a piece of equipment, a piece of land, or a building for, say, £20 million and then selling it for £5 million a year later, may raise some eyebrows but it's difficult for the authorities to do anything. The scammers can cite any number of reasons why it doesn't require the machinery any more or why it was a forced sale or whatever the excuse might be. Yes, it might be a terrible business decision, but where's the proof it was a scam?

The important thing is that £15 million of investors' cash has now been lost and left the business legally. It's now sitting in the hands of the other business which is out of reach.

Loans

Another genius way that facilitates massive 'cash extraction' are loans.

Businesses often loan money to *other* businesses. They justify the loan by telling their bond holders they have raised too much cash and because it's not all immediately required until next year, the sensible thing to do is to loan it out for twelve months and earn interest on it. Otherwise, the money would just sit in the bank and earn no return.

This not only provides a simple solution that is unlikely to raise suspicion, but it also allows for a huge capital transfer out of the business in one go. There's no limit on the size of the loan.

If the business borrowing the money says it's willing to pay say, 10% on a short-term loan to borrow the money for ninety days, that would seem like a brilliant deal for the bond scam company. That's a 40% return on capital over a twelve month window and the board of directors would pass a vote to agree to that; even the bond investors would positively encourage it too (even though they have no say in the matter).

If the initial loan is paid back after the first ninety days, then it could be renewed with an even larger amount. This shows that the directors weren't reckless by lending to an unknown firm. They have to do their due diligence, of course, so they will increase their lending money in increments to make it look credible.

After a year or two of successful re-payments and a full return of the loans, the scammers can legitimately loan a company they've built a solid relationship with a much higher figure. If it loaned, maybe, £10 million or £20 million before, it can now conceivably loan, maybe £50 million or £100 million, or even more. The sky's the limit.

The borrowing company of course must offer a security on any loan that it takes out and this is where it gets interesting.

Say, the bond company loans £100 million to another company and in return, has an IOU that is securitised against some sort of asset, like a building. The bond company conducts the relevant due diligence, checks the securitised assets, gets the papers signed off by its lawyers, passes the resolution at board level, and job done. They never involve the bond holders so, the decision is made unilaterally by the board of directors and majority owners.

So, now they've loaned £100 million to a company and they have a legal charge over an asset worth £100 million.

The business borrowing the money is, of course, conveniently located in an overseas jurisdiction which has no extradition treaties with the UK. After a few months, this business goes bust, and, because it's overseas, it's impossible to recover the funds. In addition, there's little appetite to investigate by the local authorities of any wrongdoings.

That's worthy of another WOW.

In one decisive swoop, a hundred million pounds was taken from the bond company and transferred into the business of a company in the Seychelles. The money all the investors had thought was being invested into the bond company, the company they had researched and conducted due diligence on, has now been transferred to a completely different business they've never heard of, and is in now in the control of another board of directors.

They didn't sign up to this, they weren't consulted on this, and they didn't authorise this, but it happened anyway.

£100 million of their money has now vanished into thin air.

What happened to the securitised asset that was being held as a deposit against the loan?

Great question.

This is the last piece of the puzzle. The only thing that now ties the bond company to the overseas company is that asset. But miraculously, before the borrowing company goes bust, that asset somehow wriggles free.

How it wriggles free varies depending on the type of asset and the strategy deployed by the scammers, but the end result is always the same. The asset is no more.

Sometimes, it transpires that the legal charge doesn't apply in the Seychelles or the Cayman Islands or Belize or wherever it is, so, the asset was never secured properly. The lawyers could have conveniently messed up and there was some legal oversight, some form of loop- hole in the law that the borrowing company exploited, which the lawyers failed to check etc.

Other times, the asset loses its value or was, in fact, mis-priced in the first instance. It may have only been worth £10 million and not £100 million. So, when the bond company recovers the asset, it gets back a small fraction (just 1/10th) of the loan value. The valuers, in this case, messed up.

There may even be conditions under which the board of

directors passed a resolution to *discharge* the asset. This may sound like a crazy executive decision to make but there are ways and means in which it can still be justified.

The bond company holds all the cards, they make all the decisions and they can make payments to whoever they want, when they want., They can loan out their funds to whoever they want, they can securitise their debt however they want, they can later release that debt if they want to, they can discharge assets and securities when they want to, they can hold emergency meetings and pass resolutions whenever they want, basically they can do whatever the f*ck they want.

This is all about business decisions. If a business owner does something completely stupid, like loans £100 million and for some reason loses the asset that loan was secured upon, then that's just too bad. The owner was an idiot, a buffoon, reckless, whatever name you want to give him,

But the money's gone, that's it, and he's got insurance to cover his ass.

The bond is set up in a special legal structure which means you can't take his personal assets and the business has no assets. So what are you going to do?

Remember, all of this happens *before* any coupons are missed. That's why they get away with it; the bondholders are happy so, they don't question any decisions being made. These stupid business decisions are being made and because everybody is receiving their income payments, nobody is looking at what the business is actually doing.

The trap has now been set.

Furthermore, all of these company announcements are written in a technical language so overly complicated that quite frankly it may as well have been written in Mandarin, for how useful it would be to the average investor. Unless you are keeping a close eye on company announcements, which most people aren't, it would be missed by all but the sharpest of investors. Even if they did see something, they're powerless to do anything.

The information can also be missed because if the investment is purchased through a nominee holding account such as a stock ISA or a SIPP, then it's the custodian that is notified of any announcements, not the bond holder. The custodian should technically inform the broker who, in turn, has to inform the client, i.e., the bond holder. But that's not compulsory, certainly not for general corporate announcements.

Custodians are only obliged to pass information where the bondholders are required to vote or make a decision. But all of these loans, assets, securitisations and legal charges are made at board level so don't require bondholder approval. Therefore, you're never going to know, until it's too late.

You can see why it's so easy to miss this information.

After the securitised asset has been removed from the terms of the loan, the borrowing company announces it has no money, that it's broke, and shortly afterwards, files for administration. The £100 million loan can't be repaid, and the bond company is powerless to collect any money because it's lost control over the asset. At that point, the bond starts its journey into its own insolvency.

It's a very, very sophisticated scam.

You can't disappear money like that without being sophisticated. But when the robbery involves £100 million, £200 million or £500 million, there's plenty of money to pay for the best lawyers, auditors, and tax specialists in the world. It's also enough money to grease the palms of bank managers, senior politicians, and even governments of small remote islands. It's enough to corrupt anybody who wants to make a few million pounds, which includes entire financial institutions.

It's even enough to pay off overseas regulators, local police and other authorities in those far away jurisdictions. As the prize value goes up, the level of corruption goes up with it.

It's the ultimate team of criminals.

Money *in* through loans

Loans can be used in an even better way – to get money *into* the scam business.

For example, major banks have been duped by bond scammers, in some cases to the tune of tens of millions of pounds. You would expect a scam bond firm to be able to rip off retail investors but to deceive an international financial institution seems inconceivable.

But that's what has happened in the past, and it is testament to how genuine these bonds can appear. Banking and financial institutions don't loan money to just anybody and certainly not without conducting lots of due diligence. But with the most professional scammers, the bonds are near impossible to identify so, the bank falls into the same trap as retail   investors.

The bank loans £50 million to the bond scammers and 'secures assets' owned by the bond firm as collateral. Those assets wriggle free, the bond scammers disappear, and the bank is left with nothing.

Now the bank and the group of original investors are both fighting for whatever is left over, which is not a lot.

London Capital & Finance (LCF)

One example of a bond scam that shook the markets was London Capital & Finance (LCF), which went into administration in January 2019. It had raised a staggering £237 million from nearly twelve thousand investors. That's a *quarter of billion pounds* in a scam.

More than half of the total amount raised (£136 million) was conveniently paid in dodgy loans to other companies. That's how they took their money out.

The companies that were loaned the money were later found to be connected by a network of associates which linked directly back to the directors of LCF. They all knew each other of course, and the money was just circling back to the scammers through the back door.

Thousands of innocent investors lost their life savings in one of the UK's biggest bond thefts in recent history while company directors used the cash to buy horses and helicopters.

Bonds were sold to pensioners as low risk investments where they would get a fixed interest every year and their money was supposed to be backed by property investments. But despite the promises the money was never invested into property at all. It was just a hoax.

The unique thing about LCF was that it was an FCA regulated brokerage firm so, while most of these bond scams take place with unregulated sales floors, clearly there are some which are in the regulated world. The problem is that these mini bonds are not regulated so, you're still not fully protected even though you might be buying through a regulated firm.

That said and because LCF was clearly a fraud that went bust, the FSCS was able to pay out £57 million to 2,871 bondholders who were eligible for compensation. In April 2021, the government also stepped in with of a one-off compensation payment for those who lost money.

While this is all very admirable, we need to remember that the money isn't just falling from the sky. Somebody still has to pay the bill and the question is whether that's fair?

In terms of the FSCS, that's people like me paying for it. As the owner of an FCA regulated business, my regulatory fees go up to pay for crooks like LCF. I understand that nobody is going to care about people like me, who have regulated businesses.

But what happens when the government jumps in and bails investors out? That means that YOU'RE paying the scammers once again through your taxes.

That's the point.

We all need to fight against the scammers together because we're all getting ripped off.

Blackmore bond

Blackmore is another prime example of a scam with the same storyline and with the same ending, except the difference from LCF is that Blackmore wasn't regulated. But the outcome was the same; the scammers won, and everybody else lost.

Between 2016 and 2018 Blackmore raised £46 million from selling mind-bonds to nearly three thousand investors, promising returns of between 6% and 10%. Blackmore was set up in such a way that the funds raised were loaned to a Special Purpose Vehicle (SPV), which was set up to invest eleven property developments. Their accounts later showed they had sucked nearly £10 million from marketing and management fees!

As you can see, there is no limit to what they can spend your money on. If they want to pay a 'marketing company' a few million pounds, they can do that. The money leaves the business and goes into a new business you have no control over. The money has disappeared, just like that.

Shortly afterwards, in October 2019, once they had made the various money transfers to their pals in faraway places on the globe, they stopped making coupon payments to bondholders.

In April 2020 the whole thing went down like a sack of potatoes.

Of the £46million not even a million pounds was recoverable. In fact, just the legal fees relating to the insolvency exceeded £1.8 million, which meant the bondholders got back zilch.

The bond had been sold with a "capital guarantee scheme" that was supposed to protect the bondholders in the event that Blackmore became insolvent. A fat lot of good that did. That guarantee didn't work but it was necessary for the sales pitch, it gave investors the false belief they had no risk.

So, the recurring theme with these mini-bond scams continues. Because they are unregulated the FCA can't intervene which is why you should be super cautious about going down the unregulated route.

It always sounds like a great investment opportunity when a commission hungry broker is selling it to you; lots of guarantees, plenty of asset-backed securities, many protections and blah, blah, blah. But in the end, the final scene always ends with two closing acts; 1) the money goes *whoosh*, and 2) the company goes *pop*.

Separating the wheat from the chaff

As always, there are good people, good products, and good bonds.

There are plenty of perfectly genuine bonds out there and so the question is how do you distinguish the good from the bad, and the bad from the ugly? Well, it's not easy, and with high money at stake, it's becoming even harder. Because the bond scammers have access to literally hundreds of millions of pounds, it buys them almost unlimited power and control.

However, underneath it all, they're still scams, and they do leave clues.

So, here are a few things to consider.

1. Coupon rate

One quite simplistic, crude way to avoid being scammed is to simply avoid buying any bond that pays more than, say, 10% per annum.

Of course, not every 11% bond will be fake but at least you're protecting yourself by saying 'no' to everything that *might* be a scam. That said, there are a couple of downside risks to this.

Firstly, it means you miss out on genuine bonds paying good rates of interest. It also means that those genuine companies are more likely to fail because people don't invest in them. That's not fair on those companies and that's negative for the economy as a whole if real businesses don't get access to investors.

Secondly, scammers have wised up to the fact that 10% or 12% looks 'too good to be true', so they're now actually *reducing* their coupon payments to make them more realistic.

This gives them the advantage of a) selling more bonds because they appear more genuine, and b) making *higher* profit margins. Instead of paying a 12% coupon, they can get away with paying just 6%. So, they make money on both ends – volume and profit!

It's the same reason somebody might pay £10,000 but not £500 for the same Rolex watch. They assume the £500 Rolex must be a fake. Maybe it is, or perhaps you just found a great deal.

I know of companies that in the past have paid as much as 15%, and even 20% to investors who were completely genuine, and investors got back their money in full. I also know of companies that paid 5% and were as rotten as stinking apples.

So, the coupon is a helpful starting point but it's not a reliable indicator.

2. Regulation

A better way to protect yourself is to avoid buying any bond which isn't regulated.

Buying a bond that does not trade on a listed exchange is going to be less closely scrutinised, and the risk of it being a scam therefore increases. If it's not regulated and it turns out to be a scam, then you may not be protected by the Financial Ombudsman Service (FOS) or the Financial Services Compensation Scheme (FSCS).

However, you do no need to be careful about what 'regulated' means.

I don't wish to give all unregulated bonds a bad name because again, there are some which are absolutely genuine. Just because an investment is not regulated, does not automatically disqualify the product from being genuine.

Peer to peer lending and crowd funding schemes are perfect

examples of industries which were unregulated for many years, and therefore regarded as high risk. Whilst some of the companies in this space turned out to be scams there were many which were genuine and made investors a lot of money. The returns were often between 10% and 14% which was great and couldn't be matched in the regulated world.

However, now, this market has moved into the regulated space, it means that the risk of default is much lower, the market is more established and as a result the return to investors has dropped off significantly, around 5% to 8%.

That's the downside to investing in regulated investments; because of the tighter controls, higher operational costs, increased compliance, greater overheads, saturated market conditions, more competition, and smaller margins, companies simply can't pay as much to investors.

So, there is a downside to regulated investments which is a *lower* return on investment. The upside is lower risk and greater protection. Therefore, as an investor, you need to weigh up what is more important for you.

Because most bond investors are looking for something safe and because they don't want to speculate, regulated bonds, even with smaller returns, are generally the best way to go. That said you still need to be careful because regulation comes in different shapes and sizes.

3. Inferior regulation

Even a regulated bond may not give you full protection because that varies from one regulated jurisdiction to another.

For example, some bonds trade on overseas exchanges where the regulation is very 'light touch'. Again, this doesn't mean that all companies trading on those types of exchanges are scams, but it does mean that scammers will generally find it easier to list there with fewer checks.

It also allows scammers to promote their bonds as 'regulated' which could be misleading but technically correct. The bond can have some level of overseas regulatory protection, but it's still not regulated by the UK authorities, which, as a UK investor is all that you should really care about.

It's the same for overseas investors not being protected when they buy UK regulated bonds. The difference is that UK regulation is generally regarded as the gold-standard with the best protection for consumers and retail investors.

You can see how this trick of creating the illusion that the bond is 'regulated' adds another layer of confusion to an already muddy market. The whole game for the scammers is about building credibility in the eyes of the potential investor, and most investors simply won't know about the regulatory intricacies of one exchange over another.

4. SEDOLs and ISIN codes

It used to be the case that unregulated bonds didn't have ISIN and SEDOL codes, which are identification codes for companies listed on the stock exchange.

However over recent years scammers have gone to even greater lengths to disguise themselves as official, genuine bonds and acquiring ISIN and SEDOL codes is one of the boldest moves they have managed to pull off. This allows the bond to be held electronically on nominee accounts rather than in certificated form. The big advantage of nominee holdings is that it means a bond can be invested through a stock ISA, SIPP or normal share dealing account.

That's a massive goal for the scammers because most people hold their wealth in their pensions so, it's much easier to invest, say, £50,000 or £100,000 in a bond using their SIPP, than it is to try and muster £100,000 from cash savings.

Psychologically, it's much easier to press a few buttons on a trading platform than to write a cheque for a hundred thousand pounds.

It also gives clearance for the bond to become transferable via the UK's Clearing System, CREST, and immediately raises its credibility in the eye of the investor. The assumption is always that if it can be invested in a pension or ISA, then it must be legitimate.

If an investment has a recognised identification marker such as an ISIN or SEDOL code, if it can be invested into a pension or stock ISA. If it appears to have a two-way quoted price, how can the average investor be sure if a bond is a scam or genuine?

Answer: they can't.

5. Dealing with regulated firms

Another way to reduce the risk of being scammed is to buy the bond through an FCA regulated brokerage firm. However, as we have seen even this isn't fool proof. That's because you can still buy scam bonds through FCA regulated firms.

However, there is one big benefit of dealing with a regulated firm; you won't have an aggressive sales pitch, any mistruths or deception.

An unregulated firm that's being paid a commission to sell the bond, will promote it with no concern for the investor. A decent, regulated advisor will at least tell you if he smells a rat and if you decide to proceed, he'll encourage you to be sensible in any investment that you make.

If you want to take a higher risk for a smaller part of your total portfolio as a way to diversify, and provided you know all the risks, then at least he can be the voice of reason. That's different to the unregulated firm where there is no concept of proportionality, and no real discussion of the risks.

The regulated broker also has a responsibility to ensure that the investment is suitable for you. So, if you're ninety years old, suffering from dementia and have only £10,000 of your life savings in the bank, he won't encourage you to invest it an unregulated bond. The firm has a duty of care, to you and to do what is in your best interest.

An unregulated firm doesn't have that same level of responsibility.

If a dodgy bond has managed to circumvent the system and has made its way onto a regulated custodian's platform, it's almost impossible to police. Any investor can buy that bond using their online trading portal or by giving an instruction to their broker.

Quite often investors make those decisions because they're being driven to do so, by dodgy IBs or IFAs behind the scenes. An IFA tells their client the name of the bond and telling them to call the stockbroker firm to buy it.

Of course, if the regulated firm is dodgy, as was the case with LCF, then it's a very different story. That's a classic case of the wolf dressed up as a lamb. In this case clearly the brokerage firm is in itself a scam firm.

But that's very unusual.

In most cases regulated brokerage firms are as in the dark as anybody else. The scam bonds are expertly hidden away amongst the genuine bonds, loan notes, collective investment schemes, as well as the other thousands of funds and shares in the marketplace. Unless you actually know exactly what you're looking for, you probably won't find it; it's like searching for a very small needle in a very big haystack.

Professional disguise means easy access

Because scammers have now infiltrated stock exchanges, SIPP providers, custodians, clearing houses, stockbrokerage firms, wealth management firms and regulated advisors, by extension it means you can buy a scam investment anytime and anywhere.

They're now in and amongst all the genuine, regulated investments.

If a dodgy bond has access to a trading platform, you're literally just one click away from losing your money in a scam.

There are tens of thousands of companies listed on the stock exchange, and not all directors of those companies are your friend. Some are them are your enemy, and they're there to take your money.

It may only be a very small percentage, but they're out there. Nobody really knows how many of the bonds, funds and shares currently listed on the various exchanges around the world, are scams, but you only need to be caught once for it to cost you dearly.

Like all scams, they're camouflaged, and the best ones are camouflaged so well they are indistinguishable from the genuine investments. That's why they still sit on those regulated platforms.

But there is still one card that scammers don't hold and that's liquidity.

6. Liquidity and an inability to sell

The general rule is that genuine bonds should be liquid enough to be sold within 30 days. If it can't be sold it is referred to as a 'non-standard' asset.

But liquidity is one of those things that comes and goes because it depends on the number of active buyers and sellers. If there are a lot of market participants, and plenty of buzz, the spread between the buy and sell price will be less and the bond is more likely to be tradeable. In this case, the bond might begin life as a normal, standard asset.

However, that could quickly change if the bond announces a missed coupon or some bad news. Suddenly investors might panic and want to sell their bond, in which case there are no buyers but lots of sellers. The liquidity dries up and now you can't sell, hence the bond becoming a *non*-standard asset.

If it's hard for a professional firm to know if an investment is genuinely tradeable, a retail investor really has their work cut out.

If an unregulated firm or an IB tells you the bond he's recommending is liquid and can be sold at any time, how can you verify this information? You don't hold the bond so, you can't ask for a price from a broker. The only time you will really know if it's tradeable is *after* you have bought it.

Furthermore, bonds are almost always held until maturity, at least by private investors. Professional bond traders take short-term views because they are speculating, but pensioner Bob just wants his money tucked away for five years.

Because Bob doesn't care about selling, he won't even think to ask about the liquidity of his bond. This helps the scammers because they know that if investors don't want to sell, there is little chance of the bond being uncovered as an illiquid, non- standard asset.

You might think that scammers prefer to have tradeable bonds because it's an easier sales pitch and it makes them appear more like genuine bonds. However, scammers want the opposite.

The scammers *don't* want their bonds to be tradeable for two reasons.

Firstly, any sales in the open market would depress the price of the bond which would mean they would have to lower their issuance price for new investors.

Secondly, the scammers only want people to buy from *them*. If Bob pays £10,000 to the scammer to buy a tranche of a bond issue, and John buys another tranche of the same bond say six months later for £10,000, the scammers will receive a total of £20,000.

But if the bond was tradeable, John could buy the bond from Bob and give him the £10,000 instead of giving it to the scammer. This means the scammers only receive £10,000 instead of £20,000.

The scammers want any potential new buyers to only buy from them. That's how they make their money.

At the same time, they still want the bond to *appear* liquid and ideally have a two-way price even if the price is just an illusion and for window-dressing purposes only. Ambiguity around liquidity, fake two-way prices, what's genuine and what's BS, is as confusing for professional firms as it is for retail investors.

Even for regulated firms it's not always clear which bonds are liquid because the price is controlled by the market makers. Just because a price is being quoted, doesn't always translate into the price being tradeable. A market maker may offer a temporary sell price on an illiquid bond, because he has another investor on his book who is keen to buy. So, it's easy enough to sit in the middle and match the trade between the two of them.

He might even do this multiple times completely innocently, which gives the illusion of liquidity, but fundamentally the bond might still be illiquid, untradeable and a scam.

The scammers want their bonds to be tradeable and liquid, or at least *appear* to be, so they don't get flagged by a regulated firm.

The regulatory rules on Non-Standard Assets (NSA) used to be quite relaxed but after the collapse of LCF and numerous other dodgy bonds, the rules are becoming more and more stringent. There is greater responsibility on regulated firms not to allow trades in NSAs and minibonds. This is a very good thing and I'm a strong supporter of the rules becoming tighter.

However, I can't help but think it's a much easier solution. Remember, the regulated firm is right at the *end* of the scammer's conveyor belt; it's the last line of defence.

Before a regulated firm is able to execute a purchase of an unregulated bond for a client, that bond has already been on a very long journey taking at least several months, maybe even years. It's applied for and received a listing on a stock exchange, it's been issued with an ISIN or SEDOL code, it's been approved so it can be purchased through a SIPP or an ISA, it's passed numerous due diligence checks by the custodian, and it's finally been verified so it can be executed on the trading platform.

Oh yes, I nearly forgot, it's also been approved by multiple accountants, auditors, legal advisors, compliance firms, and business consultants.

With all of those checks by a long list of professional firms, you'd have hoped that at least one of them could have identified the scam. But instead, the scam just gets rubber stamped and passed onto the next firm along the conveyor belt. Now it's the next firm's problem.

It's like allowing a terrorist to pass through all of the airport's security checks and then telling the flight attendant that it's their job to stop the plane being blown up at thirty thousand feet.

So, when can an investor sell?

Once you have invested in something, the scammers will work very hard to stop you from getting your money back. That means they'll make it extremely difficult for you to sell your investment.

However, in the case of very persistent and loud investors who could potentially bring unwanted attention to the bond, the scammers are likely to give in. Rather than run the risk of one vocal investor going to the media, write to his local MP, or telephone the regulator and report his complaint, the scammers would rather pay back his investment.

They don't want the bad publicity, especially early on in the scam. You can call it 'hush' money and returning £10,000 to somebody is a pretty good ROI (Return on Investment) if you're planning to raise a further £100 million.

The investor is happy that he got his money back and becomes very quiet. He doesn't make any more noise and the scammers continue their work without worrying about the authorities becoming alerted to the situation.

An impossible nut to crack?

As you can see this is a very difficult scam to stop.

With the millions of pounds involved, the level of complexity and detail, the overseas jurisdictions, the level of penetration in the regulated markets, the ability to invest in pensions and ISAs, the ISIN and SEDOL codes, the ability to trade on clearing houses, the ability to transfer on CREST...when you put it all together the bond scam is quite a formidable insider trading secret.

You'd be forgiven for thinking there couldn't possibly be anything more unforgiving.

But here we are, at the very end of this book.

It won't have escaped your attention there is still one final insider trading secret.

This next scam is the actually closely connected to the bond scam except it's much worse.

I hope you have enjoyed this book so far and that it's opened your eyes to what really goes on. But for this next chapter, you may want to close your eyes again. You may want to stop reading now.

Because what I'm about to share with you is not for the faint-hearted.

So, turn away now, maybe have a break for a few days and pick up this book once you're mentally prepared. Or just put it down forever and be happy that you've learned about twelve insider trading secrets.

Because what's coming next really will blow your mind.

TIP 1 –
Discretionary Fund Manager (DFM)

There are probably not many financial investments you can think of that could possibly be worse than an elderly pensioner losing his life savings in a bond scam.

But what I'm about to share with you is exactly that.

That's because for a bond scam to take effect, to hurt somebody, it requires an individual to make an investment. It doesn't matter whether it's regulated or unregulated, listed or unlisted, liquid or illiquid. In all cases, the scammers can only snare a victim if that person is willing to have a telephone conversation, fill in some forms, and send money.

Even if the investment is paper-free and available through a trading platform it still requires a conversation with the broker, a discussion about the investment, the pros and cons, some due diligence and only after all of that, can the trade be executed.

There's a process, which means the investor *must* be involved.

Even with the boiler room scam where the victim is at home minding his own business and not actively looking for investments, he must still engage with the scammer at some point. He still needs to have a telephone conversation, give his credit card details, wire a bank transfer, or post a share certificate. Something has to physically happen, an event must take place, for the scammer to make money.

That's why this last insider trading secret is the worst of all. It's the only one where no action needs to be taken by the investor.

Investors are quite literally being scammed in their sleep and they have no idea.

Wide-spread impact

This insider trading secret is also far more dangerous than the others because it's one of the most widespread as well as one of the least well-known.

Unlike many of the other scams which are now in mature markets, this one remains in a very immature market and that means plenty of growth opportunities. It's because there is a massive barrier to entry, which stops an unlimited number of potential scammers from flooding the market. Only a very few, select number of scammers are allowed into this game and they have to pass several tests to get in; they're all professional scammers who have been in the game for a long time, working up the ranks to where they are today.

They don't want amateur scammers to come in and ruin the party; right now there are no weak links in the chain. It's the best of the best, the Navy Seals, the SAS of the scam world.

The vast majority of people who work in the City don't know what's going on in the cubicles right next to them.

This scam involves a deep underground movement at the very highest level, across a sprawling, complex labyrinth of highly connected, intelligent financials. This is not your average pink diamond scammer cold calling a vulnerable, old granny or a twenty-year-old Essex kid flogging car park spaces in Liverpool's shopping centre.

This is at the highest level and totally exclusive; strictly VIP and by invitation only.

It's also not a single scam but multiple, multi-layered scams involving numerous individuals and organisations all working together in pre-defined key roles.

Between these high-powered professionals, hundreds of millions of pounds, even billions of pounds, are exchanging hands every year. Yes, that's correct. Let me say that again, *billions* of pounds.

It could be even more, because nobody knows the true numbers. Nobody knows the full picture.

There are so many layers, so many people involved, and so many cogs to this machinery that only an insider, deep in the trenches, would be able to bring the system down.

The problem is that if the scam was ever brought down, it could lead to mass panic on the streets. The financial compensation claims that would ensue could single-handedly bring down some of the biggest financial firms in the UK. There would be investment firms, market makers, and custodians who would disappear and go bust overnight if the true level of corruption was uncovered.

The government couldn't allow to that happen. There would

have to be interventions to bailout the financial institutions caught up in the dirty of all of this. Otherwise, there would be an entire generation of pensioners literally homeless and penniless on the streets.

If there was ever going to be an uprising, mass violent protests, and a full-blown civil revolution in this country, I'd put my money on it being because of the financial system. The UK is built on finance more than any other developed country in the world.

It would be like 2008 all over again. Big hedge funds would go out of business and billions of pounds would be wiped off the stock market.

The DFM scam involves a plethora of companies, directors, auditors, accountants, researchers, influencers, celebrities, introducers, and investment managers all working together with one objective – to take your money. It involves regulated companies, approved persons, celebrated hedge fund managers and reputable financial advisors all collaborating in a carefully constructed web of deceit designed to rip you off.

So many people, so many mouths to feed – this is where it all comes together – it's the cesspit of all cesspits. It's the top of the tree, the highest point of the mountain, the pinnacle of corruption.

Welcome to the financial octagon, where professional conmen congregate and conspire together to steal your money.

Remember, here in the UK, we don't have a manufacturing sector or any industrial might, we don't have a retail industry or information technology, we're not even rich in commodities or oil. We don't have any of that.

But what we do have is the most powerful financial services industry in the world. However, that comes at a cost; it means we are dependent on this one area.

That's a problem because the financial services industry isn't real, it's made up. It looks real and it feels real, but it's not. We're all living off hot air and fantasy, as the clock is about to strike midnight.

World's biggest Ponzi scheme

When people finally wake up to what's really been going on, there will be an uprising. The people just wouldn't accept it anymore and they would demand change. That's when governments are overthrown. It's when the people stand up and fight back.

The system would be so shaken up, it would spell the end of the current system and we'd have to create a new one, a fairer one.

The powers that be are already hell-bent on creating that new system; the World Economic Forum calls it 'the Great Reset'. But don't be fooled, this isn't in our interest.

Look at what happened during Covid, with restrictions on travel, lockdowns and mandatory vaccinations that didn't work. How about all of the new draconian laws that were introduced to stop freedom of speech, protests that served the interest of the powerful few but not the many. Look at how we saw the biggest transfer of wealth from the poor to the rich in living history.

Just see how the story on climate change was and is exploited, how it's being used to turn people against each other. See the new woke culture, which is driving a liberal, left-wing ideology that refuses to engage in sensible dialogue.

How was it possible that after a thousand years of using hard currency, we were able to move from paper notes and coins over to digital currency in the blink of an eye?.

All in the name of 'our safety' apparently.

It's all a clever indoctrination, with mainstream media controlling the narrative, it's all part of the bigger plan. None of these changes are in our best interest. It's always about the interests of powerful elite, it's about controlling the populous and keeping society enslaved.

The financial system is just an extension of all of the above. It sounds incredulous but it's not really.

Remember, the entire financial system is actually a scam, it's built on a pack of lies. The entire Fiat currency system, the money that we spend, the money that we earn, it's all worthless.

The money in your pocket is worth less than the paper it's printed on. It has absolutely zero intrinsic value because it's just one massive Ponzi scheme.

It's been like that since 1971 when the United States left the gold standard. Up until then you could convert your dollars into gold, so you knew that your cash was always worth something.

Now it's worth nothing.

In recent years, central banks have been only too happy to recklessly print trillions of dollars, euros, pounds and yen. As a consequence, we're now living in a time of sky-rocketing inflation. The banks could only do that because the paper they were printing is not backed by anything, it's completely worthless.

So, the system is already technically bankrupt, the system is already broken.

The only reason it still works is because only 1% of people know that it's a Ponzi scheme, and 99% of people are too busy following their local football team. Another way to control the population is through sport and building alliances. Give the poor something to think about, to channel their energies and frustrations through.

Don't let them see what's really happening.

It's the same with the DFM scam. Nobody knows that it's happening, least of all to them.

Welcome to insider trading secret number one – the most devastating of them all – it is like no other, and it wins hands down to take pole position.

Strap yourselves in for this final chapter.

DFM

As I've done throughout this book, I'm not going to simplify things because clearly there's no value in learning the technical elements of portfolio management. But I will tell you everything you need to know about this scam and how it works.

Discretionary Fund Management (DFM) is a form of professional portfolio management where all the buy and sell decisions of what goes into a fund are made at the *discretion* of the investment manager. This means that you, (the client), are not consulted; the fund manager can invest your money into whatever he or she deems suitable for that fund.

Fund managers make their money by charging an annual fee on the value of the funds they manage. For example, a typical fund might charge a 1% Annual Management Charge (AMC). If there is £10 million in a fund, the fund manager receives £100,000 for the year, and so on.

In other words, the fund charges a small, fixed percentage of the amount of money it manages, and a proportion of that fee is paid to the fund manager. For the sake of simplicity let's assume for now that the fund manager receives all of that fee.

This business model is fine and dandy if the fund manager has a well-established fund with a decent amount of money in it, let's say, £100 million. This means the fund manager will earn a million pounds to manage that fund.

But what happens if you are not an established fund manager?

What if the fund manager has only, say £10 million in the fund? This means that the fund manager earns only £100,000, so he's going to be jealous of the guys running the bigger funds.

Equally the £10 million fund manager who earns £1 million a year will be envious of the guy who runs that £1 billion fund and earns £10 million a year.

It's all about levels and each fund manager is of course trying to become the top dog.

Now, the only way for a fund manager to earn more money is either to charge a higher annual fee or to increase the Assets Under Management (AUM).

Neither of these options is easy. If you're a fund manager, simply waking up one day and deciding to increase the fee you're going to charge your clients is not a smart move. Clients will simply move their money to a more competitively price fund.

But trying to attract more investors organically is also very difficult. The fund manager has to beat the market consistently for several years for his fund to attract more funds. At the same time, he has to compete with the growing number of fund managers around him who are all trying to do the same thing.

Clearly, it's a tough gig to stay at the top of this game. That's why a new short-cut has been found.

This is the *third* way in which fund managers can massively boost their earnings.

This is the DFM scam.

Bond scammers and DFMs

In the last chapter I explained how the bond scammers

operated, mainly in unregulated markets but that some of the more sophisticated ones had been able to penetrate the less tightly regulated overseas stock exchanges.

But I intentionally left something out, which will shock you.

Bond scammers have also managed to infiltrate the *main, regulated* markets. This isn't about an illiquid, unregulated bond, that has two dodgy market makers, trading somewhere on a tiny, light-touch regulated stock exchange in Timbuktu.

This is about internationally recognised, globally listed funds, that are traded on the biggest stock exchanges in the world.

This means nobody is safe from this scam.

The most sophisticated bond scammers are now working directly with some of the most senior, reputable fund managers in the UK, US, Europe, and Japan.

It's completely covert, and hidden from the public eye, but it's happening.

On the surface it may appear to be an unlikely alliance. Why would a reputable investment firm or high-ranking, credible fund manager wants to be associated with a bond scammer? But actually, it's a match made in heaven.

You see, the scammers want to raise money for their dodgy bonds but are limited to working with unregulated sales floors. That's becoming more and more difficult as the net is closing in on the unregulated market. Many investors are wary of unregulated sales floors and mini bonds are already beginning to get the reputation of being scams.

With the collapse of LCF and other similar high-profile companies, as well as the ever-tightening regulations around mini bonds, it's going to be harder and harder for scams to generate the kind of revenue they once did.

Regulated firms, market makers, custodians, pension funds, and investment advisors are also now expected to be ever more diligent on trying to identify dodgy bonds, stopping them getting through the system. Pension funds are now obliged to actively seek out dodgy bonds and flag them to the authorities, so they can be removed from the system.

Scammers are therefore quickly losing access to the single most profitable route to raise capital, which are pensions.

SIPP providers and pension funds hold the gateway for scammers to reach millions of UK investors by allowing them to package their mini bonds through their pension schemes. But they're starting to feel the heat.

Custodians are also having to pay much closer attention. Once upon a time not so long ago, most custodians didn't really care about what was being traded on their platforms. Because they weren't directly involved in the trades, it was easy to turn a blind eye.

But not anymore; now they're guilty by association. They have a regulatory duty to police what types of investments are being traded, particularly Non-Standard Assets, which captures mini bonds.

This was going to be a massive problem for the scammers, until DFMs stepped in.

A click of a button

The problem with a dodgy bond, is that it's visible and in open view to everybody. The custodian can see it, the market makers can see it, and the investment managers can see it.

They can all see that this bond doesn't quite look like the others. There are no live trades being executed, the price doesn't move, it's listed on some far away exchange in Mongolia that nobody has heard of, and it's paying a 15% coupon which seems unrealistic.

That should be enough to set the alarm bells ringing.

But what if the bond wasn't visible at all?. What if it was hidden away at the bottom of a portfolio so that nobody could see it?

What if that portfolio wasn't just any portfolio but one with massive blue-chip companies in it, like Tesco or Facebook, or some international global funds, or maybe super low risk UK gilts or US treasuries?

Hidden underneath all of these legitimate investments, the bond is barely visible. It's there somewhere but nobody can see it because it's surrounded by genuine investments. It can't be detected.

But that's not all.

Not only is the bond now completely hidden away from prying

eyes, the scammers also don't need their massive offices. They don't need to market, advertise or promote their bond. They don't need unregulated sales floors to sell to thousands of their clients.

They just need ONE dodgy fund manager.

A fund manager can do the same job more effectively than hundreds of salespeople across London with just a single click of a button.

Instead of a bond scammer dealing with dozens of IBs and unregulated floors, with thousands of individual client application forms, thousands of ID documents, thousands of risk warnings, thousands of telephone calls, and thousands of individual trades to settle, it is; all replaced with one single transaction.

One click. That's powerful.

A hedge fund manager who controls a fund of £100 million, could invest 5%, 10%, even up to 20% of his fund (£10 million) into 'speculative' investments depending on the type and risk rating of the fund.

The fund manager would of course need to justify his investment decision by having conducted an appropriate level of due diligence on the bonds that he is buying. He would also have to document his research and analysis.

But that's not difficult; the sophisticated bond scammers already have their prospectus, the bullish analyst reports, the positive press coverage, the website, the audited company accounts, the bank accounts, the nominated advisors, they ISIN and SEDOL codes and, the listed exchange information. They have it all.

What they didn't have was the ability to raise £10 million in the blink of an eye. They didn't have the ability to partner with one fund manager and a few of his close pals, to do a single trade. But now they do.

The bond company can raise £10 million without any questions or headaches. No pressurised pitches to little old grannies and no complaints, no kickbacks, no negative online reviews, and no regulators breathing down their necks.

Instead of cold-calling tens of thousands of people out of Yellow Pages and spending several years trying to raise a few million pounds, the fund performs the same operation in just a few seconds. No fuss, no complaints. Just lots of cash.

Of course, the vast majority of fund managers are not involved in this game. They do their job properly, they work hard, and they get paid a shed load of money. They already earn millions of pounds a year, and they don't want to jeopardise that by trying a short cut.

But there are a few who think they're too smart, they think they won't get caught. They're not just the independent fund managers who you have never heard of. They are also some of the big players, that operate in the mainstream market, that work for the big company names, the big celebrity fund managers.

As I've said since time immemorial, big isn't always best. Big is just big.

These greedy DFM buffoons like the money and they like the challenge even more. When they get to that level of wealth and status, some of them don't just play God, they think they are God.

Due diligence

Most DFMs are already making big money so, in order to be involved in dodgy bonds it needs to make financial sense, which means a few things must happen.

Firstly, the scammers must make their bonds 'investable'. They need to be squeaky clean before the DFM does their due diligence. If something erroneous is uncovered in the diligence process, it's game over. The scammers can't go back and undo what has been found. That's because the DFM has to report what he and his due diligence team has found.

There may also be restrictions on the types of bonds that a DFM can invest in. Many mainstream funds are restricted to only investing in bonds that are listed on a *Recognised Investment Exchange* (RIE). This means that scammers have to put in more groundwork at the start to get their bonds listed in the right places. That takes time, effort and money but it's a necessary requirement.

The bond investment will also need the approval of several people, not just the main DFM. There will be a team of people to support the main fund manager, and quite often an entire investment committee, especially with the larger funds.

Not everybody on the committee can know what's going on, but the senior guys are in on the scam. They know the truth about those 'speculative' investments they're investing in.

The guys further down the food chain don't need to know. They add no value to the process, and it just means more mouths to feed. Besides, a low-grade analyst, a graduate intern or a part-time researcher is far more likely to spill the beans than a senior DFM. Remember, loose lips sink ships.

The due diligence must pass and that's only possible if the scammers have done their job correctly. They need to make sure there is enough 'ammunition' for the DFM and his team to give the investment a green light so they can invest.

Of course, there's always a limit. There's only so much the scammer can do to disguise his turd to resemble chocolate ice-cream.

How well the disguise is, will determine the fee the DFM will expect to pay.

Where the due diligence is light, and there is more turd than ice-cream, this increases the risk to the DFM which therefore requires higher compensation.

High quality turds

Bonds sold through DFMs are quite different to those sold through IBs on unregulated floors. That's because unregulated floors have nothing to lose in offering their clients the lowest grade bonds. They want the *worst* bonds because they pay out the biggest commission, usually between 40% and

50%, sometimes even more.

This is the worst quality of bond you can get. It has no company history, it has no track record, no ISIN codes, no listed exchanges, it's literally straight out of the cheap scam box.

However, the hedge funds can't play that game and need to invest in much higher-grade products. They're still scams but they're more sophisticated scams; they're high-quality turds.

This costs scammers more money so, the margins are lower for the DFM, maybe 20% to 30%. But that's still massive for a fund manager.

Imagine a fund manager earning 30% on funds invested - that's thirty times what he is currently paid. It's like thirty years of 1% annual fees wrapped up in that single trade!

The formula is always the same for every scam.

A dodgy bond, (or any other scam product), which is easier to sell, has a better story and looks more legitimate but, will take more time and more money initially for the scammers to set up. However, it will pay-off more handsomely in the long run. The margins are lower, but the volume is higher.

A bond which resembles a pile of dog poo is easier and cheaper to set up but much harder to sell. It increases the risk which means fewer DFMs will touch it and those who do, will demand a much bigger slice of the profit pie. That extra slice is required because of the increased risk of the DFM coming under a lot of pressure if his fund is ever investigated.

The DFM will also have to fight internal resistance from his peers and a few raised eyebrows from his colleagues, as well as compliance. He doesn't want that, but he's willing to take on the extra heat provided he's paid extra to do so.

Commissions paid by the scammer will also be based on the size and credibility of the fund and the reputation of the DFM. A big celebrity fund manager will command big celebrity money.

Business negotiation

Like all business deals there are negotiations, but with DFMs, they take place behind (very) closed doors. If a DFM is reasonably well established and runs, say, a £300 million fund, he could conceivably hide £30 million (10%) without raising too much suspicion. So, he gives £30 million in cash to the scammers which is huge. Even withstanding the extra costs involved in getting it 'DFM ready' , scammers make millions of pounds, from which they could pay up to third to the DFM, so let's say, £10 million to the DFM. Not bad.

A smaller fund of say £50 million fund might 'only' invest £5 million or £10 million into a scam bond to avoid inspection.

The negotiation is a lot of back and forth to agree terms but eventually, it leads to a 'verbal contract', there is no paperwork. In fact, there are no notes, no marks and, no records. There are no telephone calls, no emails, not even encrypted WhatsApp messages; it's all done on trust and a handshake. There can be no audit trail.

If there is any non-verbal communication it's usually conducted in pre-agreed coded language sent electronically from unregistered mobile devices, often through third parties, via the introducers who sit in the middle.

Whilst no paperwork has its obvious benefits it does put the DFM at risk from the possibility of non-payment. After the fund invests in the dodgy bond, and the trade settles, the scammer receives money into his company bank account and is free to walk away. But that very rarely happens.

That's because firstly, the DFM typically only starts off with a small investment. They test the waters to ensure their commission flows trouble-free to their offshore Cayman Island bank account.

Secondly, it's because the relationship is worth too much. A well-connected DFM is the single person who holds the keys to the unlimited printing of money, because he is the equivalent of a thousand salespeople. It's also probably taken months if not years of courting and nurturing to become part of his trusted circle.

That would have meant high-level networking, including joining private members clubs, exclusive black-tie dos, sporting shows, and charity events. That's a lot of schmoozing and brown-nosing to just throw away.

The alternative to working directly with the DFM, is for the scammer to liaise through an 'introducer', a middleman. That's often the case because it's the introducers who know how to schmooze better than anybody else. They've got the corporate boxes at Wembley football stadium, the back-stage Formula

1 passes at Silverstone and the front row Centre Court tickets at Wimbledon.

It's their full-time job to hang around expensive venues and make contact with powerful people in the financial world, specifically DFMs.

The IBs are integral to the process because they perform the critical role of giving anonymity and protection to both sides; to the scammer and the DFM. That, in itself is worth a lot of money.

Financial advisors

This scam wouldn't be complete without an appearance from our financial advisor friends. Of course, they've featured so conclusively in this book, that they would have to make an appearance in this final chapter.

The Independent Financial Advisors (IFA) is the best way to connect DFMs to bond scammers.

Whilst bond scammers will work with a number of Introducer Brokers (IBs) in the city, the IBs may not have direct access to the DFMs. Instead, the IBs will find it much easier to reach out to IFAs, thus creating two intermediary links between the scammers and the DFMs.

The IFAs are already in the financial world, rubbing shoulders with various investment firms and fund managers. They already know the DFMs who play this game and those who don't.

But that's not all. They also have hundreds of clients; in

some cases tens of millions of pounds under their control. The dodgy IFAs are already up to their necks in scam deals, they're already in bed with different wealth managers, stockbrokers and hedge funds. But, they want more scam bonds and equities, they need more 'stock' to fill their clients' stockings with.

It's much easier for an IFA to promote a new 'product' because they already have the contacts and infrastructure in place.

The IFAs are already in the same market as the DFM, they understand the game, and they speak the same language.

The scammers understand their own bond, but they don't know about the compliance and regulatory aspect. They don't have the contacts.

So, there's a chain. The bond scammers work with the IB, the IB works with the IFA, and the IFA works with the DFM. That's a lot of acronyms.

There are literally hundreds of financial advisors up and down the country who serve as the bridge between bond, scammers and DFMs.

In a market where nobody trusts anybody, and established relationships are worth their weight in gold the IFAs and IBs play critical roles as middlemen, but the IFAs play the most important role.

Whilst extra middlemen dilute the money to be made, as there are more mouths to feed, the DFM likes the extra protection because he is not dealing directly with the bond scammers, or even the IBs. But money is never a problem because there's so much of it to go around.

In fact, some established IFAs get paid not once, but twice.

Firstly, an IFA gets money from the IB for an introduction to the DFM. The IB, of course gets money from the bond scammers to pay that fee.

Secondly, the IFA can also get money from the DFM by referring his own clients into the DFM's fund.

Of course, every deal has its nuances and intricacies; no deal is off the table.

For example, a smart IFA could negotiate a third fee *from* the DFM to give him access to the bond. Dodgy DFMs need dodgy stock. They want new scams to come to the market in which they can invest their funds because they can't keep adding more and more into the same old names. That would create suspicion.

Therefore, IFAs who have access to 'new bonds' are worth a lot of money to the DFMs.

This means that the IFA makes money from the DFM for giving him access to the bond, he gets another fee for clients and funds that he refers to the DFM to invest in this bond, and he gets another fee from the bond scammer via the IB.

The IB will play his tricks, too, as will the bond scammer and the DFM.

It's a pool of sharks all trying to out-manoeuvre each other and they're all jostling for position, control and money.

Each have their own cards to play at the poker table. Some win big, some win small, but they all win. The only person who loses is you, the investor.

Making money on the AUM

IFAs work not only with DFMs who run specific funds, but also with general wealth managers who build their own 'bespoke' fund. Wealth managers can create whatever type of fund they want to; a speculative fund, adventurous fund, AIM fund, alternative fund, overseas fund or a higher risk fund.

So, when they're approached by dodgy IFAs, it's easy to create a new fund and throw some of those scam investments in there.

In this case, the wealth managers won't necessarily charge anything for putting dodgy bonds into their portfolio because their reward is an overnight and rapid increase in their AUM.

In this case, an IFA goes to a struggling wealth manager and says, "*Look, I have £50million of client money and I'll give you all of it on the condition you allow me to choose where 10% of it is invested.*"

If the wealth manager only manages a fund, of say, £25 million, he goes from £25 million to £75 million; he literally *triples* the size of his fund overnight. If it's only 10%, the DFM might take the view the risk of getting caught is low.

Of course, the DFM isn't stupid. He knows that 10% of

what he's being told to invest in is some 'alternative' or 'non-traditional' investments, aka a dodgy bond the IFA is making money on from the back end.

But without the IFA the wealth manager has nothing so either he takes the deal and makes an easy £500,000 (1% of £50m) or he gets nothing.

That deal might even suit him better because now he hasn't got the heat of an audit trail that leads back to him if things go wrong. Perhaps he doesn't want to mess around with the whole Cayman Island thing in any case or get back-handed payments. His risk is to explain how he went from £25 million to £75 million, but that's not difficult; he just says that an IFA approached him and was looking for a home for his clients.

Of course, he still bears the risk of buying the dodgy bonds in his portfolio, but he can put that down to stupidity, a bad investment decision. But if he gets caught receiving a payment into an offshore bank account from the scammers, that's a whole, different story.

If he's been building his fund for, say 10 years and so, has only reached £25 million, he could either spend another twenty years adding another £50 million or he could take the IFA's offer and turn twenty years of future hard graft into twenty days on the back of a handshake.

That's why the regulators regularly review the AUM of hedge funds and wealth managers to identify, if any, fund suddenly experiences an exceptional jump in their fund value from one year to the next.

The wealth manager counters this either by understating his true numbers on his regulatory returns, or by justifying a large jump in AUM, with increased marketing or even the takeover of another company that already has clients on their book. The IFA's business including his book of clients is basically bought out by the wealth manager.

The wealth manager could also fly under the radar by introducing the IFA clients *gradually* over a period of time. This might take a few years so isn't ideal but it's a lower risk strategy.

Another option is simply to set up a new fund, a new spin-off business, or even a new regulatory licence. An established fund manager can put a new fund together relatively quickly and sign up all the new IFA clients straight into that vehicle without raising suspicion.

They could even do trade shows and online marketing to launch a new fund. They then get all the clients to sign up at that show, either in person or online as if they are new investors. A single landing page with a new 'opt-in' makes it appear like it's not a referral but that the clients are making a new enquiry. New funds are expected to have 'pent up' demand from investors who want to buy on the first day of trading so, it could potentially add tens of millions of pounds at inception.

There are lots of different ways to get funds under management.

You don't even need to say 'yes please'

This scam is so devastating because the people who invest in the funds, have no idea what they're buying into. There's no consent, no discussion, no paperwork signed and, no risk assessment.

As an investor, you wouldn't expect a high profile, reputable fund manager to be performing dodgy dealings behind your back. When you put your money into a particular fund it was on the understanding that the DFM managing that fund would buy investments that he believed would make money. You didn't give consent to the DFM intentionally buying things which he knew were worthless but, that's exactly what is happening.

The fund manager has full discretion of what goes in and out of his fund.

Therefore, you, the investor, are not scammed once, or twice, but maybe three times, or ten times, or twenty times. For as long as you are in that fund, the DFM can do what the hell he wants, and you have no knowledge or control over it.

You don't even get to see any details about the investment. This means you can't do any due diligence or research on those companies. It's a complete unknown entity and yet you're investing your pension and life savings into it.

The fund simply lays out a risk rating, a broad overview of the types of investments, and the overall composition. The individual investments are down to him, not you.

That's pure genius, if you want to be a DFM scammer.

It's unlike all of the other scams where the client has to be offered the product and then has to decide on whether to invest. If the client suspects something is not right, that it perhaps looks a little dodgy, that the directors behind the company are a little shady, that the figures don't add up, or he spots anything remotely suspect, he simply walks away from the investment. That's it.

If he did decide to invest, he gets to choose how much he commits based on how risky he thinks it is. In other words, he's in control.

On the other hand, a DFM invests what he wants, when he wants, and how much he wants.

The investor has zero control.

Monitoring

The DFM scam also severely impacts the investor's inability to *monitor* their position. If I invest in a dodgy bond, I can see the performance clearly and without interruption. I can see the value of my investment, I can see the price, I can see the coupons being paid and critically, I can single out that one investment from the others in my share portfolio. I can keep an eye on it, especially if I'm a little dubious about it.

In a fund, I can't do that.

The ability to monitor investments *individually* is critical and the DFM scam prevents that.

A hedge fund is a type of Collective Investment Scheme (CIS) so, the money from investors is simply pooled together into a great big, melting pot of shares, funds and bonds. You throw your money into a great big mixer and take your chances.

You can't monitor, you can't assess, and you can't control. Just what the scammers were praying for.

Multiple bonds

Bonds are great fee generators for DFMs but there are restrictions in dealing with single entities.

It would be quite reckless for a DFM to lump, say, more than 10% of his fund into a single bond; even 5% is probably too high. What would be far better is to split 10% across maybe four or five bonds, giving a weighting of around 2% per bond.

Diversification is important from a compliance perspective. It looks as though the portfolio is being diversified to reduce risk for the investor, but actually the benefit is to the DFM.

It means less focus is brought on a single investment. If a DFM invests 10% into a single bond it will get attention but if he packages several 'alternative bonds' into a single investment of 10%, then it's less scrutinised. In fact, he could even invest 20% or 30% of the total fund into dodgy bonds, depending on the risk rating of the fund.

If the fund is marketed as a speculative fund in 'alternative' investments, and it already states this would include unregulated investments, then in theory, a DFM could invest 100% of his fund into dodgy bonds. That would be a very aggressive investment move and unlikely because there's a good chance the whole thing would just collapse and trigger an investigation.

What's more likely is that a fund would be diversified into

several different, unrelated scam investments. Each of those investments will be added to the portfolio at different times so they appear unrelated. They will also be chosen with different maturity dates so they fail at different times.

They would also be in different sectors, industries, geographical locations, with different histories, and of course, there must be absolutely no connection between the directors of each company.

That's why IFAs are so useful; an IB who works exclusively for one scam company is limited to bringing just that one investment to the table, but a dodgy IFA will have access to multiple IBs who each have access to their own unrelated, scam products.

Dodgy equities

Diversification doesn't stop with bonds. It also takes place across other asset classes, including equities.

Remember, the underlying *company* is a scam, it's not the investment vehicle. In other words, a 'bond' is not the problem, it's the *company* issuing the bond that is the problem.

The scam company simply chooses the vehicle that best suits their goal of maximum money extraction. Some scammers use bonds, others use equities, and the professional scammers often use both.

DFMs often invest in dodgy equities which is good because it gives them the opportunity to appear to be diversifying again. Unsurprisingly, these equities are the typical, low value, lightly regulated, illiquid penny shares we talked about in previous chapters. They have a huge spread and to put it bluntly nobody wants them (except Dodgy Dave, the fund manager).

The equity scam works in the same way as the bond scam. Instead of issuing shares through a placing or principal dealing and hiring multiple brokerage firms to sell stock to their clients, they can do a single deal with a DFM.

Just like with bonds, it's quick, easy, and highly profitable. There's no fuss.

The DFM snaps up these obscure little penny shares and puts them into his fund as part of his 'speculative' portfolio. Those particular shares are not purchased through the open market but, instead, directly from a market maker who is holding those shares on his trading book (having previously bought them from the directors of the dodgy company).

It's like the kids' game, 'Pass the Parcel', except nobody wants the music to stop when they're holding it. That honour is bestowed on the end investor. The game is played like this:

The directors of the scam company 'sell' shares to a friendly, scam market maker. The DFM rings the market maker and says he's looking for shares in company ABC. Wow, would you believe it, the market maker has some of those very shares on his trading book, what a coincidence.

The market makers know the DFM is going to buy the shares so, there's no risk to him buying them from the company directors. The market maker makes money with the spread, plus he receives a big, fat, brown paper envelope the following day from the IB who set up the deal, when he's out for lunch at his favourite City restaurant.

So, the directors offload their worthless shares and get paid from the market maker. The DFM buys those shares from the market maker and the market maker gets his money back plus a profit on the spread and an envelope. The DFM gets paid through the back door via an IB by the company directors, and you my friend, are now the proud owner of a big pile of dog poo that sits proudly in your pension.

Everybody wins again, except you.

Optimal diversification

The trick for the DFM is to get the right balance between dodgy and legitimate investments, because this is what helps with the disguise.

The dodgy investments pay out massive back-handed commissions to the DFM, but they also increase the risk, whilst the legitimate stuff pays no commission (except for the annual management fee) but means significantly less risk to the fund and the DFM.

As you'd expect with the human emotions of greed and fear, some DFMs find it difficult to strike the right balance. Some become too greedy and that's when things go wrong for them. But most fly well under the radar and get away with this unchallenged. They've been doing it for years.

They are now the real experts in hiding their scam investments in and amongst other well-known shares and funds. The fund gives the impression to its investors that everything is legitimate.

If 90% of a fund is held in world-recognised indices like the S&P500 Index, in triple AAA rated government bonds like UK gilts and US treasuries, in some of the world's biggest investment and unit trusts, and in some of the most profitable companies on the planet, like Amazon and Apple, it's really not that difficult to hide a few dodgy bonds and illiquid penny shares right at the bottom where nobody is paying any attention.

The 5% or 10% speculative part of the portfolio generally doesn't raise any red flags and if investors don't make a noise, the regulators are less likely to investigate. In other words when the scam bonds and equities eventually go bust (which they always do in the end), and provided the rest of the fund has done well enough to cover the loss, no alarm bells will need to ring.

It's part of the risk game and because the 10% is covered nine times over by the 90% of genuine investments, it's often completely missed.

Think about it; if a fund made a 10% profit in one year but lost 2% because some of its speculative investments and went bust, investors would still make 8% profit. Do you think those investors would complain? Would you complain?

No, of course not – because you won't see the 2% that disappeared.

All you get to see is the total return at the end of the year of the fund which was 8%. You could dive into the numbers and see which investments did well and which didn't do so well but most people won't care about that. They only want to know how much money *they* made.

They don't even care if they could have made 10% but only made 8%.

Coulda, shoulda, woulda... – it's irrelevant.

Investors just think, "*The fund manager will make some good investments and some poor investments but overall, I'm just interested in how much money I make...if he makes me 8% profit, I don't care how he makes it, I'm happy with that.*"

Nobody cares about the 2%, and here's the thing. Even if somebody did look at the 2%, and see those companies went bust, so what?

Companies go bust all of the time and that's what happened here. Investors already knew that 10% of the fund was going to be invested in highly speculative, unregulated, alternative investments and they were happy with that risk.

Because the bonds and companies are going bust at different times the impact is spread over a number of years. DFMs can even disguise things further by adding a few genuine, high-risk bonds and penny shares. They're not scams and so are less likely to go bust. So, now it balances out the scam investments that are disappearing.

We come back to the same problem of knowing what is true and what is fake.

Because let's remember this: every day, somewhere on the global stock market, there will be at least one genuine, company that goes bust. They're not scams, there were no commission kickbacks and no brown, paper envelopes. They just failed, like so many small businesses do, and it's not just small businesses.

Over the years, there have been many big companies that have failed, from Northern Rock to Carillion, from Debenhams to NMC Health, and from Toys R Us to Blockbuster.

So, who's to say that a DFM was investing in a scam company or if he actually invested in a genuine company and just got unlucky?

Total fund performance

Because investors rarely analyse the individual components of the funds they buy, and they only care about how much money they make, the question is, 'Does it really matters if a DFM is doing something dodgy?'.

I mean, if you still make 8% profit, who cares if the DFM is feathering his own nest, right?

Even when individual shares or funds fail completely, it's only the overall portfolio that really matters to most people. There is no incentive for investors to dive deep down the rabbit hole and investigate every investment within the fund.

It would be counter productive, time-consuming and unnecessary. The whole reason that investors buy a fund is for a fund manager to do the hard work of analysis and research for them. That's what they're paying their DFM for!

Should an investor even care if their DFM is buying scam investments? If he's still making 8% profit and he's happy with that, does it even matter that the DFM is doing some dodgy dealings?

What if another DFM wasn't doing any dodgy dealings but was only making 6%, which fund would you prefer? Would you go for the 8% dodgy fund?

Perhaps you might think the 8% DFM deserves to earn extra money from his back, handed deals because he's outperforming on the rest of his investments?

Is that a sensible position to assume? Sounds almost rationale but the answer is definitely not.

No, no and no again. I'll explain why.

Why you *should* care

There are two reasons why it matters if a dodgy DFM makes 8% profit instead of 10% because it lost 2% in scams.

Firstly, if a fund makes 8% because it loses 2% in dodgy investments that go bust, then assuming that the 2% made no money at all, the fund would be worth 10%. However, if that 2% actually made money, then the fund might be worth say 10.5% or even 11%. Remember, the 2% is speculative so, the returns should be much higher than on the rest of the investments within the portfolio.

So, the difference between the 8% and the 11% is significant; that's 3% more profit for you or think of it another way, you would have made 40% more profit than you did! That's a lot of profit to give away.

Secondly, the 8% disguises one critical thing - the **higher** level of risk you are taking. It's all well and good when the fund is performing well, the stock market is going up and you're making a decent profit across your other investments, you can absorb the loss from the scam investments. But what happens when the market isn't so kind?

Your fund is making 8% and therefore it feels kind of 'acceptable' because the performance is okay, but actually, the genuine investment, i.e., the 90% is doing all the hard work and it's being pulled down by the dead-weight that is the 10%.

This means the risk of your entire portfolio is being ramped up. You are being exposed to unnecessary high levels of risk.

You're not being rewarded for that risk. That's a big problem. Think of it like this.

Your pension is best described as a lifetime of your work distilled into money. It's an exchange of your time on this planet for money, an exchange of your total number of hours that God has blessed you with for pounds and pence.

Your pension is a hurtful reminder of all the things you didn't get to do, the people you didn't get to see, and the places you didn't get to go, because you had to work. It doesn't matter if you enjoyed your work, or hated it. It doesn't matter if you worked for a company or ran your own business, it still controlled you, it still gave you stress and, it still dictated your life.

It took away your freedom, in the same way it takes away mine.

So, your pension is simply this.

It's all of those times you couldn't come home early to put your kids to bed. It's that embarrassing time when a boss ten years your junior, gave you a humiliating and public dressing down, you couldn't respond because you were fearful of losing your job. It's that time when you missed your son's school Nativity play where he was playing the star role of Joseph, because you couldn't get anybody to cover your shift. It's the two-hour daily commute you spent doing every single day for decades being stuck in traffic or stood on a packed train next to the fat, sweaty man who refused to use deodorant.

Your pension is all of *your* hard-earned work and sacrifice converted into cash; it's not mine, it's not your IFAs and it's not your DFMs.

Now after forty years of work, it's just sitting there, just a number on a trading platform. It doesn't even matter what that number is; it could be £10,000 or it could be £10million.

It's your hard work and you should be proud of it. But even more than being proud of it, you should protect it.

Because some tos*er right now is using it to feather his own nest. He's using your sacrifices and the sacrifices of your children and your family, so he doesn't have to make any of his own.

It's *your* bloody hard work, it's *your* savings and it's *your* life.

How dare somebody put your financial future at risk for their own financial gain? How dare somebody take food out of the mouths of your children and grandchildren, so they can buy a new luxury car or travel first class while you sit at the back of the plane?

Should you be angry? Yes, you should be furious.

Somebody has taken your money but they're not even investing it, and they're not even gambling with it. Even gambling could be forgiven, at least you'd have a chance of winning.

They're just taking it. They're literally throwing it down the pan, so, you lose everything, and they always make something.

It's not just the DFM but a whole group of people your hard work is being used to paid for. The directors of the bond company, the IB, the IFA, as well as all the legal team, auditors, accountants, marketers and all the employees who played their part in setting the whole thing up.

You're paying for all of them, for their holidays, their cars, their homes, for everything.

It's a scam – a one-way bet – they will always win, and you will always lose.

Now the 8% doesn't seem so fair, does it? Angry yet? Damn right, you should be angry.

Do the DFMs ever get caught?

The DFM scam is really quite unique.

Most scams enjoy a honeymoon period for a few years where the early entry scammers make lots of money without suspicion. It's the benefit of being the first early birds into a new, fresh market.

Over time, more and more scammers from other industries will see and hear about the profit being made and join, making the market not as new or fresh anymore. As more scammers join, it's not long before the market becomes saturated. The profit margins fall, as the scammers earn less and less, until eventually they become desperate.

In order to make the same sort of profit they once did, scammers have to take bigger risks. They go wider on their pitch, they become reckless with their marketing, make bigger and bigger promises, and finally, when everybody senses the market is about to implode, all hell breaks loose. Now there's a race to the bottom. The scammers know the good times are coming to an end and throw all caution to the wind. Now they don't care, they just want to take whatever they can and run.

The scammers become obsessed with making money. They've become too greedy and look for instant gratification. Investors start to make complaints, the press begins to post negative articles, pressure piles on the regulatory body to take action, investigations take place, companies are fined and shut down, then new laws and regulations are brought in. The industry grinds to a halt, and the scam product is suffocated of oxygen.

Some scammers who didn't leave quick enough, are caught with their snouts in the trough, oblivious to the net that had closed in on them. They get caught and hit with penalties, they're struck off as directors, and in some cases they're even jailed.

But the majority of scammers make their money, and get out of that scam before the proverbial hits the fan. They saw the writing on the wall and fled. A few of them will return later when the heat dies down, then hang around and feed off whatever scraps are leftover, but the majority will search for new hunting ground to rip off investors.

That's the full circle. That's how all scams play out, except for one; the DFM scam.

The DFM scam is different because the scammers belong to an elite profession, i.e., regulated portfolio fund management. That's something like 0.00001% of our society. It's a very exclusive club, which means that unlike every other scam, there isn't free access for others to join.

To work in the City of London is not an easy thing to do, but to become a qualified fund manager, then head up a fund so that you have autonomy and control over the buying decisions is almost impossible; it takes lots of networking, an Oxbridge education, and decades of hard work. If it was easy everybody would do it.

This means the barriers to entry are extremely high and therefore the market can never become saturated. New, novice scammers can't just one day say they're going to be a discretionary fund manager or wealth manager and join the party. Because they can't join the party, they can't ruin it for everybody else due their greed and inexperience.

Fund managers are very intelligent.

Unlike Bob and his mates doing a little side hustle from their run-down office in Covent Garden by, selling pink diamonds, the guy who runs a multi-billion pound fund is cut from a different type of cloth. He's called Giles, studied Politics at Eton, and is surrounded with the best advisors as well as lawyers, in the country. He won't be young, inexperienced, or the slightest bit wet behind the ears.

He moves in exclusive circles. As one of the most highly paid professions in the world, fund management naturally attracts the finest talent in the world. Giles is one of them.

This guy will be sharp as a nail and very well-positioned in society. He will move in very small groups of trusted people. He'll be a member of the most exclusive clubs only, and he'll be ferociously suspicious of any outsiders. He'll also go to great lengths to keep his identity anonymous.

He's the polar opposite of the inexperienced twenty-year-old Essex kid who left school at fifteen and blows money on strippers and champagne, and openly boasts about how much money he makes.

All of these factors play a part in why the DFM scam is different and so hard to stop.

Of course, not all funds are hidden away; some fund managers are high-profile and well-publicised. In those cases, the fund managers have become mini celebrities in their own right. They use their personal brand and reputation to promote the fund and attract more investors. They rub shoulders with the rich and famous and are happy for the attention.

But whether they're hidden away or in full show, it's impossible to imitate a DFM.

This means that supply of DFMs is tiny but demand for what they do by scammers is huge.

There's a disproportionate amount of power concentrated within a small number of DFMs, making it more difficult to detect any wrongdoing. Across a relatively small group of DFMs that work independently up and down the country, they're jointly responsible for controlling many *tens of billions* of pounds of pension money for everyday investors.

But they still can, and do, get caught sometimes. That usually happens when they become too greedy. When a DFM buys too many dodgy bonds and shares, he over-exposes his fund.

Then there is the increased risk that if a single, large investor or a group of investors simultaneously want their money out, the fund may not have enough liquid investments within it to sell without collapsing the share price. In this case the fund would be suspended and that, in turn, will set off the alarm bells for other investors, who will be queuing up to sell as soon as the fund resumes trading.

Remember, these funds aren't made up of just 'individual' investors. Private investors are the small guys; the biggest investors are large organisations, including banks, pension funds, charities, local councils and other government bodies.

Any organisation that holds a large amount of cash for more than a few months, will feel pressure from its shareholders and investors to make that money work. Even if the money is in a gilt or parked in a low-risk fund making 3%, that's better than have it withering away in a bank account.

So, right now, there are billions of pounds from local authorities, charities and organisations that has been invested into dodgy funds, and neither they, nor the people they represent, have any clue what they've got themselves into.

Mediocre fund managers with non-mediocre fees

It's an interesting statistic to consider that 75% of funds in the marketplace *underperform* the benchmark index. It's a crazy number when you think about it. In technical terms, most fund managers are basically 'rubbish' and you'd be better off sticking your money into an index rate tracker.

But you don't, and do you know why? It's because you're programmed and brain-washed into thinking you need a financial advisor, a wealth manager, a fund manager, a portfolio investment manager, an account manager, a stockbroker, and a thousand other people to manage your money for you.

If you find a good money manager, then great, you've hit the jack pot. But realistically, what is the probability that you can find him?

It's unlikely to happen and you're far more likely to end up attracting a long list of commission-hungry vultures who will feed off your portfolio for years. They will take whatever the stock market would have given to you, keep at least half of it and give you whatever's left over.

Most funds and fund managers are mediocre at best, some are terrible, and a few are downright crooks. So, you've got your work cut out to find somebody half decent.

When you add our lovely, paper-pushing, middleman IFA into the mix, you've now got double trouble. Instead of dodging one bullet, you must dodge two.

If you manage to miss both bullets without landing on your ass, well done to you. The next challenge is to avoid getting whacked with the market risk of your investments going down, as well as the volatility and risk of a stock market crashing. You've got to beat the professionals at their own game by picking the winning stocks and avoiding the losing ones, and, it's not an easy task.

If you get through all of that, you'd better cross your fingers and hope that your broker doesn't go bust, wiping out your entire portfolio.

If, amazingly, you are still standing, then finally your next task is not to get clobbered by the taxman.

There are a lot of things that can go wrong, and unfortunately, they can only go wrong from one person, you.

It's all your fault

As for the bond scams themselves, even I couldn't tell you with all my years of experience what is or isn't a scam. I could make an educated guess if I spent enough time researching something, but it would be just that, a guess.

The best scams today are now indistinguishable from genuine companies.

The speculative penny stocks that disappear are just that speculative. When they go pop, like so many do, that's it another one has gone under. There are probably at least a hundred companies that go bust or are suspended each year in the UK alone.

There are many more on the unlisted market that disappear too.

Another collapse, another failure, another investment gone wrong.

It won't raise any eyebrows, much less any complaints.

You're none the wiser because the stock market keeps going up and so does your portfolio.

"At least it's better than the bank", you tell yourself. Hmmm...is it?

If the fund does lose money, then, of course, who else can you blame but yourself? Your IFA was doing what he thought was best.

Besides, *you* were the one who opted for that 'adventurous' part. Don't you remember?

You play back the conversation in your mind, as your IFA was sat on your sofa, gobbling down those delightful, chocolate digestives.

"Yes, that's right" you remember, *"I did choose that fund".*

Your IFA had given you a choice of three different funds, a cautious, balanced or speculative.

You chose the balanced one, of course you did, everybody does. The IFA knew your answer before he had even asked you the question.

He also knew that in the fund, there would be something special, a little bit of healthy 'high growth stock. After all, that's what balanced means, a little bit of everything but not too much of anything.

"What were those special investments called again?" You ask yourself. *"That's right...exotic, alternative investments. It was only 5% of the fund so that was okay..."*

That 5% was a big enough number to make the DFM very rich but a small enough number not to make you cry.

Yep, you remember it very clearly. The IFA had nothing to do with this, no fault whatsoever.

YOU chose that fund, remember?

And YOU signed all the risk warnings, filled in all those forms. You read the prospectus, you knew the downside, it was all you.

Nobody to blame, not the IFA, not the fund manager, not the wealth management firm, nobody to blame but YOU, my dear friend. If things go wrong, that's just your bad luck.

Isn't that correct? Isn't that what everybody thinks?

That's exactly what they want you to believe. They want you to believe that it was all your fault. It was, all your decisions that led to where you were before to where you are today.

From the secure company pension being converted to a SIPP to the wealth management firm you used, from the funds that you chose to invest into, to the performance of those funds.

Even though everything was already pre-planned, they made you believe that all of the decisions were yours, from start to finish.

That was their final and greatest trick; to convince you it was all down to you.

Positive steps forward

I know that I've laid it on a little thick in this last chapter but what did you expect? This isn't a romantic love novel, that you're reading. This is your life we're talking about here.

But that doesn't mean you should leave this chapter feeling defeated. That may be your first reaction, but you should be more positive. In fact, you should be proud of yourself. I'm proud of you. I'm proud of me, too, we did this together.

By some small miracle, you have stumbled across this book, agreed to buy it, and have now read it to the very end. That means you know more about the financial scams plaguing our society than 99% of the population.

So, well done to you. You invested your time into learning something you can now take to protect you, your family, and your loved ones.

Don't worry about the DFM Scam.

As strong and impenetrable as it is today, it's time will come. It will eventually break; they all do in the end. This one might just take a while.

But one day the regulators will catch up with it, rules will change, and loopholes will close. The fines and penalties will increase, sentences will be served and eventually, the rewards won't justify the risks.

That's when the scammers will move onto their next magic show. Old scammers will retire, and new ones will take their place. That's the circle of life.

So, no, I'm not worried about the DFM scam. In fact, I'm not worried about any of the scams I've written about in this book. That's because I know them all.

Now so do you.

I'm more worried about the scams that I don't know about.

For sure, there are plenty of them

BONUS TIP –
The Financial Redress Scam

Before I go, let me leave with you one final scam that will definitely help you.

With all the scams going on in the world, there's a good chance that, at some point you will get scammed. I really hope this doesn't happen, but it probably will and you should be prepared for that happening.

That's why this final bonus chapter is so important.

Because once you are scammed, your name will be targeted again and again. The scammers will share your information with other scammers for a price. That's because you've now become a 'hot lead'.

Your details are worth a lot of money to other scammers, which includes your name, address, email, telephone number, the scam product you bought, how much you invested and when, and detailed notes of previous conversations.

Of course, the original scammer won't be able to speak to you again, but his colleagues can, and so can other scammers; be ready for that next phone call.

It's like bees to a honeypot. The scammers can't help themselves.

If you've been caught out once, you are an irresistible target, to be aimed at, over and over again. They see you as the weakest link. If you were tricked before, they know there is a decent probability you will fall for again. Certainly, better for them to try on you than somebody new.

Sometimes the second scam will be direct.

The new scammers will just go in hard and try to sell you new scam products, something that you've not bought before. However, if that fails a few times, you'll find another company will call you who specialise in the seeking 'financial redress' scam, it works like this.

Because they already know exactly how you were scammed, what you bought and, how much money you lost, they have the information that equates to power. They also know you're desperately looking to get your money back.

You're feeling stupid and they know you want redemption, closure, to end this sorry chapter.

So, at this precise moment in time, when you are at your lowest ebb, they give you what you want more than anything else in the world.

They give you an opportunity to get all of your money back. To get your honour back, to save your pride.

This saviour, a knight in shining armour, will represent a no win-no fee, claims compensation company.

You will of course, be very wary to begin with, but your guard quickly drops when they say they don't need any money from you. In fact, you don't need to pay them at all because they get paid from the money they recover.

You have nothing to lose so, of course you say 'yes'. That's when they start probing and asking more questions. You'll go down the path of building a relationship with the new scammers until eventually, after a few weeks, they say something like this:

"Ok, John, we've looked into your case. It's pretty complicated and it turns out that the company that scammed you was run by a gentleman by the name of Tony Fletcher. We did some digging around and he's got a long history of scams.

Unfortunately, he's disappeared because the police are after him but, in his haste, to get away, he was unable to completely empty the bank accounts of two of his scam operations. That's now been seized and in total there's around £2.6 million that the administrators now have access to. I can send you the links if you want, it's all over the internet.

The problem is that there are a lot of investors who he scammed so we don't know at this stage what you might get back. It won't be the full amount but I'm hoping you should get back at least 30% of what you put in. You invested £40,000 so 30% of that is still £12,000. It's not bad all things considered.

We of course will take our agreed 20% but that still leaves you with £9,600. I know it's not the full amount but it's better than nothing. Besides this is just the first step and we haven't exhausted the other options we discussed previously so there's probably more to come.

I've helped other clients like you, of course so my best advice is *that we claim what we can now and then keep pushing to see what we can recover through the other channels.*

However, we need to apply quickly if you want a chance of recovery. There are hundreds of other people out there who are going to be applying soon so we need to get your application off now.

Don't worry, I'm going to send you the forms by email to complete this evening and we can submit them by tomorrow morning if you can send them back to me tonight.

Now, one final thing. For us to do this, you can appreciate that it's quite time-consuming and this falls outside of our normal work. This means that if you want me to do all of the paperwork and make the application for you, you will need to pay an administration fee. It's normally £1,995 + VAT, but if you want to move quickly, we can agree a discounted rate of just £995.

Alternatively, if you want to try and chase this up yourself, you can do that but it's not a straightforward process...."

Can you see what's happened? After weeks of courting, John is already committed to the process. He's rebuilt trust and believes that this new company will help him.

Now, he's faced with a dilemma. To pay £995 to recover nearly £10,000 or to just walk away.

Doing the forms himself is too difficult. He hasn't got the information, and the firm, whilst pretending to help, actually won't give it to him. That's because the story is a load of baloney, it's all made up.

The initial agreement had always been that John wouldn't have to pay up front for anything but that eventually morphs into a small fee upfront. If that fee is paid, the scammers will then ask for another fee for something else, and so it goes on.

It's the same cycle.

From robbery to recovery

There's another redress scam where the scammers actually become the heroes. They genuinely *don't* take any money up front. It's like being robbed at knifepoint and your assailant then donning a suit and tie to become your attorney to help you recover the money.

This was massive with CFD firms and principal brokerage firms.

During the time when dozens of CFD and principal firms were put out of business for mis-selling practices, many of the directors of those companies, transitioned into the 'financial recovery' industry. They, of course, hid their identities by using moles to front their new companies but look into the records on Companies House and you'll see the connection between those different people; you just need to join up the dots.

It was another genius stroke. After all, the directors already had all the data, and details about their clients, tens of thousands of them. They also knew about the mis- selling that had taken place because they were the ones who did it!

They also knew the complaints process better than anybody else, and how to recover the money.

So, literally tens of thousands of CFD and penny share investors up and down the country, were sent letters, asking if they wanted to recover their losses on a no-win, no-fee basis. Of course, they pretty much all said yes.

But because the original firms were previously regulated and had now been liquidated, the complaint couldn't go against the directors of those firms so, it had to go to the Financial Services Compensation Scheme (FSCS). Because the cases were so strong and the evidence so compelling, thousands of investors were paid out tens of millions of pounds for those mis-selling practices.

Just rewind and consider what has just happened here.

The CFD and penny share scammers mis-sold their products, made false claims, pressurised old grannies to part with their life savings, churned portfolios through spreads and made massive commissions. They did that for several years and made tens of millions of pounds. When the FCA started investigating, they took their money and quickly wound up their businesses, disappearing into the sunset so they couldn't be touched.

They then set up brand new 'financial redress' companies, and took all of that valuable client information, which only they would know, to make perfect complaints against the same CFD and penny share firms they previously owned! Because those CFD firms were insolvent, the complaint was passed over to the FSCS. Because the complaints were so perfect, the FSCS had to uphold them.

In the process the financial redress companies would take as much as 50% from the total sum recovered!

So, if a client lost, say, £20,000 with a CFD or principal dealing scam, the scammers would have made £20,000, give or take, on the first scam. When they recover £20,000 for their victim from the FSCS, they would make another 50%, which is £10,000!

So, the scammers make £30,000; £20,000 from the victim and £10,000 from owners of regulated firms, like me, that fund the FSCS!

There's no pitch or hard sale required. There's no marketing costs or expenses. There's no product to set up or create. There's nothing but full co-operation.

Most of those scammed had no idea they could even claim, let alone, how to claim effectively. They would rather receive 50% of something than 100% of nothing and it involved no work or effort on their part.

Besides, they didn't know how to write a proper complaint letter, or how to organise their files correctly, or present it to the FSCS in the best possible way. Many didn't have the full documentation in any case.

The scammers, however, had everything. They had the telephone call recordings, the account forms, the transactional history and, suitability questionnaires.

They had everything because it was their job to have everything. Because they committed the crime, they knew better than anybody else how the crime was committed.

It's like asking a murderer who was exonerated from the crime, to solve his own murder case. If anybody knows where the murder weapon and disposed body is, it's him!

What a scandal; scammers make money not once but TWICE on the same scam.

The people who get back 50% are also over the moon.

Little do they know that the people they're sending thank you letters and boxes of chocolates to, are the people who scammed them in the first place!

However, we're still not finished yet; there's one financial redress scam which will shock you even more.

From scammed to scammer

There is a horrible situation where the scammed can become the scammer; it's where the prey becomes the predator.

When people hit a brick wall and are out of options, they might feel they have no choice.

If it means having to choose between losing their marriage, their home and their children, it's understandable that people will do just about anything to stop that from happening. Sometimes that means becoming the scammer yourself.

There's nothing sadder than being scammed, and then recovering your money, by scamming somebody else. But that's what happens.

The scammer tells their victim that if they want to recover their money, the only way to do that is to convince a friend or family member to buy the same scam product they had originally lost their money on.

For example, if John lost £10,000 in a scam, the scammers would give him the opportunity to recover all of his money if he could get somebody else to invest £20,000 into the same product he was scammed in.

To make the story more convincing, the scammer tells John exactly how to pull off this deal. He tells John the exact script and what to say. John tells his friend that he's going to put £20,000 into the same deal but needs another investor in the deal. This is because the minimum investment is £40,000 and he can't afford to do the deal on his own. His friend thinks it must be a good deal because John is also putting his money into the deal. Official papers will be signed; the scammers and John now collude together to scam his friend.

But it's just a hoax. John never puts in the £20,000 and his friend loses his £20,000.

It's hard to think that somebody might throw somebody else into the lion's den in order to save their own skin, but it happens, and an entire industry is built around this. This happens to anybody from work colleagues and acquaintances to friends and even family members.

People who have lost money in scams become desperate and desperate people do desperate things.

I'm not condoning it. It's completely wrong but I understand why it can happen.

If you had a small lifeboat, and either your children or your neighbour's children had to survive, who would you choose? Well, for some people losing their life savings in a scam can become a case of life and death.

Some feel that they may as well be dead. Some even kill themselves.

If their 'friend' happens to be rich and affluent, they will rationalise it and justify that their friend can afford to lose the money more than he can. When the whole thing collapses, he must, of course, play along and feel cheated. Damn, he lost his money, too, right?

I understand that it's still not right, it's not fair and it shouldn't happen. But this is a twist to all scams that are happening right now.

Sometimes, the scammed victims won't take the bait as, they'd rather take the hit themselves. But in other cases, they feel they have no other choice but to throw somebody under the bus if it means they can save their family and themselves from being knocked over.

The lesson is very simple.

If you've been scammed once, understand that the money has most likely gone. Forget about it. Don't pass your scam onto somebody else, no matter how rich they are. Even if they can absorb that loss, it's not theirs to take. It's yours.

You don't need karma like that in your life.

If you scam a friend or family member, you're even worse than the scammers.

Don't be tempted by these financial redress conmen. You should only try to recover money from a legitimate firm, like the FCA, the Financial Ombudsman Service (FOS), the police, the government, or another recognised body that you know genuinely has your best interest at heart.

If you're approached by anybody else, just run a mile.

Administrator scam

There is one final, final piece of the scam jigsaw. Right at the end of the scam, at the very end, when everything blows up, you have the administrator. You would think that after all of the money was extracted, after the last bit of blood had been extracted, this would be enough.

But no, it's never enough.

After all the money has been taken out by the scammers, the business will still usually have a few million pounds left over in assets. Those assets need to be sold and the money distributed to the shareholders.

Because the assets are usually very specialist, such as a piece of machinery, or a building, there is no single quoted price and there isn't a big market with lots of willing buyers. The administrators are expected to move quickly, which means they are expected to make a fast sale at a *low* price.

This makes it easy for an appointed administrator to sell £10 million of assets at a fire-sale price of, say just £5 million and that means the ability for yet one more final scam.

The administrator can sell a distressed asset to a firm that it's 'friendly' with, at a massively discounted price. Nobody questions it because the bond has already lost, say, £100 million, so, it makes no difference to the remaining investors if the final asset is sold for £5 million or £6 million or £7 million. They're going to get such a small percentage of the final money raised, they're not concerned about the final asset sale.

They've already got their hands full trying to fight the original scammers. They are not expecting the administrators to also screw them over.

I've personally seen administrators of failed stock brokerage firms, sell an entire client book, consisting of more than 10,000 clients and £100 million under management, for a tiny fraction of the true value. I'm not suggesting that anything dodgy happened on this particular occasion, but you can see how it is open to abuse, especially as the business is not sold to the highest bidder.

The business is sold to the firm who is deemed to be the 'best fit', which means it's based on other factors outside of just money. It's no free competition, which means it's open for abuse.

Imagine I'm an administrator and having dinner with a good pal of mine who is the CEO of a large firm. I'm currently working on a project to wind up a business and my pal happens to be in the same industry. He tells me that he'd be happy to buy the distressed assets or even buy the whole company out. So, I want to sell and, he wants to buy. There is no market price, there's no competition, there's nobody except me, him and a bottle of red wine.

How do you think that conversation might go? Exactly.

I'm sure there are many administrators where things are sold correctly, to the right people for the best price, under the best terms and, in the best interest of their shareholders.

But, as we have seen, there are always a few you have to watch out for.

So, there you have it, corruption from the start, to quite literally, the finish.

You don't know what you don't know

So that's it, we are at the end. It's been quite a journey and I thank you for sharing it with me.

I hope that it's not just been educational but entertaining. I hope that you now regard me as your friend.

If you ever need help and you want to protect yourself from being scammed, just drop me a line at info@londonstonesecurities. co.uk.

Because, unfortunately what you have learned in this book isn't even half the full story.

There are scams that exist and impact people every day which I have not written about because I don't know about them.

Even I don't even know everything about the scams I *have* written about.

Nobody really does, except those who are full-time scammers, who live and breathe in that murky world.

The scam business is like any other businesses, forever changing, growing and learning.

There are financial scams in binary options, crypto currencies, blockchain technologies, and in Non-Fungible Tokens (NFTs) that I have no clue about.

There are countless banking, technology, internet, and telecoms scams where your telephone is tapped into, where your computer is breached, and where your credit card details are extracted.

The old scams haven't died but now there are plenty of new ones to think about, too. The scam market just gets bigger, wider and deeper. It's never-ending.

With the explosion of the internet and technology, the physical location doesn't even matter anymore. The market is now truly global which means there are billions of potential victims to target anywhere around the world, at any time.

Armed robberies used to take place on the high street, but now the biggest theft takes place inside your living room.

Like they say, you don't know what you don't know.

This small insight I have shared with you should be the beginning of your journey in learning about scams and not the end.

But please don't become paranoid, bitter, or resentful. Just be aware.

If you've been scammed don't worry, you're in good company.

You join a long list of people who have been scammed, me included.

We'll all get caught at some point. We can't beat mathematical probability. There are too many people out there looking to scam us, it's what they do.

Never feel sad if you've lost money or you if lose money in the future. Don't even feel anger towards the scammers. That's wasted energy and emotion.

Just stay positive, learn from your experiences and move on. Life is too short to dwell on yesterday's darkness when we know that tomorrow the sun will shine even brighter.

Waheguru Ji Ka Khalsa

Waheguru Ji Ki Fateh

Ranjeet Singh is a professional investment manager who lives in Richmond, Surrey with his four children. As a passionate Sikh, he is compelled to fight for the underdog not least because, for a long time, he was one.

He was born in Coventry in 1974, growing up in tough working class conditions but was fortunate enough to break out of the mold. Unlike some of his childhood friends who ended up on drugs or in prison, he excelled academically. He graduated in Economics and Business Finance with Honours at several prestigious universities including Nottingham, Kingston and Brunel.

He soon found his way into the City of London working for one of the largest, global investment banks in the world, Deutsche Bank. But as a young, adventurous and restless twenty-three year old, he found it difficult to settle. As he moved from one firm to another, he noticed the same recurring pattern over and over again; corporate greed and corruption.

With each experience, he became increasingly disillusioned with the financial system and its politics. In 2008, he set up his own business and for the first time, he can now finally tell his story.

His uncle once described him as a maverick. His friends call him a loose cannon. His mother says that his brain is like a computer. They might all be right.

Whoever he is, he's fighting for you, the man on the street. Love him or hate him, you can't ignore him

Printed in Poland
by Amazon Fulfillment
Poland Sp. z o.o., Wrocław

22497936R00292